Africa Human Development Report 2016

Accelerating Gender Equality and Women's Empowerment in Africa

Foreword

This 2016 Africa Human Development Report on gender equality follows the 2012 Africa Human Development Report, which looked at the importance of assuring food security for all Africans. Both reports share a common objective of addressing what might be considered two unfinished agenda items on Africa's development trajectory. Both have long been recognized as important priorities for the governments and citizens of African countries.

This year's report on gender equality reviews the ongoing efforts of African countries to accelerate the pace of assuring women's empowerment through all spheres of society – in the home and community, in health and educational attainment, in the workplace, and in political participation and leadership. While significant progress has been made across numerous fronts in most countries, gender equality for African women and girls is still far from satisfactory. To address the gender gap, this report adopts a political economy approach to gender equality and women's empowerment in Africa.

A key message of this report is that giving more concerted attention to gender equality will be an important and long overdue stimulus to faster and more inclusive human development and economic growth for the entire continent. A policy and programming focus on harnessing the potential of women is an important economic and social driver for more inclusive and sustainable development. Policies and programmes that unintentionally leave out or disenfranchise women will never be successful over the long term. Nor can inclusive growth be achieved if women's empowerment is compartmentalized, or seen as a separate activity from what are traditionally perceived as the core functions of government.

Simply stated, accelerating gender equality is a core function of government, involving multi-sectoral efforts that include national and local government entities, non-governmental actors, civil society organizations and the private sector. Similarly, addressing gender equality in such a holistic way dovetails with, and reinforces, the ambitious agenda of the Sustainable Development Goals (SDGs), which African governments and the international community as a whole have set for the coming 15 years. A holistic approach to gender equality will also bolster the achievement of Agenda 2063 of the African Union. This 2016 Human Development Report therefore provides a framework for operationalizing SDG 5 on gender equality, in particular, and all the SDGs, in general.

Finally, it is important to emphasize that this report has been written to encourage policy debate and discussions on what further steps are needed to ensure that gender equality is more fully integrated into national agendas and ongoing policy dialogues across Africa. The report has been prepared with diverse audiences in mind – African policymakers and practitioners, other development organizations, the private sector, civil society, academia, and Africa's citizens, young and old. It is hoped that the report will engage and stimulate active discussion and consensus on the different pathways each African country can take in addressing this critical development challenge and fundamental human right – gender equality.

Helen Clark

Administrator
United Nations Development Programme

Preface

On behalf of the UNDP Regional Bureau for Africa, I am pleased to present this second Africa Human Development Report on the topic of Accelerating Gender Equality in Africa.

Gender equality is not a new development priority for African countries. Indeed, its importance has long been recognized, with the African Union and its predecessor, the Organization of African Union, taking a leading role in espousing the rights of women and girls dating back several decades. The African Union has designated 2016 as the year of Human Rights with a focus on Women's Rights, while 2015 was the year of Women's Empowerment and Development. However, progress in achieving gender equality has been slower than hoped and inconsistent for many African countries.

This report on gender equality is thus aimed at refocusing attention on what continues to be a critical development challenge, at a time when Africa has been undergoing a period of significant and unprecedented economic, social and political change. The fast pace of economic growth in some African countries only a few years ago has been dampened by the recent global downturn in demand for many primary commodities. Political and civil unrest driven by inequality, localized disputes and unmet expectations continue to affect many countries in Africa. Also, the Ebola epidemic of 2014 and drought in East, West and Southern Africa in 2015/16 demonstrate how vulnerable and fragile even rapidly improving African societies can be to unexpected shocks and downturns. Under such conditions, African women often bear a differentially greater burden as mothers, caregivers and family providers.

In the analysis that follows, the report highlights where progress has been made in addressing gender equality and what and where the remaining shortfalls and challenges are. It first provides a synopsis of Africa's human development progress using UNDP's different human development indicators, with particular attention to the two indicators that measure gender development and gender inequality. The report further analyses gender trends and comparisons in terms of health, education, economic opportunities and barriers, as well as political representation and leadership. Attention is also given to the underlying and root causes of persistent gender inequality, including negative social norms in slowing the pace toward gender equality and the policy dilemmas that African governments face in reconciling legal norms and precedents with detrimental social customs and traditions.

The report further reviews the policy and institutional approaches that African governments have used to address gender inequality and accelerate the pace of women's empowerment and access to equal economic, social and political opportunities. Throughout the report, comparisons are made between African countries and between the Africa region and other developing regions, notably Asia and Latin America and the Caribbean.

The final chapter of the report offers an agenda for action through a policy and strategic framework that places gender equality at the centre of the development agenda. Four broad 'pathways' are suggested that offer a policy and programme framework to accelerate gender equality and fully integrate gender into the broader development agenda.

These four pathways entail:

- supporting the adoption of legal reforms, policies and programmes to advance women's empowerment;

- supporting national capacities to promote and increase the participation and leadership of women in decision-making in the home, economy and society;

- supporting capacity to implement multi-sectoral approaches to mitigate the impacts of discriminatory health and education practices; and

- supporting women to gain ownership and management of economic and environmental assets.

The rationale for these pathways is that only by ensuring that women receive the same economic, social and political opportunities by shifting from legal to substantive gender equality can governments assure that their progress in economic growth and human development is fully inclusive for all their citizens and sustainable in the long term.

We hope that this report stimulates discussion and debate on what remains a critical challenge and unexploited opportunity for Africa's future.

Abdoulaye Mar Dieye

Abdoulaye Mar Dieye

Assistant Administrator and Director of the Regional Bureau for Africa

Acknowledgements

The Africa Human Development Report (2016 AfHDR) was prepared by UNDP Africa experts. It benefitted from the overall guidance of Abdoulaye Mar Dieye, the UNDP Africa Regional Director, with a special contribution to and direction on the theoretical framework from Selim Jahan, the Director of UNDP's Human Development Report Office. The strategic support from Ruby Sandhu-Rojon, Deputy Regional Director, is duly acknowledged.

The report preparation process was coordinated and directed by Ayodele Odusola, Chief Economist and Head of the Strategy and Analysis Team, UNDP Africa. The AfHDR project team was led by Angela Lusigi. Key team members included Eunice Kamwendo, Yumna Omar, Ahmadou Mboup, James Neuhaus, Khady ba Faye, Yechi Bekele, Jonas Mantey and Yihua Lyu.

The project was informed by research and analysis from nine background papers prepared by authors listed in Annex A. Selected UNDP Country Offices supported the investigative study with fieldwork in Gabon, Mali, Niger, Sierra Leone, Rwanda and Zimbabwe, and case studies from Angola, Benin, Kenya, Malawi, Morocco, Togo, Tunisia and Zambia that contributed to the report. Lamine Bal, Sandra Macharia and the UNDP communication team translated key messages into communication products, including data visualization by Daniel Sauter and the team from The New School in New York, USA.

The project benefitted from the oversight and guidance of the AfHDR Report Advisory Board, co-chaired by UNDP and the African Union Commission, including Leymah Gbowee, Amy Jadesimi, Ndioro Ndiaye, Jeni Klugman, Geraldine Fraser-Moleketi, Aminata Diba, Justine Diffo Tchunkan, Beatrice Hamusonde and Ayo Ajayi. A UNDP internal oversight team provided technical inputs with representation from the Human Development Report Office, the Bureau for Policy and Programme Support, the Regional Bureau for Asia and the Regional Service Centre for Africa. A UNDP Africa field sounding board composed of selected resident coordinators and economic advisers peer-reviewed the document and provided inputs to the process.

The work on the AfHDR project team greatly benefitted from the valuable contributions of United Nations sister agencies through a UN Readers' Group including Moa Westman (United Nations Environment Programme) and Simonetta Zarrilli (United Nations Conference on Trade and Development). Thoko Ruzvidzo (United Nations Economic Commission for Africa), Fatime Christiane N'Diaye (International Labour Organization) and Euphrasie Kouame (United Nations Capital Development Fund) facilitated regional consultations. The project also benefitted from the assistance provided by *Centro de Alianzas Para el Desarrollo* (Global CAD) and Forcier Consulting, which supported the synthesis of background papers and an interactive field study, respectively.

During regional consultations on this report in Addis Ababa, Dakar, Johannesburg and Lusaka, the inputs and comments from numerous representatives of regional organizations, civil society groups, the private sector and academia included in Annex A were extremely valuable.

The dedication of the lead writer, editing, translation and proofreading team was essential to the timely production of this report. Thomas Stephens provided invaluable support to the drafting of the report, and Barbara Hall edited it. The proofreading from Prime Production and Leah Brumer is also appreciated.

Generous grants from the Government of Japan and the Open Society Initiative of West Africa were essential to the research, consultations and writing of the report.

Contents

FIGURES

TABLES

Abbreviations and acronyms

ACHPR	African Commission on Human and People's Rights
AfDB	African Development Bank
AfHDR	Africa Human Development Report
AU	African Union
AWIB	African Women in Business Initiative
CARMMA	Campaign on Accelerated Reduction of Maternal Mortality in Africa
CCT	Conditional cash transfer
CEDAW	Convention on the Elimination of All Forms of Discrimination Against Women
ECOSOC	United Nations Economic and Social Council
FAO	Food and Agriculture Organization of the United Nations
FGM	Female genital mutilation
GBV	Gender-based violence
GDI	Gender Development Index
GDP	Gross domestic product
GII	Gender Inequality Index
GNI	Gross national income
HDR	Human Development Report
HDI	Human Development Index
HIV/AIDS	Human immunodeficiency virus/acquired immunodeficiency syndrome
ICESCR	International Covenant on Economic, Social and Cultural Rights
ILO	International Labour Organization
IHDI	Inequality-adjusted Human Development Index
IMF	International Monetary Fund
IPV	Intimate partner violence
LAC	Latin America and the Caribbean
MDG	Millennium Development Goal
M&E	Monitoring and evaluation
MPI	Multidimensional Poverty Index
NEET	Not in employment, education or training
PPP	Purchasing power parity
SADC	Southern Africa Development Community
SDGEA	Solemn Declaration on Gender Equality in Africa
SDG	Sustainable Development Goal
SIGI	Social Institutions and Gender Index
SME	Small and medium-sized enterprise
STEM	Science, technology, engineering and mathematics
TBA	Traditional birth attendant
UDHR	Universal Declaration of Human Rights
UNDP	United Nations Development Programme
UNECA	United Nations Economic Commission for Africa
UNESCO	United Nations Educational, Scientific and Cultural Organization
UNICEF	United Nations Children's Fund
UNIFEM	United Nations Development Fund for Women
UN WOMEN	United Nations Entity for Gender Equality and Empowerment of Women
WHO	World Health Organization

Overview

Overview

Report rationale

From the Universal Declaration of Human Rights, 68 years ago, to the Millennium Declaration 15 years ago, and to the Sustainable Development Goals today, global attention remains focused on promoting human rights and eliminating discrimination and inequitable outcomes for women, men, girls and boys. However, despite widespread recognition of women's rights and the benefits that accrue to all of society from equitable treatment and access to resources and opportunities for women and men, inequalities persist. At the regional and national levels, there is growing recognition that as African women attain higher measures of economic and social well-being, benefits accrue to all of society; despite this growing understanding, removing inequalities for women has not kept pace. Significant gaps between men's and women's opportunities remain a major challenge and a severe impediment to structural economic and social transformation that is still the goal of all African countries.

The evolving development landscape – with its emerging opportunities, vulnerabilities and shocks – makes it imperative for Africa to accelerate the advancement of sustainable and equitable human development. This can be achieved by building economic, social and environmental resilience for women and men, enhancing their productivity, and accelerating the pace of structural economic transformation in the region. This report explores where and how progress in gender equality has been made and how best to accelerate the pace of gender advancement in Africa. Its focus on gender equality comes at a time of tremendous change across the continent, including recent dynamics of social and economic transformation that have resulted in significant strides in Africa's human development.

This report pinpoints the intersection between political and economic processes, and presents a clear agenda for action. The agenda provides an approach to help African countries more forcefully confront the challenge and accelerate progress on gender equality and women's empowerment. The agenda on gender equality can support progress toward Africa's Agenda 2063 and the Sustainable Development Goals (SDGs). While SDG 5 focuses specifically on gender equality, addressing gender issues more vigorously and comprehensively will expedite efforts by governments and other stakeholders to achieve many, if not all, of the other SDGs due to the role and position that women play across all of society and all sectors.

Analytical approach

From UNDP's perspective, gender inequality from the standpoint of human development is addressed by improving women's capabilities and opportunities, and contributing to better outcomes for present and future generations. The nexus between gender equality and human development is based on three overlapping concerns:

- **economic**: more productive work at home and in the marketplace as employers, employees and entrepreneurs;

- **social and environmental**: better health, education, cessation of physical and sexual violence against women, and sustainable resource use for present and future generations; and

- **political**: more equal voice and representation in decision-making and resource allocation.

The analytical approach taken in the report is to examine the challenge of gender equality by pinpointing the interaction between political, economic and social processes that either impede or contribute to advancing women's empowerment. A 'political economy' perspective is used to understand the way ideas, resources and power are conceptualized, negotiated and implemented by different social groups in relation to gender inequality – whether in the workplace, the marketplace, or at home.

It is important to emphasize that the preparation of this Africa Human Development Report was a highly collaborative effort between the UNDP Regional Bureau for Africa and many different agencies, institutions, practitioners and researchers. It was also prepared in close collaboration with the African Union Commission. As a result, it not only focuses on sub-Saharan Africa, but also includes the Arab states of North Africa. The report preparation process included in-depth quantitative research and analysis, a qualitative interactive study, consultations with numerous organizations throughout Africa as well as an Africa-wide online survey.

The sections below highlight some of the key points found in the chapters of the report.

Progress and challenges in African human development

The report reviews current progress in African human development using the different indicators that UNDP has constructed to capture various aspects of human development, including gender inequality. Using UNDP's different human development indicators, there is wide variation in values and ranking across the African region and between the different African sub-regions. Overall, Africa has one of the fastest rates of improvement in human development over the past two decades but also has the lowest average levels of human development compared to other regions in the world. At the same time, not all African countries have low human development. Seventeen African countries across the five sub-regions have attained medium and high human development – five countries each from Southern and North Africa, four in Central Africa, two

in West Africa, and one in East Africa. The highest human development levels in Africa are in Algeria, Libya, Mauritius, Seychelles, and Tunisia. Thirty-six African countries (out of 44 countries worldwide) are classified in the low human development group.

Countries with initially low levels of human development are making large gains. The following countries have made the largest gains since 2000: United Republic of Tanzania, Burundi, Mali, Zambia, Niger, Angola, Sierra Leone, Mozambique, Rwanda and Ethiopia. Countries that began with initially low levels of human development are growing faster, on average, which indicates that they are catching up. However, the pace has slowed since 2010.

Calculations using the UNDP gender indices indicate significant gender inequality in almost every African country. Gender gaps in income and non-income dimensions mean that women often experience lower human development outcomes than men. On average, African women achieve only 87 per cent of male human development levels.

Social dimensions of gender equality

The social dimensions of gender equality involving trends in health and education are key determinants of women's equality and empowerment. Overall, gender inequality in social services translates into fewer opportunities for women, in particular, and society, as a whole, to achieve well-being. During the last decades, many African countries have seen the expansion of their citizens' capabilities in the basic areas of health, education and other social services. These improvements have included women and girls, and today they have greater access to education at all levels, have better health, safely give birth to their children, and achieve higher life expectancy. Yet, many women face severe deprivations in their health due to such factors as early age marriage, sexual and physical violence, and the continued unacceptable high incidence of maternal mortality.

The spectrum of violence affecting women includes domestic violence, intimate partner

Inequality in how women and men have different health and education outcomes is still evident across and within sub-regions. Gender inequality in social services translates into lower opportunities for the well-being of women in particular and society as a whole.

violence, rape, genital mutilation, intimidation, and additional threats to women´s personal security in periods of war and conflict.

With respect to education, it is remarkable that near gender parity has been achieved in primary school enrolment. However, gender discrimination is still significant in secondary and tertiary education. The reasons why children do not attend school vary, but they are often associated with poverty, ethnicity, social exclusion, living in a rural area or slums, geographic remoteness, disasters, armed conflict, lack of basic facilities and poor-quality education. These barriers often interact with gender to create even greater disadvantages in learning opportunities.

Women in African economies

Another key determinant of gender equality is defined by women in the workplace and economic decision-making. Significant economic and workplace disparities between men and women continue to be the norm rather than the exception in many African countries. These inequalities are found across Africa in terms of access to economic assets, participation in the workplace, entrepreneurship opportunities, and use of and benefits from natural resources and the environment.

In addition, women are more likely to be found in vulnerable employment with weak regulation and limited social protection due to differences in education and the mismatch between women's skills and those demanded by the labour market. This in turn pushes women into the informal economy. It is estimated, using survey data for 2004 to 2010, that the share of non-agricultural informal employment in sub-Saharan Africa is about 66 per cent of all female employment.

Increased female participation in the labour market has not meant increased opportunities in high paying jobs or enterprises. A gender wage gap outside agriculture is pervasive across all labour markets in sub-Saharan Africa, where, on average, the unadjusted gender pay gap is estimated at 30 per cent. Thus, for every $1 earned by men in manufacturing, services and trade, women earn 70 cents. Gaps in earnings between women and men are influenced by parameters such as age, occupation type, education, parenthood and marriage.

Because social norms and beliefs assign African women and girls the primary responsibility for care and domestic work, women, on average, spend twice as much time as men on domestic work - child and elderly care, cooking, cleaning, and fetching water and wood. In sub-Saharan Africa, 71 per cent of the burden of collecting water for households falls on women and girls.

As the economic status of women improves, so does the economic status of entire families – a major factor in reducing the blight of inter-generational poverty and low human development. For example, ownership or title to land represents an important source of equity and collateral for women in obtaining credit and accessing other forms of productive assets. Lack of access to land deprives African women of an important economic tool for improving their livelihoods.

There is a high economic cost when women are not more fully integrated into their respective national economies. Gender inequality in the labour market alone cost sub-Saharan Africa about USD 95 billion annually between 2010 and 2014, peaking at USD 105 billion in 2014. These results confirm that Africa is missing its full growth potential because a sizeable portion of its growth reserve – women – is not fully utilized.

African women in politics and leadership

Another key driver in advancing gender equality is the role of women's political voice and leadership. Women's political participation and representation in governance have long been taken as key indicators of the general level of public sector effectiveness and accountability in a country. When more women are involved in politics and leadership positions, women's rights, priorities, needs and interests are less likely to be ignored or silenced.

Significant progress has been made in advancing women's participation in holding elective office and in positions of leadership in

Far too many African women are trapped at the lower end of the spectrum of economic opportunities, which often perpetuates the same socio-economic status for their own families.

the public and private sectors. Some countries have seen the successful election of women to their parliaments and other elected offices, but existing social and political structures still proscribe women's full potential in helping to equally shape the national and local economic, social and political agenda.

In addition to making progress in politics, women have also made advances in leadership positions in such areas as the civil service, trade unions and the private sector, but here again progress in achieving gender equity is still lagging due to a combination of political, economic and social resistance to change.

In the private sector, the general perception that male enterprises out-perform female ones is not supported by data nor does it justify the gap in leadership. Although the trend is improving, the percentage of firms with a female top manager still ranges between 7 and 30 per cent. Narrowing the private sector leadership gender gap relies on increasing the pool of women with tertiary education in science and technology-related fields.

Peace processes are another principal ground for decision-making and for the exercise of power and influence. However, historically women's formal participation has been limited despite the profusion of peace agreements across the continent. In the last decade, women's roles in conflict resolution and peacebuilding have shifted considerably from when women could only informally impact negotiations for cessation of hostilities or peace agreements. There is a growing recognition that women should be an integral and formal part of any peace negotiations process, given women's role in securing and maintaining peace.

The role of legal and social norms in gender equality

Existing legal and social norms, and their interactions have a major effect on gender equality and women's empowerment. The underlying importance of legal and social norms cannot be overstated in such areas as access to economic services, health and education, as well as the role they play in influencing gender-focused violence, childhood marriage and other socio-cultural barriers to gender equality.

African states and regional bodies have put in place a wide array of legal norms, precedents and legislation promoting gender equality. The challenge is not in fine-tuning existing legal standards, but rather, in ensuring that standards are advocated, accepted and integrated into national laws and regulations, and then fully implemented and enforced. It is the gap between legal rights and expectations, on the one hand, and prevailing practices and behaviours embodied in social and cultural norms, on the other hand, that pose a fundamental challenge for accelerating gender equality and women's empowerment.

Many social norms have very important and positive roles in creating strong family and community bonds, as well as establishing conditions for trust and support in times of crisis and hardship. Other social norms, however, continue to have a negative impact on the attainment of gender equality, despite existing laws and standards. Such prevailing social norms and gender stereotypes that assign different standings, roles and privileges for women and men prevent progress towards gender equality. About one quarter of Africans did not embrace the concept of gender equality, i.e. they disagreed or strongly disagreed with the fundamental notion of equal rights between men and women. This calls for proactive awareness and advocacy on gender equality in Africa.

The impact of social norms that limit women has also been shown to have deleterious effects on men and boys, and communities as a whole, essentially holding everyone back from achieving higher human development and impeding societies from realizing their full development potential.

Policy and programme approaches to addressing gender inequality

African governments have used a range of policy and programme approaches to address gender inequality. These include broad

Closing gender gaps in public administration helps to ensure democratic governance, restore trust and confidence in public institutions, and accelerate the responsiveness of government policies and programmes.

The challenge is not fine-tuning existing legal standards, but rather, ensuring standards are advocated, accepted and fully implemented and enforced.

macro- and sectoral-level efforts that have sought to address gender inequality through a combination of policies and institutions. Examples include fiscal policy (including public expenditures and subsidies), legal and regulatory measures and set-aside programmes, as well as other targeted interventions. But the record of success is mixed, and there is ample room for expanding such efforts, both in scope and scale. In this regard, much can be learned from the experience of Latin America and Asia.

Most African countries have followed international practice by setting up institutions for the advancement of women. These new organizational mechanisms for gender issues have taken many forms, including thematic ministries or ministerial departments for women, designated in some countries as lead institutional mechanisms. Developing effective institutional models towards more equal societies must be understood as a shared responsibility across multiple ministries and involving the private sector and civil society.

African governments have begun using various kinds of social protection programmes (including cash transfer and subsidies) to promote gender equality and poverty reduction. Still, there is considerable room for expanding a number of cash transfer and social service programmes that would have a direct impact on improving women's economic and social well-being. These include paid maternal leave, provision of childcare services, and some form of income support or cash transfers for women's unpaid work, usually taking place in the home or in the farm field.

Gender-sensitive reviews of existing legislation in the areas of family law, land law, labour and employment law, and customary law are necessary to identify and remove ongoing gender discrimination.

Likewise, the legal environment within which women and men engage in society underscores the fact that more effective non-discriminatory labour institutions, family-friendly policies and work environment standards could contribute greatly towards reducing women's economic and social disadvantages. In an estimated 28 per

cent of African countries, customary law is considered a valid source of law – even if it violates constitutional provisions on non-discrimination or equality.

In order to better apply international and regional legal norms for gender equality, many African countries may therefore need to more fully articulate, implement and enforce existing laws, statutes and regulations that could have a profound impact on improving women's access to equal rights and entitlements. Reconciling national laws and regulations with customary laws and traditions remains a monumental challenge.

An agenda for action to accelerate gender equality

The 2016 Africa Human Development Report offers some key conclusions and overriding themes that provide a strategic framework and agenda for action aimed at a more results-oriented and comprehensive approach to addressing gender inequality. Four broad 'pathways' are suggested that offer policy and programme guidelines to accelerate gender equality and fully integrate gender into the broader human development agenda and help achieve the Sustainable Development Goals and the African Agenda 2063.

Pathway 1:
Supporting the adoption of legal reforms, policies and regulations to advance women's empowerment through the formulation and full implementation of a combination of laws and regulations, policies and programmes that provide equal opportunities for all, regardless of sex.

Pathway 2:
Supporting national capacities to promote and increase the participation and leadership of women in decision-making in the home, economy and society. In this regard, public and private sector institutions as well as civil society organizations (CSOs) should commit to implementing UNDP's Gender Equality Seal (GES) in Africa.

Pathway 3:

Supporting capacity to implement multi-sectoral approaches to mitigate the impacts of discriminatory health and education practices can generate collaboration across ministries and with the private sector and civil society.

Pathway 4:

Supporting women to gain ownership and management of economic and environmental assets can help tackle factors that propagate socio-economic exclusion, poverty and inequality.

With these four pathways in mind, there is an overriding strategic question facing African governments wishing to accelerate women's rights and entitlements: Assuming the political commitment to do so, how can African leaders and policy-makers more forcefully address gender inequalities in the face of other competing national priorities?

Due to the pressure on leaders and policy-makers to maintain the pace of economic growth, diversify the economy for integration into global markets, meet the rising demands of a growing middle class, address shocks and vulnerabilitys and meet national security concerns, policy-makers must take tough and often competing decisions on the use of scarce resources.

To provide some policy guidance for African leaders concerned with this ongoing dilemma, six strategic considerations are offered as an organizational framework for action in addressing gender inequality. This organizational framework coincides with the argument put forward that accelerating gender equality and women's empowerment simultaneously represents a practical operational approach for African governments to tackle the challenge of achieving the SDGs and move forward on the AU's Agenda 2063. To the extent that gender inequalities are addressed, then, in effect, progress will be made across the wide spectrum of development goals found in the SDGs. Addressing gender equality is not separate from addressing the SDGs.

From this perspective, the six strategic considerations are outlined below.

Using gender equality as an organizing policy lens for formulation, planning and implementation of the development agenda. It is a false assumption that giving higher priority to gender equality means giving lower priority to other development priorities. Focusing on gender issues is not a zero-sum choice, where choosing one priority comes at the expense of another. Whatever the policy objective – inclusive growth and economic diversification, revitalizing the agricultural sector, improving national health services, eradicating extreme poverty, tackling climate change – if 50 per cent of the population, that is, women and girls, are not benefitting equally from the policies and programmes, then the latter cannot be considered a success. Discarding this false assumption and addressing gender equality is no longer about 'adding' in special policies and programmes for women or having separate women's ministries or agencies, but, instead, ensuring that all policies and programmes are intended to achieve equal outcomes for both men and women.

Tackling destructive social norms directly. Reversing the social norms that impede women's and girls' equal opportunities will be a long-term and difficult process. Pushing to deconstruct harmful social norms and cultural barriers is no doubt a morally demanding, socially difficult and politically risky course of action, or more precisely, multiple and overlapping courses of actions. African leaders and policy-makers therefore need to understand the long-term nature of deconstructing harmful social norms and replacing them with positive social norms. In many instances, the approach will entail reconciling legal and social norms.

Using plans and budgets to prioritize gender equality. African governments will invariably need to identify and then implement a strategic set of policy and programme choices that are deemed priorities in the

Gender equality may in theory be mainstreamed in laws, policies, programmes and institutions, but the test of commitment is ultimately a function of resources made available and how effectively they are used.

Development, if not engendered, is endangered. All policies and programmes must be intended to achieve equal outcomes for both men and women.

national context, that have the highest likelihood of making important changes, that can work synergistically, and that have the best chance of being successfully implemented. The objective is to suggest that African governments must have a prioritization process for achieving gender equality given the tremendous needs and resource constraints facing each country. The task does not necessarily entail selecting and implementing a wide range of policy options, but instead, prioritizing, in an orderly and transparent process, among multiple (and often contending) policy options—all of which place competing demands on scarce public resources.

Three guiding questions are suggested for linking short- and long-term prioritization:

- What policies and programmes have the highest likelihood of improving the lives of women and bringing them into the economic mainstream through productive employment opportunities and improved social welfare?

- In what ways are the views and concerns of women, stakeholders and other recipients being factored into the decision-making process?

- In situations where resources are shifted from one programme or initiative to another, can the shift be justified in terms of improved economic and social outcomes for women and girls than would otherwise have been the case?

Strengthening adaptive policies and institutional capacities. Achieving gender equality and accelerating the pace of human development will require African governments to incorporate a commitment to a strong, proactive and responsible social framework that develops policies for both the public and private sectors – based on a long-term vision and leadership, shared norms and values, and rules and institutions that build trust and cohesion. At the same time, governments will need the capacity for flexibility and adaptation. In complex societies

such as in Africa, the outcome of any particular policy is inevitably uncertain. African governments will need to follow a governance framework that is pragmatic and able to problem-solve and adapt collectively and rapidly – as opposed to abandoning a course of action in the face of unintended effects.

Adding value to data for improved decision-making. For African governments to fully address gender inequalities and understand the outcomes of chosen policies and programmes, more robust data collection and monitoring systems will be required. Effective capacity in statistics and monitoring and evaluation is the 'lubricant' by which governments are able to perform as an adaptive state and undertake necessary policy change and mid-course corrections. Data collection and analysis should not be considered an afterthought, but rather a core function of governmental services, which require commensurate financial and political support.

Assessing capabilities for monitoring national development plans and budgets, and the SDGs, together with traditional economic and social statistics, is an imperative. This represents a window of opportunity for African governments to evaluate how their statistical agencies and line ministries can improve their data gathering, management and analysis functions in order to fully capture the gender implications of current policies and initiatives, and how, over time, they can be modified and improved.

Prioritizing regional and South-South cooperation. It is important to underline the importance of regional and South-South cooperation in designing and implementing gender-focused policies and initiatives. African countries have much to learn from each other – both what has worked and what has not. There are also many useful lessons that can be learned from the Asian and Latin American and Caribbean (LAC) experience. The focus of such cooperation should be on sharing tools, strategies and experiences across sectors, from large infrastructure projects to community-based interventions –

> Data collection and analysis should not be considered an afterthought, but rather a core function of governmental services, which require commensurate financial and political support.

all need to drive innovation, learning and upscaling. There is considerable scope for expanding cross-national training and study tours, secondment of staff and other kinds of experiential learning opportunities that place managers and policy-makers more directly in the fulcrum of on-the-ground change.

In summary, the report focuses on the continuing problem of gender equality facing African women and girls. A key conclusion is that gender equality is not achieved by having gender-specific ministries or women-only projects and programmes (although they can be important), but rather, by tackling gender equality as a wide-ranging effort across multiple sectors that engage all segments of society. The report further emphasizes the inter-linkages between the social well-being of women and their economic opportunities for more productive lives. Underpinning all of these efforts will be the necessary but understandably difficult task of breaking down harmful social norms and cultural barriers that have a particularly serious impact on women and their families.

Another conclusion is that accelerating gender equality will entail highly collaborative efforts involving not only national and local governments, but also non-governmental organizations, the private sector, advocacy groups and effective community-based organizations.

Finally, it will be important for African governments to articulate time-bound benchmarks to measure progress, make adjustments as needed, and maintain a national vision of the important ramifications that achieving gender equality has for the entire society. The peoples of Africa must hold themselves and their governments accountable for making progress on improvements within a sufficient timeframe that does not dilute the urgent need for action. The 15-year timeframe of the SDGs and the first ten-year implementation plan of Agenda 2063 represent a viable timeframe to which African governments have already pledged themselves.

Breaking down harmful social norms and cultural barriers that have a particularly serious impact on women and their families is pivotal.

Gender Equality is essential for human development in Africa

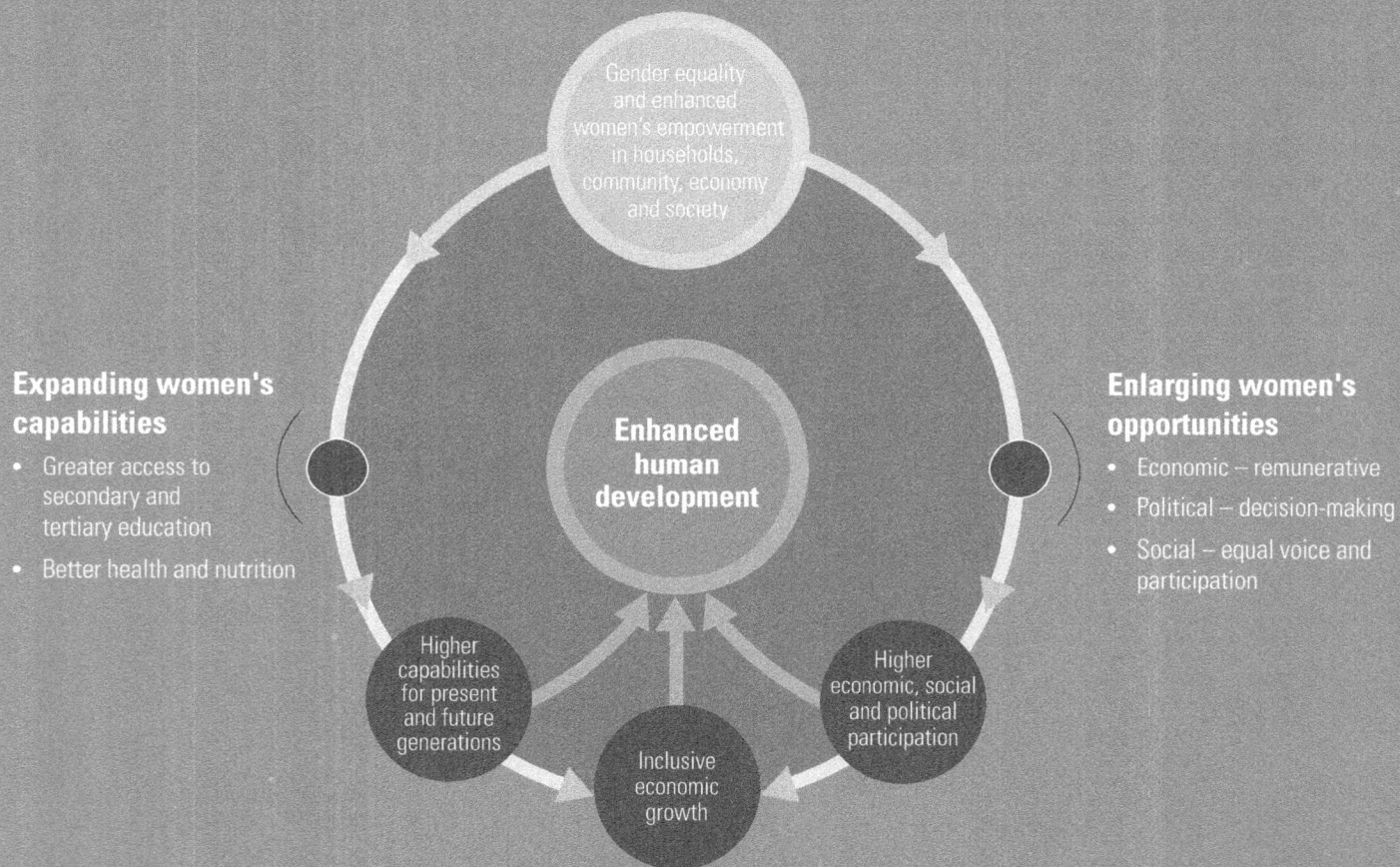

Gender equality and enhanced women's empowerment in households, community, economy and society

Enhanced human development

Expanding women's capabilities

- Greater access to secondary and tertiary education
- Better health and nutrition

Higher capabilities for present and future generations

Inclusive economic growth

Enlarging women's opportunities

- Economic – remunerative
- Political – decision-making
- Social – equal voice and participation

Higher economic, social and political participation

Chapter 1

Introduction

Chapter 1
Introduction

The 2016 Africa Human Development Report (AfHDR) focuses on the continuing problem of gender inequality facing the women and girls of the Africa region. At the national, regional and international levels, there is growing recognition that as African women attain higher measures of economic and social well-being, all of society benefits. Improvements in women's and girls' education, health and workplace opportunities result in economic and social progress, and a leap in productivity for an entire country and for the Africa region as a whole. Despite this growing understanding, removing inequalities experienced by women has not kept pace. Significant gaps between men's and women's opportunities remain a major challenge as well as a severe impediment to achieving structural economic and social transformation, which is the goal of all African countries.

'There is a growing recognition that as African women attain higher measures of economic and social well-being, all of society benefits. Despite this understanding, removing inequalities experienced by women has not kept pace.

It is important to recall that widespread recognition that more gender equality promotes human development is not recent. Gender equality and women's empowerment have been a concern of the international community dating back at least three decades, and even longer when declarations on human rights are included. International and regional declarations on gender equality and women empowerment abound. The goal of reducing gender inequality has held a prominent place on the international development agenda. Global attention to the issue of gender inequality was reflected in Millennium Development Goal (MDG) 3, which provided direction for governments focusing on education, employment and political participation. More recently, Sustainable Development Goal (SDG) 5 calls on the international community to "achieve gender equality and empower all women and girls". In addition, many of the other SDGs have a strong focus on inequality, including ending poverty and hunger, and assuring access to clean water and sanitation, affordable and clean energy, meaningful workplace opportunities and reduced gender inequality.

With this understanding, international and regional statements of solidarity for women's empowerment must be more quickly translated into concrete actions on the ground. While progress has been made in certain areas and within many countries, the pace of change has been slower than hoped and more inconsistent than desired. The objective of this report is therefore to explore where and how progress in gender equality has been made and how best to accelerate the pace of gender advancement in Africa. This report sets out to examine this dilemma of limited success in narrowing the gender gap and exploring ways that African governments can more forcefully confront the gender equality challenge.

This report's focus on gender equality comes at a time of tremendous change across the Continent. The optimism of double-digit economic growth in some African countries only a few years ago has been dampened by the recent global downturn in demand for many commodities, such as oil, gas and minerals, upon which many African economies depend. The economic gains of the first decade of this century have been notably impacted. Political unrest and civil discord continue to affect many countries in North, East and Central Africa. The Ebola epidemic of 2014 in West Africa demonstrated how vulnerable and fragile African societies can be to unexpected shocks, which have set back economic and social advances in the affected countries of Guinea, Liberia, and Sierra Leone. At this writing, drought in the Sahel and the Horn of Africa, and a heat wave in Southern Africa are causing major hardships for the peoples of the

FIGURE 1.1

Gender equality and enhanced women's empowerment in households, communities, economies and society

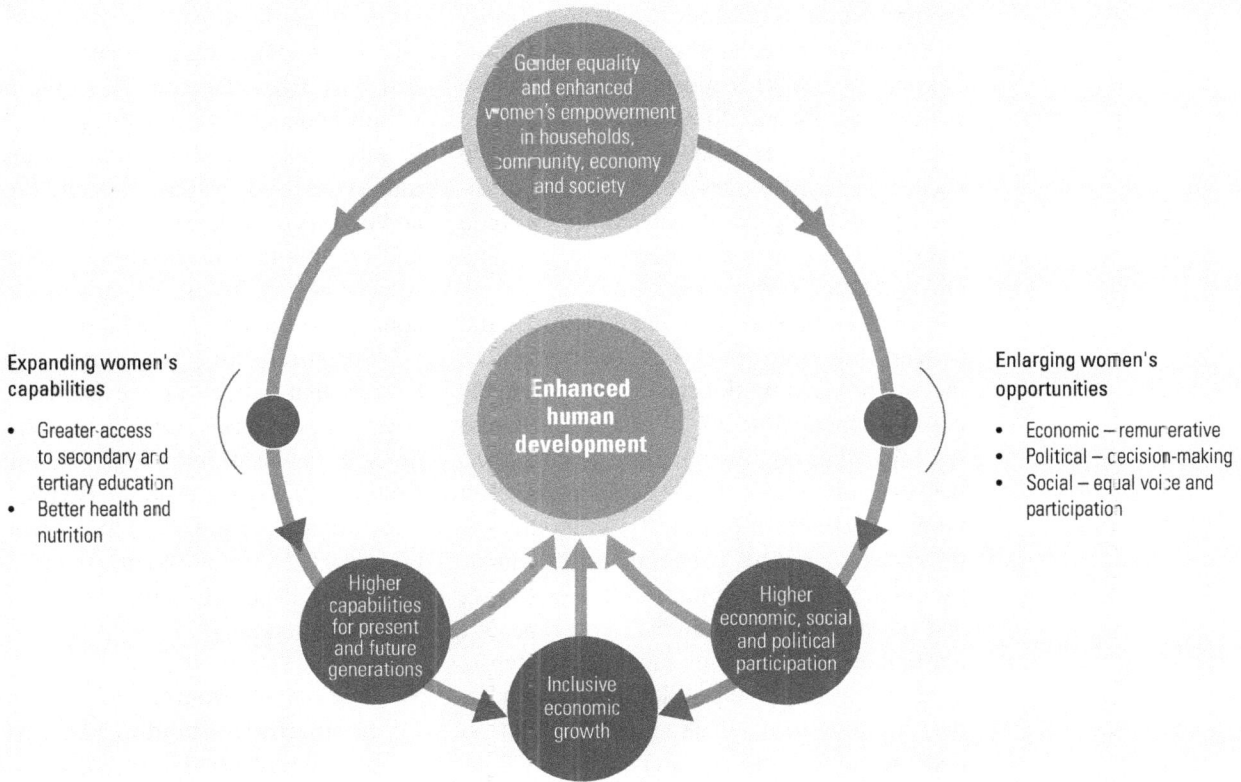

Source: Contributed by Selim Jahan, Human Development Report Office (HDRO), 2016.

affected countries. Similarly, the fight against terrorism and religious extremism can have devastating effects on civic and social order. All of these crises have significant gender dimensions because women inadvertently bear the brunt of the adjustment given the socially constructed roles they play in providing food and care for the young, sick and aged while dealing with lost livelihoods, health and security-related threats.

These recent circumstances require more concerted attention to addressing women's inequality. Greater focus on gender equality and empowerment can mitigate the negative impacts of such events by distributing economic and social benefits across the entire population as part of the structural transformation process, and not by simply improving women's well-being in isolation

from the overall transformation being sought. Using gender equality as an organizing policy lens not only promotes inclusive economic, social and political partcipation for the current generation, but also leads to high capabilities for present and future generations, as illustrated in figure 1.1. This is a long-recognized argument for gender equality and remains a key message of this report.

Human development and gender equality: contextual issues

Before turning to the progress and specific challenges of gender equality in Africa, it may be useful to first establish the policy context and conceptual underpinnings of human development and gender equality.

Since the concept of human development was first introduced by UNDP in 1990, the term has gained widespread acceptance. 'Human development' was formally defined in the first Human Development Report (HDR) as "a process of enlarging people's capabilities and choices". The most important of these wide-ranging capabilities are to live a long and healthy life, to be educated, and to have access to the resources needed for a decent standard of living. Additional choices include political freedom, guaranteed human rights and personal self-respect. In later reports and in work outside the United Nations,[1] the concept has been refined and elaborated to include broadening the choices and strengthening the capabilities of all individuals. An important contrast was thus established between, on the one hand, the long-standing view of economic prosperity, embodied in the measurement of economic achievement by gross national income (GNI) per capita, and on the other hand, human development, i.e. human achievements measured in terms of capabilities – what people can do and what they are able to do. This wider approach to understanding economic and social development is now a well-recognized tenet of the international community.

Another accepted principle is that human development and human rights are closely intertwined. The expansion of human choices and capabilities, and the enjoyment of human rights for women and men are inextricably linked. Human development is thus built on a commitment to human dignity and freedom that has a human rights-based foundation (UNDP, 2000). Without such a foundation, equity and social justice as well as the effective use of institutions, capacities and resources for promoting human development will be constrained.

In examining human development and gender equality, the next chapter will explore how Africa has fared over time by using the human development indicators that account for inequalities between male and female outcomes, including the Gender Development Index (GDI) and the more recent Gender Inequality Index (GII) introduced by UNDP in 2010. Beyond the correlation between indicators of human development and gender equality, this report also reviews the challenge of gender equality in the context of the complex web of socio-cultural, economic, political and legal barriers that have a direct bearing on advancing gender equality – factors that vary from one country to the next and within countries. Achieving gender equality is ultimately based on family- and community-level decisions that are supported and enforced by national-level policies, laws and programmes in the context of changing societal norms. Box 1.1 elucidates some basic concepts on gender-related issues.

More specifically, what are some of the lessons that can be drawn from a growing body of evidence that demonstrates the linkage between human development and gender equality in Africa? Below are five trends that have impacted and will continue to impact on progress in gender equality, which are discussed in more detail in subsequent chapters.

- **The recent dynamics of social and economic transformation have resulted in significant strides in Africa's human development**. Africa as a whole has seen more than a decade of robust economic growth and increasing integration into the world economy. This growth has resulted in more concerted attention to sound economic and political governance as well as the expansion of social investments. This has led to notable strides in human progress and human rights, including women's rights, despite the recent economic slowdown in some countries.

- **Africa's transformation has not been pervasive across national economies**. Economic and social transformation is leaving many behind, with large disparities at the regional, sub-regional and national levels in addition to a significant gap between outcomes for women and men. Until the ongoing transformation reaches all segments of society, inequalities could be exacerbated. Similarly, continuing gender inequality has measurable economic, social and development costs that can further impede Africa's transformation.

- **There is a growing recognition that gender equality has multiplier effects across the spectrum of development from health, education and labour markets to greater productivity, resilience and intergenerational mobility**. Seeking to achieve gender equality is not only the right policy, but also an economically and socially sound one. In addition, there is also a track record of successful initiatives and programmes in many countries. Scaling up and improving on these foundational initiatives is the overriding challenge. For most African countries, this challenge is moving beyond codified legal gender equality to gender equity and substantive gender equality so that women are practically and tangibly benefitting from these rights through corresponding actions to level the playing field.

- **The next 15 years represent a time of either tremendous opportunity or tremendous peril for African countries**. During the 15 years of the SDGs, significant opportunities for growth in human development from greater economic diversification and structural transformation are possible if based on national efforts to make growth and transformation fully inclusive and gender-neutral. Such an approach is much broader and more comprehensive than simply focusing on SDG 5 on gender equality. Through a broader focus, African governments will be much better positioned to address the expected changes in global development financing, deepen the benefits from democracy and effective governance, and leverage global trends from technology change and connectivity. They will also more likely be capable of addressing the still-evolving implications of climate change. Conversely, the African countries that fail to make concerted efforts for the transformation process to be more

inclusive and gender-neutral are less likely to make the transition to strong economic growth and full integration in the global economy, and lag behind progress achieved by other countries in the Africa region.

Methodology for report preparation

This report adopts a 'political economy' perspective to understand the way that ideas, resources and power are conceptualized, negotiated and implemented by different social groups in relation to gender inequality – whether in the workplace, the marketplace, or at home. 'Political economy analysis' (UNDP, 2012c) is concerned with the interaction of political and economic processes in a society, including the distribution of power and wealth between groups and individuals,

---

BOX 1.1

Definitions of some basic gender-related issues

Sex refers to the biological and physiological characteristics that define men and women.

Gender refers to the socially constructed roles, behaviours, activities and attributes that a given society considers appropriate for men and women.

Gender equality denotes women having the same opportunities in life as men, including the ability to participate in the public sphere.

Gender equity denotes the equivalence in life outcomes for women and men, recognizing their different needs and interests.

Gender division of labour is the socially determined ideas and practices that define what roles and activities are deemed appropriate for women and men.

Gender mainstreaming is an organizational strategy to bring a gender perspective to all aspects of an institution's policy and activities through building gender capacity and accountability equality.

Source: Reeves and Baden, 2000.

There is a growing recognition that gender equality has multiplier effects across the spectrum of development from health, education and labour markets to greater productivity, resilience and intergenerational mobility.

and the processes that create, sustain and transform these relationships over time. This definition recognizes that power is essentially about relationships – between the state, social groups and individuals, or between the state, market forces and civil society.

The preparation of this Africa HDR has been a highly collaborative effort between the UNDP Regional Bureau for Africa and many different agencies, institutions and individuals, who are mentioned in the Acknowledgements. Here it is relevant to note that the report has been prepared in close collaboration with the African Union Commission. As a result, it not only focuses on sub-Saharan Africa, but also includes the Arab states of North Africa.

The report preparation process included in-depth quantitative research and analysis, a qualitative interactive study, and consultations with development practitioners, women and youth organizations. The nine background papers prepared for the report deepened the evidence on the human development costs of gender disparities in work, markets, leadership and social outcomes. These studies used country benchmarking and regional analysis to identify development areas, examples of successful reforms and proposed institutional responses. This analysis was complemented by qualitative analysis of the role of social norms and institutions in perpetuating the cycle of gender inequality using in-country investigative interviews, focus group discussions and country case studies as well as an Africa-wide online survey.

These qualitative and quantitative findings were discussed, validated and complemented by regional consultations in Addis Ababa and Dakar, as well as two policy dialogues in Lusaka and Johannesburg, in close collaboration with the African Union, United Nations organizations with participation from civil society organizations, regional economic institutions, and representatives from women and youth organizations across Africa. These debates have created a network of change agents who will contribute to advocacy and the implementation of the policy agenda from this report. The report has benefitted from the oversight of a diverse, high-level Advisory Group with representation from the African Union Commission, regional institutions, civil society and academia, an internal oversight group with experts from across UNDP, and an external readers' group with representatives from United Nations agencies.

Annex B contains a technical note on methodology covering the report's preparation.

Report organization

This report is organized in eight chapters in order to examine the progress towards gender equality and accelerate its pace as well as the remaining challenges. Following the introductory chapter is **Chapter 2**, which reviews current progress in African human development using indicators that UNDP has constructed to capture various aspects of human development, including gender inequality. The chapter offers a general assessment of human development trends over time using the Human Development Index (HDI), the Inequality-adjusted Human Development Index (IHDI), the Multidimensional Poverty Index (MPI), the Gender Development Index (GDI) and the Gender Inequality Index (GII).

Chapter 3 focuses on the social dimensions of gender inequality. These data sources – different from the various human development indicators per se – include social trends involving health and education as well as other welfare determinants of women's equality and empowerment.

Chapter 4 turns to women in the workplace and economic decision-making. The chapter explores how women are faring in accessing economic assets and participating in labour markets, as well as other determinants of economic decision-making.

Chapter 5 explores the role of women's political voice and leadership in advancing gender equality. The chapter looks at women in African politics, government service and trade unions, as well as in leadership positions in the private sector.

> This report adopts a 'political economy' perspective to understand the way that ideas, resources and power are conceptualized, negotiated and implemented by different social groups in relation to gender inequality

Chapter 6 reviews both legal and social norms, and the ways they interact to affect gender equality and women's empowerment. The underlying importance of legal and social norms cannot be overstated in such areas as access to economic services, health and education, as well as their role in influencing gender-focused violence, childhood marriage and other socio-cultural barriers to gender equality.

Chapter 7 examines the policy and programme approaches adopted by African governments to address gender inequality. The chapter looks at how, at the broad macro- and sectoral level, African governments have sought to address gender inequality through a combination of policies and institutions. Attention is given to cross-regional comparisons with Asia and Latin America and the Caribbean (LAC). Examples include fiscal policy and public expenditures, legal and regulatory measures, subsidies and set-aside programmes, as well as other targeted interventions.

The final **Chapter 8** offers some key conclusions and overriding themes that provide a strategic framework and agenda for action aimed at a more results-oriented and comprehensive approach to addressing gender inequality.

A number of annexes have also been included that provide supporting data, summaries of specialized topics, as well as references.

Human development levels
in Africa

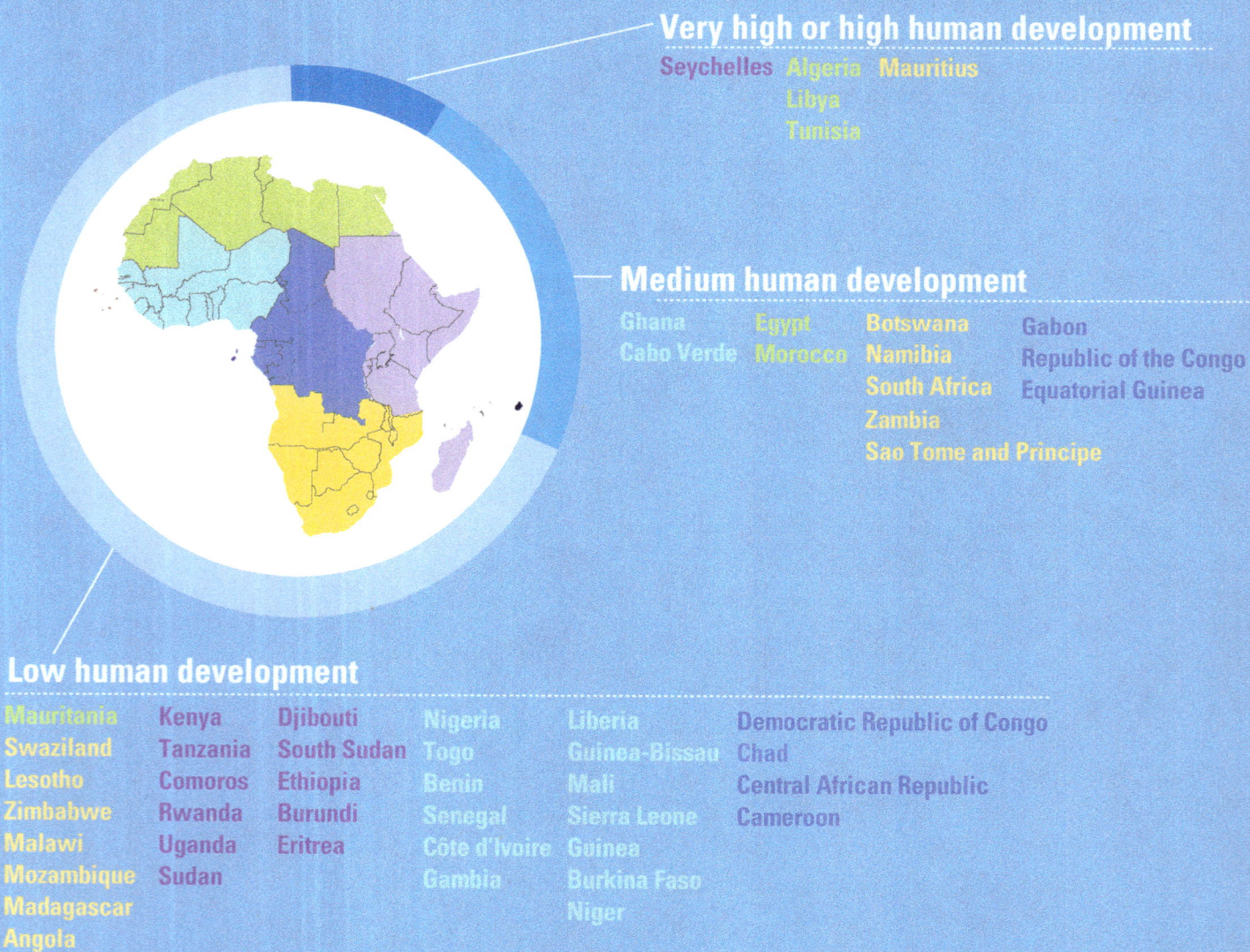

Very high or high human development

Seychelles   Algeria   Mauritius
Libya
Tunisia

Medium human development

Ghana   Egypt   Botswana   Gabon
Cabo Verde   Morocco   Namibia   Republic of the Congo
                South Africa   Equatorial Guinea
                Zambia
                Sao Tome and Principe

Low human development

Mauritania	Kenya	Djibouti	Nigeria	Liberia	Democratic Republic of Congo
Swaziland	Tanzania	South Sudan	Togo	Guinea-Bissau	Chad
Lesotho	Comoros	Ethiopia	Benin	Mali	Central African Republic
Zimbabwe	Rwanda	Burundi	Senegal	Sierra Leone	Cameroon
Malawi	Uganda	Eritrea	Côte d'Ivoire	Guinea	
Mozambique	Sudan		Gambia	Burkina Faso	
Madagascar				Niger	
Angola					

Chapter 2

Review of Africa's Progress in Human Development and Gender Equality

Chapter 2
Review of Africa's Progress in Human Development and Gender Equality

This chapter reviews the status and trends of African countries using UNDP's different human development indicators, including comparisons with other developing regions. Particular focus is given to using the specific human development indicators capturing gender development and gender inequality.

The concept of human development, first introduced by UNDP in 1990, has undergone several modifications and refinement over the years. UNDP's human development indicators have become a widely accepted tool used by governments, civil society, researchers, analysts, and the donor community for estimating a country's economic and social progress and making cross-country comparisons of relative progress on human development.

As with any quantitative calculation, the indicators are not without their limitations. This led UNDP to develop a set of complementary indices in order to better capture the notion of human development from different perspectives and adjust for shortfalls found in some of the indices. Currently, there are five indices: the first and most commonly cited index, the Human Development Index (HDI), which ranks 188 countries; the Inequality adjusted Human Development Index (IHDI) – 151 countries; the Gender Development Index (GDI) – 163 countries; the Gender Inequality Index (GII) – 159 countries; and the Multidimensional Poverty Index (MPI) – 91 countries. For purposes of this report, data and comparisons are taken from the 2015 Human Development Report based on country data available as of 15 April 2015.

In this context, this chapter turns to examine Africa's development progress using UNDP's different human development indicators. The analysis focuses on using the indices to show trends in African human development over time and to offer cross-regional comparisons. The last section of the chapter looks specifically at the GDI, the GII and other human development data that shed more light on gender equality and women's empowerment.

For purposes of the analysis that follows, the review of human development indicators breaks the region down into five sub-regions – North, East, West, Central and Southern Africa – in order to facilitate more useful comparisons.[2]

Overview of African Human Development

The Human Development Index

The HDI is a summary measure for assessing long-term progress in three basic dimensions of human development: a long and healthy life, access to knowledge and a decent standard of living. A long and healthy life is measured by life expectancy. Access to knowledge is measured by: (i) mean years of education among the adult population, which is the average number of years of education received in a life-time by people aged 25 years and older; and (ii) expected years of schooling for children of school-entry age, which is the total number of years of schooling a child of school-entry age can expect to receive if prevailing patterns of age-specific enrolment rates stay the same throughout the child's life. Standard of living is measured by gross national income (GNI) per capita expressed in constant 2011 international dollars, converted using purchasing power parity (PPP) rates.

TABLE 2.1

Global HDI comparisons by region

Region	HDI mean value by Region 1990	HDI mean value by Region 2000	HDI mean value by Region 2014	Change in HDI value (1990-2014)
East Asia and the Pacific	0.516	0.593	0.710	1.34
Eastern Europe and Central Asia	0.651	0.665	0.748	0.58
Latin America and the Caribbean	0.625	0.684	0.748	0.75
South Asia	0.437	0.503	0.607	1.38
Africa	0.426	0.449	0.524	1.09

Source: Compiled by the AfHDR Team.

The following tables and figures used in this chapter are derived using data from the 2015 HDR. Table 2.1 compares the Africa region with the other regions around the world. The comparison is based on the HDI mean value of the 53 African countries used in this Report's analysis compared with the HDI mean values of the developing and emerging market regions between 1990 and 2014. Africa has shown one of the best improvement in HDI between 1990 and 2014 but also has the lowest average levels of human development compared to other regions in the world. However, there are also large variations within Africa, as discussed below.

Annex H shows the individual country HDI values, rankings and trends, which vary considerably from country to country. Part of the African HDI shortfall compared to other regions can be explained by the large number of African countries – a total of 36 – found in the *Low Human Development* group. No African countries are found in the *Very High Human Development* group, which consists of the top 49 countries by rank, with Norway, Australia, Switzerland and Denmark being the top four. Five African countries (out of a total of 55 countries worldwide) are found in the *High Human Development* group. Twelve African countries (out of a total of 39 countries worldwide) are found in the *Medium Human Development* group. And as noted above, 36 African countries out of 44 total worldwide are found in the *Low Human*

Development group. In the global ranking, African countries hold the bottom 19 places out of the lowest 20 rankings.

In addition to this 'snapshot' of African countries' HDI values and rankings from the latest global HDR, Annex H shows the HDI trends over time, including data points from 1990 up to the most recent calculations using 2014 data. Figure 2.1 highlights the percentage changes in HDI values between 2000 and 2014 for the 20 African countries with the largest positive change in value. This list of 20 countries is instructive because 17 countries are classified in the *Low Human Development* group of countries, which suggests that many countries are making significant progress in human development even though they remain in the *Low Human Development* category. Only three countries in figure 2.1 fall into the *Medium Human Development* category – Zambia, Botswana and Republic of the Congo. Figure 2.2 shows the average annual HDI growth rates of African countries within the different HDI categories over different timeframes. It is interesting to note that the African countries in the *Low Human Development* group showed the largest changes in 2000-2010 and again from 2010-2014. The figure also shows African HDI growth rates in comparison with all developing countries, suggesting that African countries have generally kept up with, if not surpassed, changes in HDI growth for all developing countries as a whole.

FIGURE 2.1

Top 20 African countries with highest percentage change in HDI values, 2000-2014

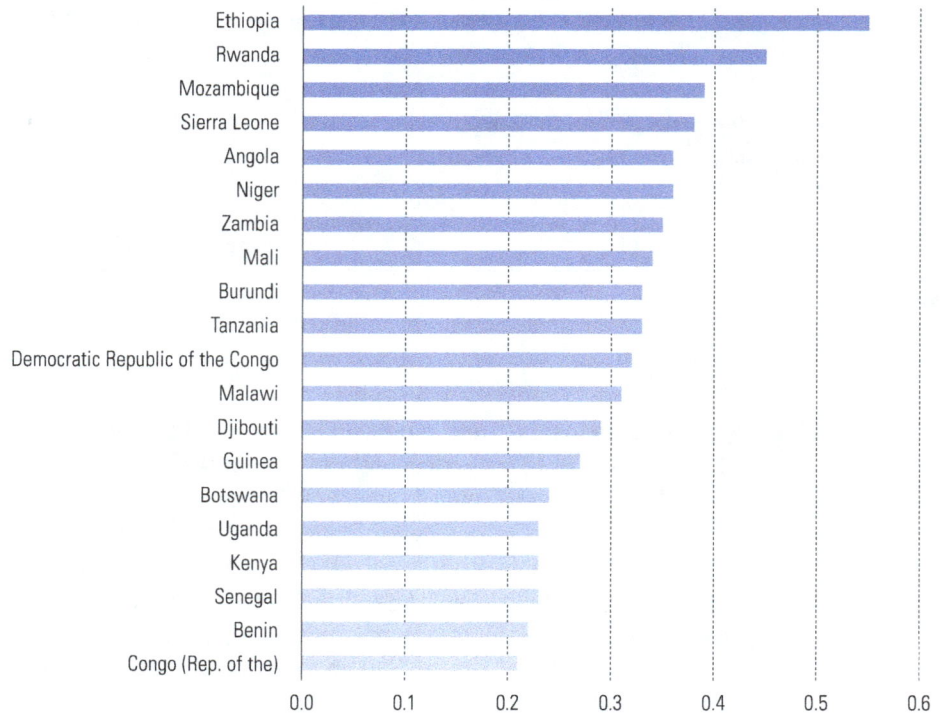

Source: Compiled by the AfHDR Team.

FIGURE 2.2

Average annual HDI growth rates, by human development group, 1990-2014

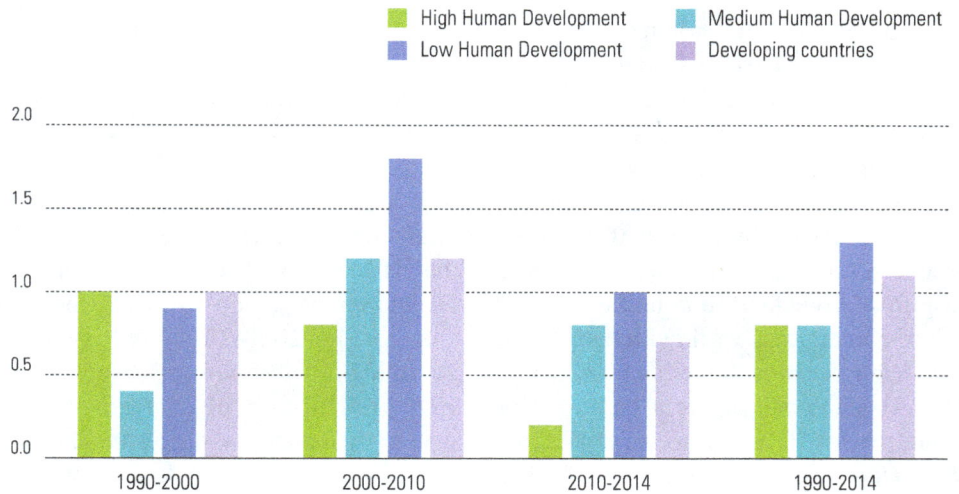

Source: Compiled by the AfHDR Team.

Table 2.2 is summary table of the average values of each of the five sub-regions. It highlights the considerable differences in HDI values among the African sub-regions and within the sub-regions. As noted in the table, North Africa is significantly above the African HDI mean, and even with Mauritania included, is above South Asia in a global regional comparison. Southern Africa is the only other sub-region above the African regional mean HDI value. As would be expected, there are also considerable variations in HDI values within sub-regions. In East

Africa, for example, Seychelles and Kenya have HDI values of 0.772 and 0.548, respectively, compared to Burundi and Eritrea of 0.400 and 0.391, respectively – both well below the African average. Similar comparisons are noted in the other sub-regions, such as Cabo Verde (0.646) and Niger (0.348) in West Africa, and Gabon (0.684) and Central African Republic (0.350) in Central Africa.

It is also instructive to compare changes in HDI values over time by region. Figure 2.3 shows changes in HDI values for different time periods dating back to 1990. In addition,

TABLE 2.2

Average HDI value by sub-region

Sub-region	HDI Value 1990	HDI Value 2000	HDI value 2014	Change in HDI value, 1990-2014 (%)
North Africa	0.533	0.613	0.668	20.209
East Africa	0.337	0.423	0.497	32.193
West Africa	0.333	0.352	0.461	27.766
Central Africa	0.453	0.439	0.507	10.651
Southern Africa	0.481	0.478	0.570	15.614
Mean (average) HDI value for the Africa Region	0.426	0.449	0.524	18.702

Source: Computed by the AfHDR Team.

FIGURE 2.3

Change in HDI by region: 1990-2014 (average annual %)

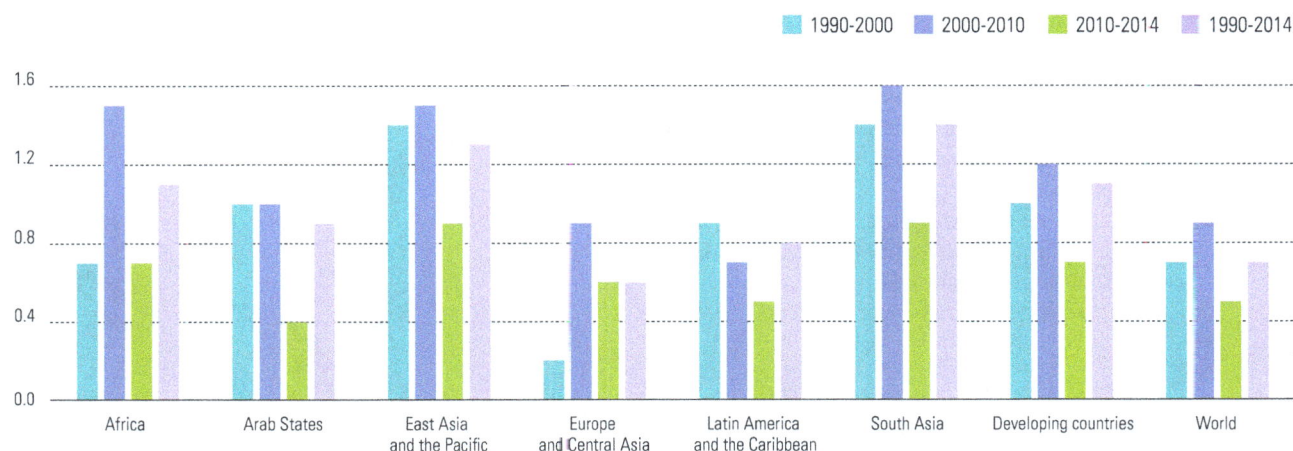

Source: Compiled by the AfHDR Team.

FIGURE 2.4

IHDI loss from HDI from highest to lowest values (overall loss %)

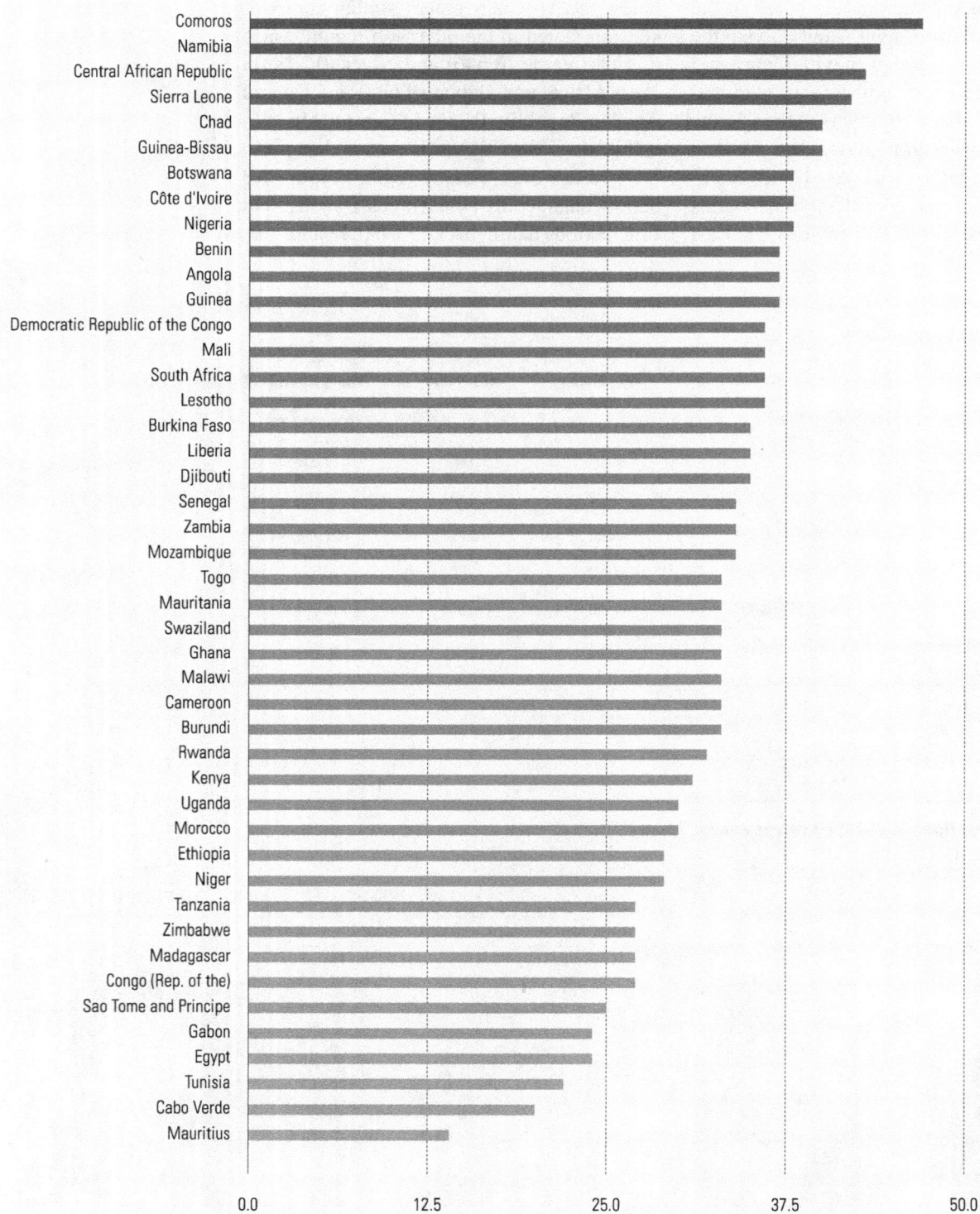

Source: Compiled by AfHDR Team from UNDP, 2015.

TABLE 2.3

IHDI comparisons by Region

Region	Human Development Index (HDI)	Inequality-adjusted Human Development Index (IHDI)	Overall loss in human development (from inequality) %
Sub-Saharan Africa	0.52	0.35	33
South Asia	0.61	0.43	29
Arab States	0.69	0.51	25
Latin America and the Caribbean	0.75	0.57	24
East Asia and the Pacific	0.71	0.57	19
East Europe and Central Asia	0.75	0.65	13

Source: Compiled by the AfHDR Team.

the Africa Region has made progress at a faster rate than Latin America and the Caribbean (LAC), the Arab States, Europe and Central Asia, and developing countries as a whole. For the 2000-2010 period, Africa's change in HDI was equivalent to the rate of change in East Asia and the Pacific, just behind South Asia and well above the average for all developing countries.

Evidence from this report provides some illumination on structural factors impinging on progress on HDI in Africa. Reduction in adolescent birth rate, increase in female population with at least secondary school education and expansion of female labour participation help to accelerate HDI. See Annex M.

The Inequality-adjusted HDI

The HDI is an average measure of basic human development achievements in a country. Like all averages, the HDI masks inequality in the distribution of human development across the population at the country level. UNDP's 2010 HDR introduced the IHDI, which takes into account inequality in all three dimensions of the HDI by discounting each dimension's average value according to its level of inequality. The IHDI is basically the HDI discounted for inequalities. The loss in human development due to inequality is given by the difference between the HDI and the IHDI, and can be expressed as a percentage. As inequality in a country increases, the loss in human development also increases.

The table in Annex I shows the IHDI ranking for the countries of the Africa region and provides useful insights into the stark inequality – both male and female – that exists in many African countries. Of the 53 countries listed, only 20 countries show positive gains from their HDI values, another eight countries have insufficient data to make a calculation, and two countries showed no net change, indicating that 23 countries had negative differences in their HDI values. In this regard, countries with higher HDI values do not necessarily fare better than countries with lower HDI values. For example, Botswana, South Africa and Namibia are three of the top four countries with the highest negative differences with their HDI values, 23, 15 and 25, respectively due to higher inequality in these countries.

On the positive side, Tunisia (22), Ethiopia (7), Uganda (6), Republic of the Congo (6) and Sao Tome and Principe (6) show the largest gains in HDI value. In addition, several countries achieved gains of four per cent or higher, including Cabo Verde (5), United Republic of Tanzania (4), Madagascar (4), Rwanda (4), Zimbabwe (4) and Burundi (5). Addressing inequality in education, health and job opportunities helps to accelerate human development in Africa.

TABLE 2.4

The Multidimensional Poverty Index

African countries with the highest and lowest population percentage living in multidimensional poverty

Country	MPI: Intensity of deprivation (%)	Population near multidimensional poverty (%)	Population in severe multidimensional poverty (%)
Niger	65	5.9	73.5
South Sudan	61.7	8.5	69.6
Chad	62.7	8.8	67.6
Ethiopia	60.9	6.7	67
Burkina Faso	61.3	7.6	63.8
Somalia	61.1	8.3	63.6
Guinea-Bissau	61.6	10.5	58.4
Mali	58.2	10.8	55.9
Zimbabwe	44.1	29.3	7.8
Swaziland	43.5	20.5	7.4
Morocco	44.3	12.6	4.9
Gabon	43.4	19.9	4.4
South Africa	39.6	17.1	1.3
Egypt	37.4	5.6	0.4
Tunisia	39.3	3.2	0.2
Libya	37.5	6.3	0.1

Source: Compiled by the AfHDR Team from UNDP, 2015.

In comparing the HDI and IHDI values, it is also instructive to note the ratio of these two values for each of the different human development groups. For the Medium Human Development group, the mean difference is 30.0 per cent; for the Low Human Development group, the mean difference is 35.5 per cent. (There is no computation for the High Human Development countries for lack of sufficient data.) Figure 2.4 captures the loss in HDI when adjusted for inequality.

With respect to disparities in HDI-adjusted inequality, it is useful to show comparisons across different regions. Although regional aggregations must be treated with care, table 2.3 is instructive in showing that the loss in IHDI is greatest in Africa (33 per cent), and at the same time, the Region's HDI mean value is the lowest.

The Multidimensional Poverty Index (MPI), introduced in UNDP's 2010 HDR, measures poverty by identifying multiple deprivations in the same households in education, health and living standards.[3]

The ten African countries with the highest percentage of their population in multi-dimensional poverty are all low human development countries. Yet, not all countries with the lowest proportion of the population near or in severe multidimensional poverty are in the high human development category. Table 2.4 provides a computation of the eight African countries with the highest percentage of their population who are near multi-dimensional poverty and in severe poverty, and the eight countries with the lowest per cent of their population in severe multidimensional poverty. Annex 6 shows the MPI rankings for all African countries for which data were available.

Table 2.4 suggests that countries with the highest MPI scores – for example, Niger, South Sudan, Chad and Ethiopia – are note-worthy for the small percentage of near poor compared to the percentage of those in severe deprivation. There is a strong correlation between HDI and MPI - 0.71. Almost all countries with an MPI of 50 per cent and above fall into low HDI group. For the African countries scoring lowest on the MPI, such as Libya, Tunisia, Egypt and South Africa, most of the deprivation is found in the group near multi-dimensional poverty, with a much smaller percentage found in severe deprivation. Countries with severe deprivation should focus more on system-wide social protection, while those with deprivation around near multidimensional poverty should focus on managing vulnerability – social protection targeted at people near the MPI cut-off line. The existence of a high correlation between high levels of deprivation and low values across both the HDI and IHDI measures is further confirmed in Table 2.5. This tends to suggest that frontally tackling severe MPI is critical to addressing HDI and IHDI in the Continent.

As the newest of the HD indicators, the MPI is an important complementary tool in trying to capture the many dimensions of human development. As additional data become available from more countries, the value of the MPI will grow proportionally.

Gender-specific Human Development Indicators

This section now examines the two gender-related HD indicators, the Gender Development Index (GDI) and the Gender Inequality Index (GII). The GDI was first introduced by UNDP in 1995, and the GII, in 2010.

The Gender Development Index

The GDI measures differences between male and female achievements in three basic dimensions of human development: (i) health, measured by female and male life expectancy at birth; (ii) education, measured by female and male expected years of schooling for children, and female and male mean years of schooling for adults ages 25 and older; and (iii) equitable command over economic resources, measured by female and male estimated earned income.

The GDI reveals that, on average, women in sub-Saharan Africa achieve 87 per cent of male human development outcomes. The region performs better than South Asia and Arab States, but is among the poorest performers. Annex K provides the GDI for all African countries and by sub-region. Table 2.6 shows the GDI values by region, in which sub-Saharan Africa has a higher GDI value than both the Arab States Region and the South Asia Region, but lower than the other three regions.

Do countries with a better GDI also tend to be countries with higher HDI? There is no clear-cut answer, since the GDI measures of women's and men's outcomes are the same, but countries with a lower HDI could have better distribution between both sexes.

In addition, gender gaps in income per capita contribute to lower achievement of human development by females. On average, African women living in countries with lower levels of gender inequality in income tend to achieve higher levels of human development than African men (30 countries). For countries with low gender inequality in income and lower female-to-male HDI ratios, the implication is that there is higher inequality in education and health outcomes, which cancels the benefit of more equal distribution income. Countries in this category include: Democratic Republic of the Congo, Sierra Leone, Togo, Central African Republic, Guinea, Liberia and Chad. For six countries with high female-to-male HDI and high gender inequality income, the gap in income inequality seems to be overcome by more equal distribution in health and education outcomes. These include Egypt, Tunisia, Mauritius and Libya.

TABLE 2.5

Correlation among HDI, IHDI and MPI

	MPI	Population in severe MPI
HDI	-0.838	-0.823
IHDI	-0.785	-0.758
Loss in HDI values	0.369	0.304

Source: Computed from UNDP 2015 Human Development Report.

TABLE 2.6

Gender Development Index values by region, 2014

Region	Human Development Index (HDI) value		Gender Development Index value (female HDI value/male HDI value)
	Female	Male	
Arab States	0.611	0.719	0.849
East Asia and the Pacific	0.692	0.730	0.948
East Europe and Central Asia	0.719	0.760	0.945
Latin America and the Caribbean	0.736	0.754	0.976
South Asia	0.525	0.655	0.801
Sub-Saharan Africa	0.480	0.550	0.872

Source: UNDP 2015 Human Development Report.

FIGURE 2.5

The Gender Development Index (female/male HDI) and income gap (female/male GNI per capita)

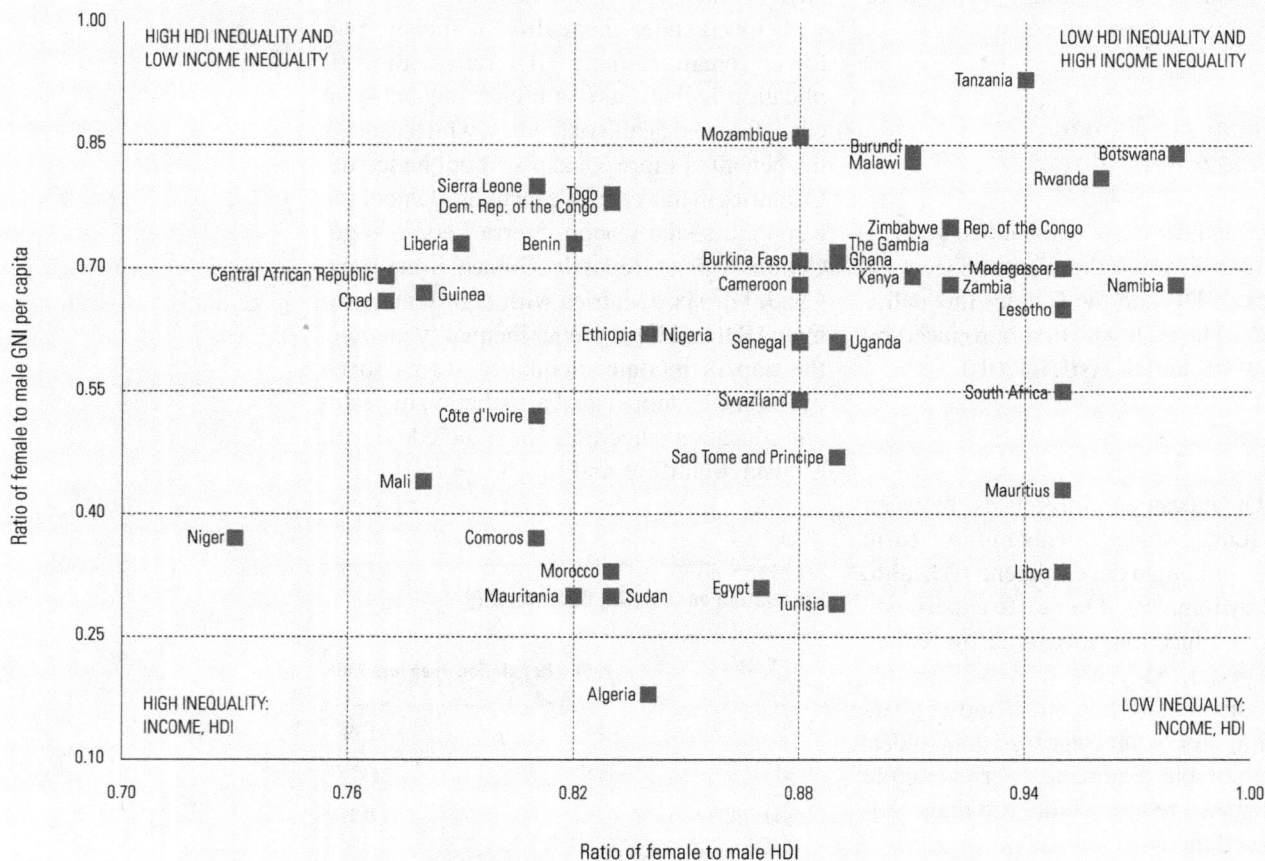

Source: Computed by the AfHDR Team from UNDP 2015 Human Development Report.

Turning specifically to Africa, figure 2.5 captures one aspect of the GDI when measured against income across the entire African region. The spread of the countries across the scatter plot shows, among other things, the wide range of possibilities between countries with high inequality and low income inequality or, conversely, low inequality but high income inequality. Looking at three outliers, United Republic of Tanzania has low HDI inequality and low income inequality. By contrast, Niger has high income inequality and high HDI inequality. Libya has low HDI inequality but high income inequality.

In terms of Africa's sub-regions, women in East and Southern Africa show the highest achievements in terms of human development relative to men, followed by North and Central Africa and least in West Africa.

Figure 2.6 presents the GDI values for each of the African sub-regions. As shown, there are notable differences in HDI values for men and women in each of the sub-regions, with men having a higher HDI value than women in all sub-regions. Southern Africa has the highest female-to-male ratios, at over 0.92, followed by East Africa, at 0.90.

Figures 2.7 to 2.9 show the sub-regional comparisons for each of the three dimensions measured by the GDI: health, education and income. The most significant variation between men and women is shown in income

FIGURE 2.6

GDI values by sub-region

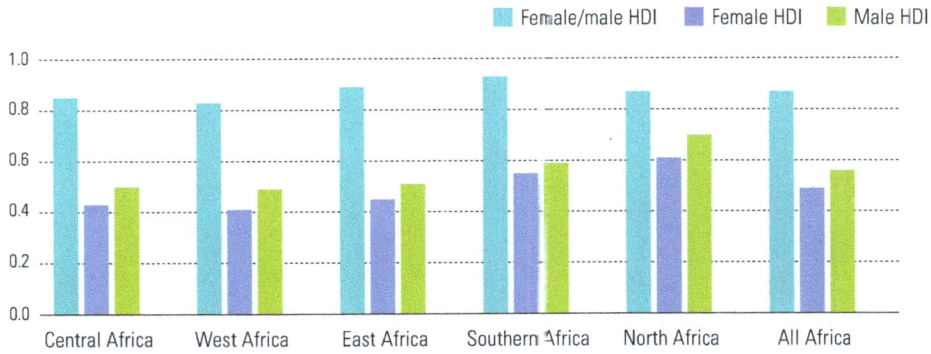

Source: Computed by the AfHDR Team from data in UNDP, 2015.

FIGURE 2.7

Life expectancy at birth, 2014

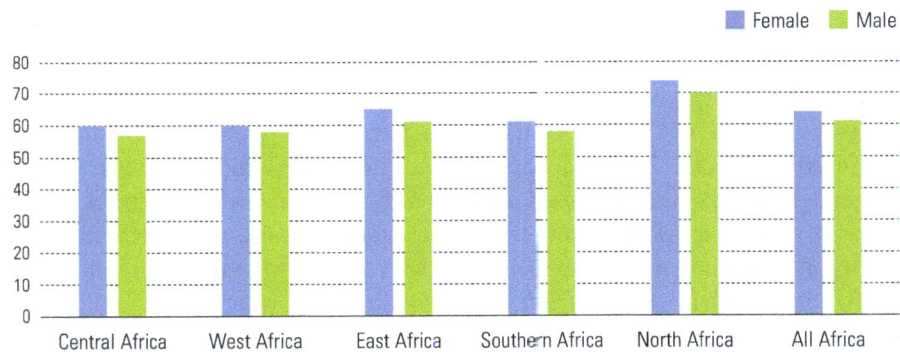

Source: Computed by the AfHDR Team from data in ILO, 2015d.

FIGURE 2.8

Expected years of schooling, 2014

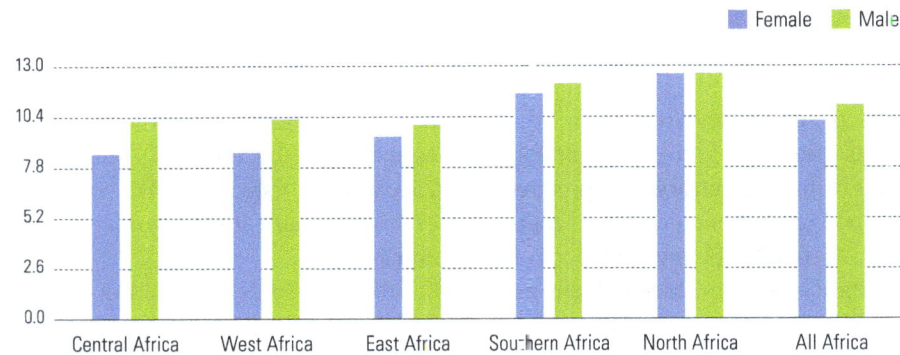

Source: Computed by the AfHDR Team from data in ILO, 2015d.

FIGURE 2.9

Differences in sub-regional income as measured by GNI per capita, 2014 (PPP, 2011, US$)

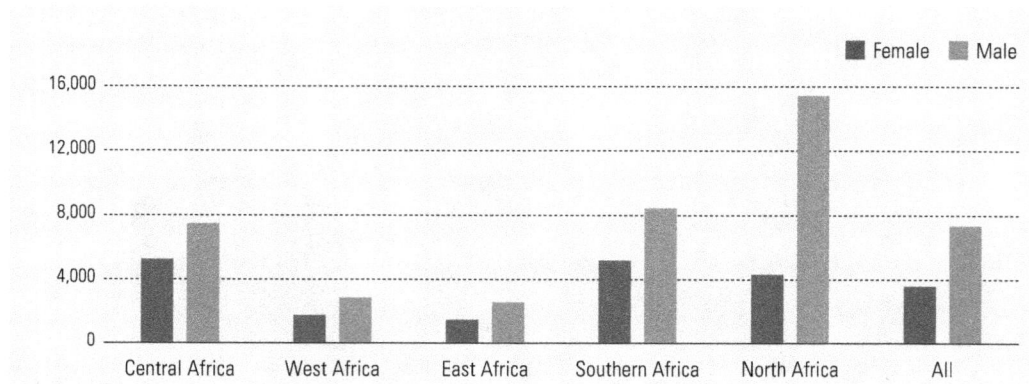

Source: Computed by the AfHDR Team from data in ILO, 2015d.

differentials in figure 2.9, which is true for all sub-regions; North Africa has the most income inequality. The low female labour force participation rate in North Africa, especially among youth, at 19.7 per cent in 2014 compared to 52.1 per cent for sub-Saharan Africa (ILO, 2015), accounts for high gender income inequality in this region. It is only in North Africa that there is gender parity in expected years of schooling (figure 2.8). It also has the longest life expectancy at birth for both sexes among all the sub-regions (figure 2.7). The system-wide social protection institutions focusing on better education and improved health care make North Africa stand out in life expectancy at birth and expected years of schooling compared to other regions in the continent.

The Gender Inequality Index

The GII is the second index on gender differences and reflects gender-based inequalities in three dimensions – reproductive health, empowerment and economic activity. Reproductive health is measured by maternal mortality and adolescent birth rates; empowerment is measured by the share of parliamentary seats held by women and attainment in secondary and higher education by each gender; and economic activity is measured by the labour market participation rate for women and men. The GII can be interpreted as the loss in human development due to inequality between female and male achievements in the three GII dimensions.

When observing GII tables, it is useful to briefly explain how to interpret the GII value and rank. Regarding the GII value, the closer the value is to zero, the higher the gender equality. For example, UNDP's 2015 HDR for all countries where data are available shows that Libya has the lowest (best) GII value among all African countries, at 0.016, whereas Niger has the lowest score, at 0.713. With respect to the GII ranking, only 154 countries are included (in contrast to the 188 for the HDI) due to data limitations.

Annex L provides the complete table of African countries with their GII values and rankings by their HDI ranking. It is important to note that all but six countries have meaningful gender inequality problems as measured by their GII ranking. In total, 25 countries listed have GII values of 0.500 or higher, indicating significant gender inequality.

Table 2.7 gives the ranking of the top ten and bottom ten African countries by GII values (bearing in mind that 14 African countries are not included in the GII calculation for lack of data). The list of GII scores is instructive by showing that countries that have lower (better) GII values significantly boost their rank when compared to their HDI rank. For example, Libya's rank on the GII scale improved by nearly 60 places. Similarly, Rwanda's GII score was 83 places better than the country's HDI ranking. Conversely, Niger, Chad and Côte d'Ivoire saw their GII ranking drop by some 30 places compared to their HDI ranking. These gains or losses in ranking, however, can be misleading to some extent since there were 188 countries in the HDI ranking compared to only 154 countries in the GII ranking. In both rankings, Niger was at the bottom. Yet, when Niger is compared to Rwanda, the differences are significant, even though both countries are found in the bottom 20 per cent of the HDI ranking of all countries (188 vs. 163).

GII is impeding HDI performance across African countries. Evidence from this report shows that 1 per cent increase in GII reduces HDI by 0.75 per cent. See Annex M.

Low expected years of schooling contribute to high gender inequality in Africa (Annex M). Gender inequality is driven by discriminatory social institutions. High gender inequality countries are also rated as having highly discriminatory social institutions in the Social Institutions and Gender Index. In recent years, the Organisation for Economic Co-operation and Development has developed the Social Institutions and Gender Index (SIGI). The SIGI measures gender gaps in social institutions across a number of variables related to discriminatory family codes – restricted physical integrity, son bias, restricted resources and assets, and restricted civil liberties. Higher SIGI values indicate higher inequality.

Discriminatory codes refer to social institutions that limit women's decision-making power and undervalue their status in the household and the family. Restricted physical integrity captures social institutions that limit women's and girls' control over their bodies, increase women's vulnerability, and normalize attitudes toward gender-based violence including female genital mutilation

TABLE 2.7

GII calculations for top ten and bottom ten African countries

HDI rank 2014	Country	GII value 2014	GII rank 2014
188	Niger	0.713	154
185	Chad	0.706	153
172	Côte d'Ivoire	0.679	151
179	Mali	0.677	150
176	Congo (Dem. Rep. of the)	0.673	149
187	Central African Republic	0.655	147
177	Liberia	0.651	146
181	Sierra Leone	0.650	145
183	Burkina Faso	0.631	144
175	The Gambia	0.622	143
155	Zimbabwe	0.504	112
184	Burundi	0.492	109
106	Botswana	0.480	106
63	Mauritius	0.419	88
83	Algeria	0.413	85
116	South Africa	0.407	83
126	Namibia	0.401	81
163	Rwanda	0.400	80
96	Tunisia	0.240	48
94	Libya	0.134	27

Source: Compiled by the AfHDR Team from data in UNDP, 2015.

(FGM). Social bias captures unequal intra-household investments in caring for, nurturing and allocating resources to sons and daughters, reflecting the lower value given to girls. Restricted resources and assets capture discrimination in women's rights to access and make decisions over natural and economic resources including land, assets and financial services. Civil liberties refer to discriminatory laws and practices that restrict women's access to public space, their political voice, and their participation in all aspects of public life.

FIGURE 2.10

Correlation between GII and SIGI values

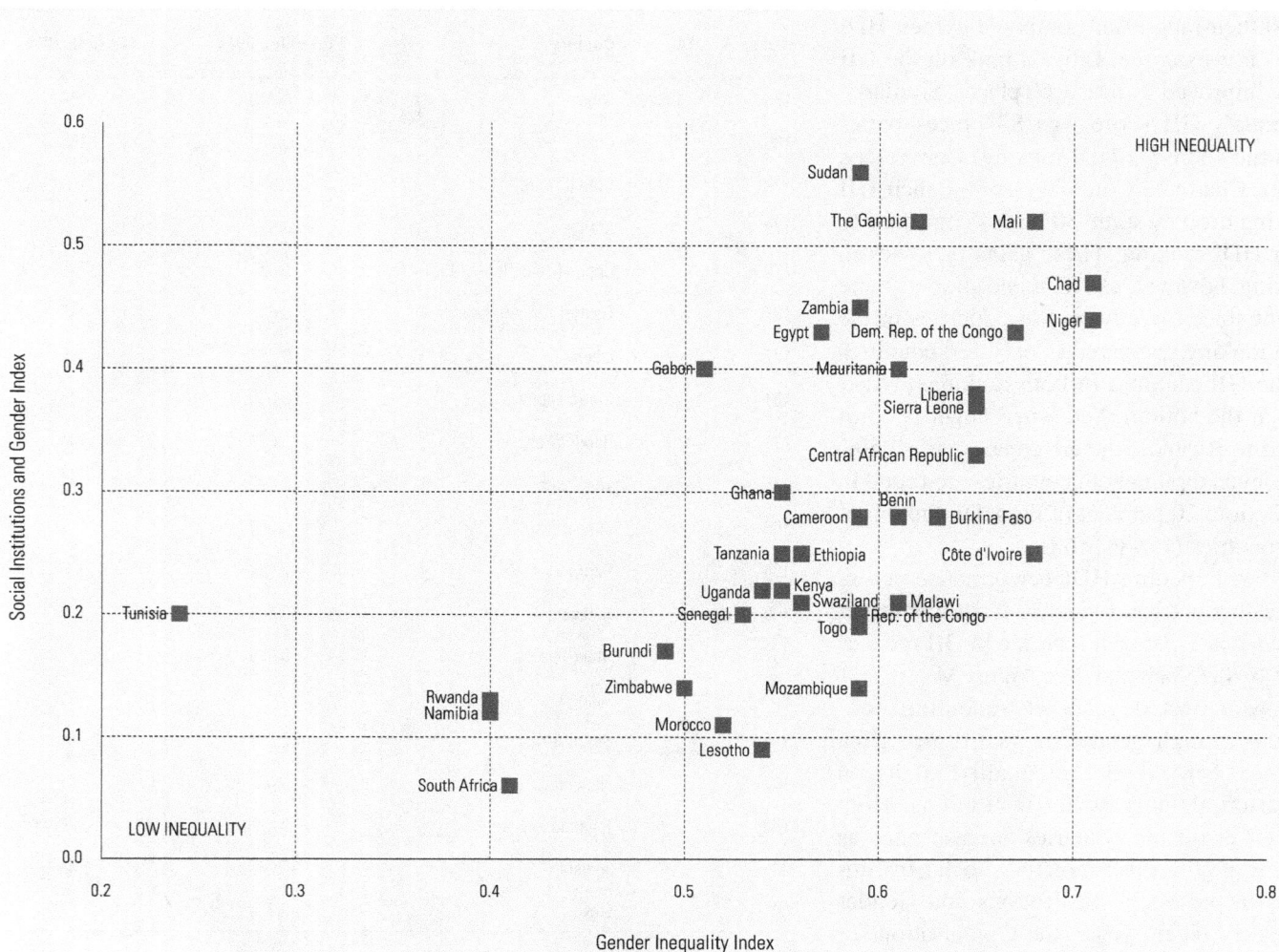

Source: Computed by the AfHDR Team from data in UNDP, 2015o and OECD, 2014.

Countries with lower gender inequality also have lower discriminatory social institutions. Figure 2.10 examines the correlation between GII and SIGI among African countries where data is available. The different placement of the countries is clearly evident when four of the countries with the lowest (best) GII values are found in the lower left quadrant (Tunisia, Rwanda, Namibia and South Africa), which denotes less socially discriminatory institutions. However, nine of the ten countries with the highest (worst) GII values are situated in the top right quadrant with the highest levels of discriminatory social institutions. The implication of the scatter plot suggests the high correlation between gender inequality and the efficacy and role of social institutions in addressing it. This has direct relevance on the kinds of social institutions and services that are brought to bear in addressing gender inequality and women's empowerment.

Summary, Conclusions and Policy Observations

Using UNDP's different human development indicators, there is wide variation in values and ranking across the Africa region and between the different African sub-regions. In general, however, the vast majority of African countries are clustered in the Low Human Development group with notable gender differences.

- Even though several African countries, including Ethiopia, Rwanda, Mozambique, Sierra Leone and Angola, fall into the Low Human Development group, they have made significant progress in increasing their HDI values.

- Calculations of the IHDI reveal serious inequality issues. Only 20 countries show positive gains from their HDI values, whereas 23 countries had negative differences with their HDI value.

- Calculations using the UNDP gender indices imply notable gender inequality in almost every African country. This suggests a clear correlation between countries with low HDI values and high gender inequality.

- In addition, African countries that are not in the Low Human Development group do not necessarily have better gender inequality scores.

- Discriminatory social institutions seem to perpetuate unequal outcomes. Rapid progress in tackling challenges associated with multi-dimensional poverty and inhibiting social institutions help accelerate human development.

- Gender gaps in income drive disparities in human development outcomes for women and men, but disparities in education and health also matter.

Child marriage prevalence
by Africa sub-region

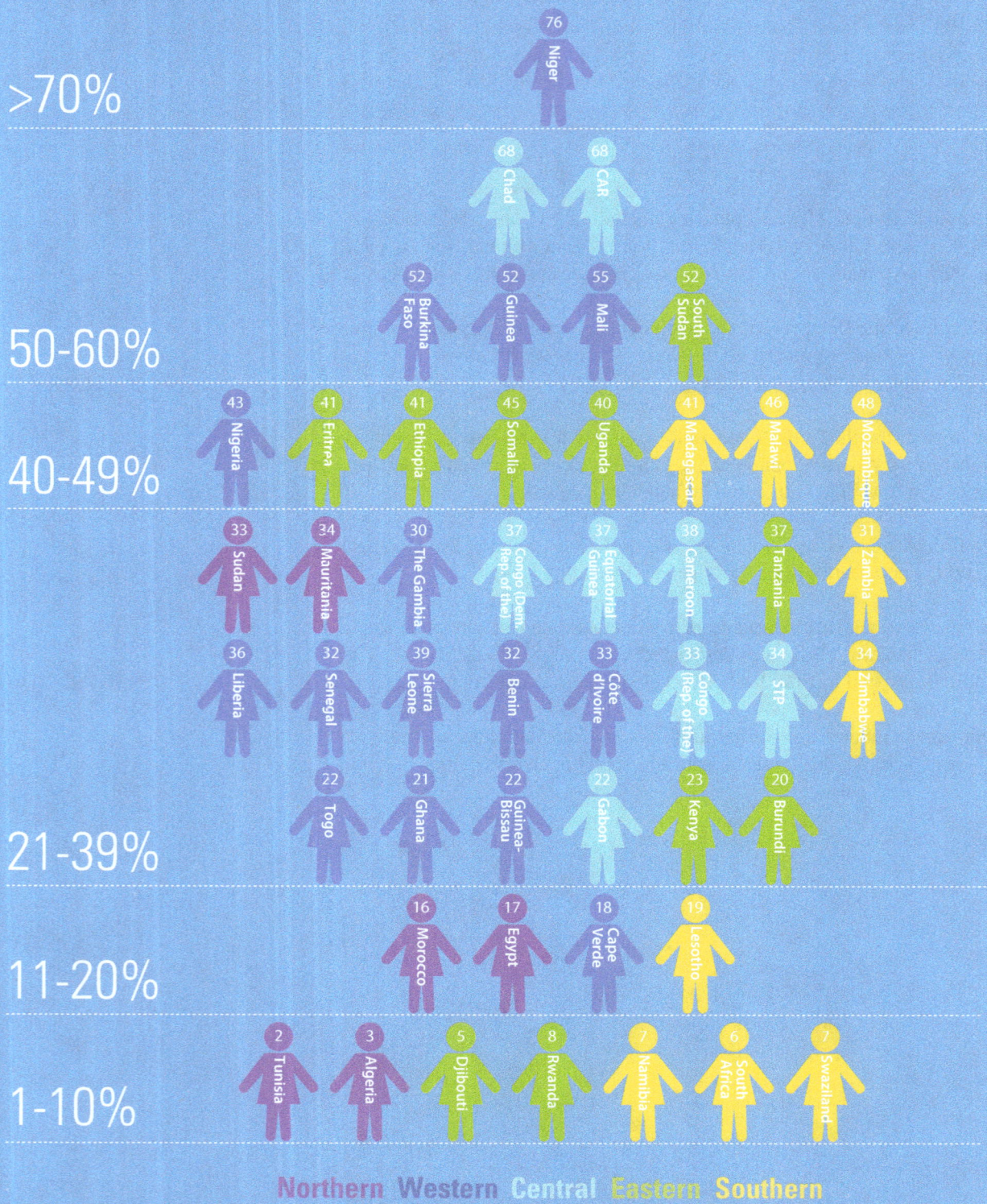

>70%

Niger 76

50-60%

Chad 68 · CAR 68

Burkina Faso 52 · Guinea 52 · Mali 55 · South Sudan 52

40-49%

Nigeria 43 · Eritrea 41 · Ethiopia 41 · Somalia 45 · Uganda 40 · Madagascar 41 · Malawi 46 · Mozambique 48

Sudan 33 · Mauritania 34 · The Gambia 30 · Congo (Dem. Rep. of the) 37 · Equatorial Guinea 37 · Cameroon 38 · Tanzania 37 · Zambia 31

Liberia 36 · Senegal 32 · Sierra Leone 39 · Benin 32 · Côte d'Ivoire 33 · Congo (Rep. of the) 33 · STP 34 · Zimbabwe 34

21-39%

Togo 22 · Ghana 21 · Guinea-Bissau 22 · Gabon 22 · Kenya 23 · Burundi 20

11-20%

Morocco 16 · Egypt 17 · Cape Verde 18 · Lesotho 19

1-10%

Tunisia 2 · Algeria 3 · Djibouti 5 · Rwanda 8 · Namibia 7 · South Africa 6 · Swaziland 7

Northern Western Central Eastern Southern

Chapter 3
The Social Dimensions of Gender Inequality

Chapter 3
The Social Dimensions of Gender Inequality

This chapter explores African gender equality by examining how the Continent has progressed on gender equality and women's empowerment by looking at the social sectors and highlighting the differences in social outcomes that are still commonly prevalent between men and women.

Unequal health and education outcomes for men and women is still evident within and across sub-regions.

In general, important advances across numerous dimensions of human development can be seen throughout the Continent. During the last decades, many African countries have seen the expansion of their citizens' capabilities in the basic areas of health, education and other social services. These improvements have benefitted women and girls, who today have greater access to education at all levels, expect better health, safely give birth to their children and achieve higher life expectancy. However, inequality in women's and men's different health and education outcomes is still evident across and within countries, communities and households. Gender inequality in social services translates into fewer opportunities for the well-being of women in particular and society as a whole.

This chapter is organized into three sections. The first section reviews some of the trends around specific health indicators, including maternal mortality, 'missing' women, early age marriage, and violence against women. The second section turns to women's education and the impediments to gender parity in access to educational opportunities. Finally, the third section explores some of the policy and programmatic implications that African governments must address in closing the social gender gap as well as the challenges being faced in their implementation.

Health-related gender issues

Maternal mortality

The African continent made spectacular progress from 1990-2015 in improving women's health, based on a growing commitment by African governments and their donor partners to invest heavily in human capital development. The maternal mortality ratio is a useful indicator to assess women's health status. This indicator also gives an indication about the accessibility, sufficiency and effectiveness of a country's health service system. Over the 1990-2015 period, there was a reduction in maternal mortality by 45 per cent in sub-Saharan Africa and 59 per cent in North Africa. Despite the progress of the last two decades, however, there are still major risk factors for women's health. More than 60 per cent of the world's maternal deaths occur in the African continent. In 2015, there were 546 maternal deaths per 100,000 live births in sub-Saharan Africa (70 in North Africa), compared to the world average of 216 maternal deaths per 100,000 live births, with developed countries having achieved an average of 12 deaths (WHO, 2015: 17, 20). Of the 18 countries in the world with the highest maternal mortality ratio (between 500 and 1,100) globally, 16 are in Africa (UNECA et al., 2014: 61). Poor, uneducated and rurally remote women are at most risk.

Adolescent birth rate is a major impediment to advancing maternal health in Africa. A 10.0 per cent increase in adolescent birth rate increases maternal mortality by about 2.0 per cent (Annex M).

There are severe differences in maternal mortality among Africa's sub-regions. North Africa leads the Continent's achievements in reducing maternal mortality in absolute terms, at 113 deaths per 100,000 live births. Southern Africa is the next lowest, at 248 per 100,000, but still at more than double the rate of North Africa. Trailing far behind are the remaining three sub-regions with rates well over 400 deaths per 100,000 live births, illustrating the extreme severity of maternal mortality for a large part of the Continent (figure 3.1). If the goal of ending all preventable maternal deaths by 2030 remains an urgent and critical challenge in these sub-regions, special attention is required to achieve these targets.

Another health-related aspect of gender equality was manifest in the Ebola epidemic that affected Guinea, Liberia and Sierra Leone in 2014. For women, the effects included direct impacts on their health and lives because of their added responsibilities in their traditional roles in caring for the sick and dying. In addition, the Ebola outbreak affected women through the loss of livelihoods attributable to reduced productivity in agriculture, trade (including cross-border trade), small businesses and service sector activities. Maternal deaths increased because of reduced antenatal and neonatal care. In addition, gender gaps in education widened with school closures and because of girls' increased dropout rates,

owing to teenage pregnancies and early marriages. The responsibility to care for the Ebola-orphaned children also falls on women. Toward the end of 2014, it was estimated that there were more than 30,000 Ebola-orphaned children in the three countries (UNDP Africa Policy Note, 2015a).

Women's premature death ('missing women')

Closely related to maternal mortality is the growing recognition of 'missing women'. Amartya Sen introduced the concept of 'missing women' by analysing the differences in the ratio of women to men. The objective is to understand and explain why this occurs and then react to it. Thus, the concept of missing women relates to the female population that could be expected if men and women received similar care in health, medicine and nutrition. In short, this concept represents the deficit of women and girls who have died prematurely compared to a benchmark population distribution.

FIGURE 3.1

Sub-regional trends in maternal mortality ratio (maternal deaths per 100,000 live births)

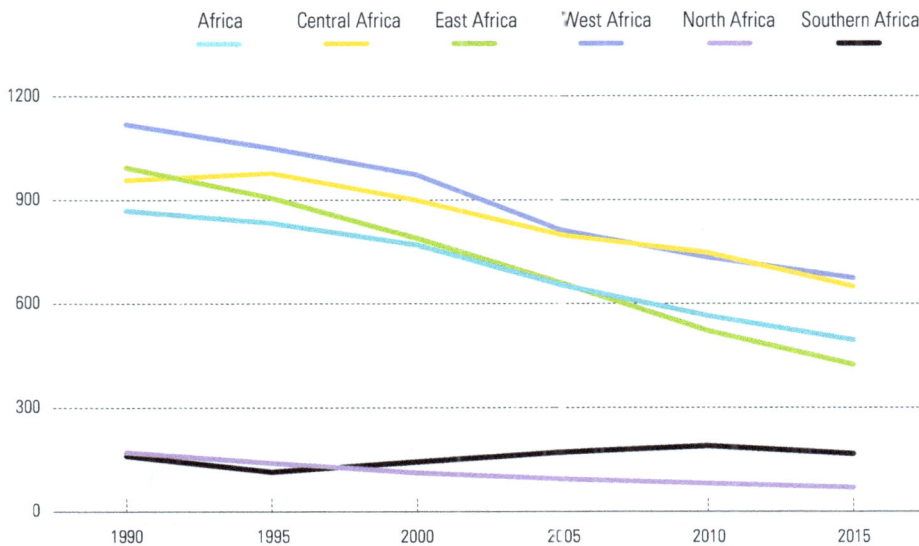

Therefore, as illustrated in table 3.1, excess female deaths in a given year represent women who would not have died in the previous year had they lived in a high-income country, after taking into account the overall health environment of the country they live in. Every year, excess female mortality after birth and 'missing girls' at birth account for an estimated 3.9 million women below the age of 60; about two-fifths of whom are never born; one-fifth goes missing in infancy and childhood, and the remaining two-fifths die between the ages of 15 and 59 (World Bank, 2012). Figure 3.2 shows missing women in Africa by sub-region.

Between 1990 and 2008, the total number of missing girls at birth and excess female mortality after birth did not change appreciably in sub-Saharan Africa. Declines in infant and childhood mortality were actually offset by

dramatic increases in the number of women within the reproductive age cohort due to population growth. Africa, as a whole, is one of the biggest contributors to the global population of missing women, and its numbers are increasing. This could even be more challenging in the years ahead given the high fertility rates in sub-Saharan Africa: 5.1 percent in 2011 compared to 2.5 percent for the world (UNFPA, 2012). This trend requires rapid and profound action to slow it down and then reverse it. By contrast, the number of missing women in all the other regions of the world is diminishing.

From a sub-regional perspective, data through 2010 show that East Africa was the region with the highest number of missing women and the number is increasing; West Africa was the second highest. Central Africa and Southern Africa also registered

TABLE 3.1

Excess female deaths in the world, by age and region, 1990 and 2008 (thousands)

	Girls at birth		Girls under 5		Girls 5-14		Women 15–49		Women 50–59		Total no. of women under 60		Change (1990-2008)
	1990	2008	1990	2008	1990	2008	1990	2008	1990	2008	1990	2008	
China	890	1 092	259	71	21	5	208	56	92	30	1 470	1 254	-216
India	265	257	428	251	94	45	388	228	81	75	1 255	856	-399
Sub-Saharan Africa	42	53	183	203	61	77	302	751	50	99	639	1 182	543
High HIV prevalence countries	0	0	6	39	5	18	38	328	4	31	53	416	363
Low HIV prevalence countries	42	53	177	163	57	59	264	423	46	68	586	766	180
South Asia (excluding India)	0	1	99	72	32	20	176	161	37	51	346	305	-41
East Asia and Pacific (excluding China)	3	4	14	7	14	9	137	113	48	46	216	179	-37
Middle East and North Africa	5	6	13	7	4	1	43	24	15	15	80	52	-28
Europe and Central Asia	7	14	3	1	0	0	12	4	4	3	27	23	-4
Latin America and the Caribbean	0	0	11	5	3	1	20	10	17	17	51	33	-18
Total	1 212	1 427	1 010	617	230	158	1 286	1 347	343	334	4 082	3 882	-200

Source: Compiled by the AfHDR Team from World Bank, 2012.

an increase in number of missing women although with less intensity. By contrast, in North Africa, the situation relatively stabilized between 1990 and 2010. North, Central and Southern Africa are seen as numerically less important in terms of their contribution to the total number of missing women in Africa, which may reflect both cultural differences, higher access to social services and more economic opportunities.

These trends suggest that, unlike in Asia, most African countries saw little change over two decades. The rise in absolute numbers of missing women is worrying and may have arisen from a number of different factors. The sub-regional differences may mirror those countries with high HIV/AIDS rates. It may further reflect discrimination in the household, resulting from the combination of strong preferences for sons combined with the spread of technologies that allow parents to know the sex of the foetus before birth, or it may reflect high rates of maternal mortality in certain countries. The high fertility rates in Africa are another factor. It is obvious that progress in reducing missing women and human rights associated with protecting

their lives has not been commensurate with income growth. In certain African countries such as Chad, Guinea-Bissau, Liberia, Mali, Niger, Sierra Leone and Somalia, at least one of every 25 women dies from complications of childbirth or pregnancy, and a much larger fraction will suffer long-term health consequences from giving birth (Carresco, 2015).

Early age marriage and HIV/AIDS

A third indicator of gender health issues relates to early age marriage. By all accounts, child marriage remains a dominant problem, with some 50 per cent of girls married under the age of 18 years in East, West and Central Africa. More than 58 percent of marriages among women age 20-46 years in Niger, Chad, Ethiopia and Guinea occurred under the age 18 years – ranging from 58 percent in Ethiopia to 77 percent in Niger (UNICEF, 2013:2). If the current trend persists, it will not be fast enough to offset population growth, and early child marriage will double by 2050. In Mali, for example, the maternal mortality ratio for women aged 15-19 years is 187 per 100,000 live births,

Between 1990 and 2008, the total number of missing girls at birth and excess female mortality after birth did not change appreciably in sub-Saharan Africa. Declines in infant and childhood mortality were actually offset by dramatic increases in the number of women within the reproductive age cohort due to population growth.

FIGURE 3.2

'Missing women' in Africa, by sub-region

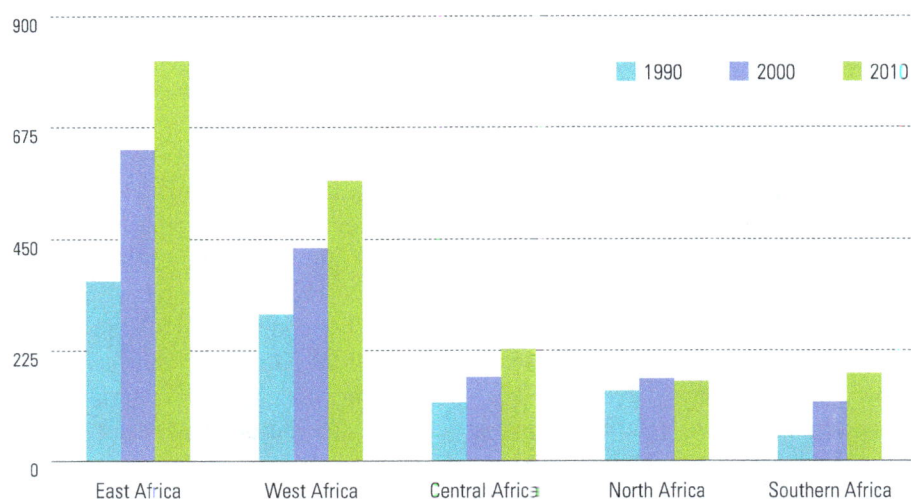

Source: Computed by the AfHDR Team based on UN Statistics Division database.

Chapter 3 The Social Dimensions of Gender Inequality | 39

FIGURE 3.3

Incidence of child marriage, by African sub-region

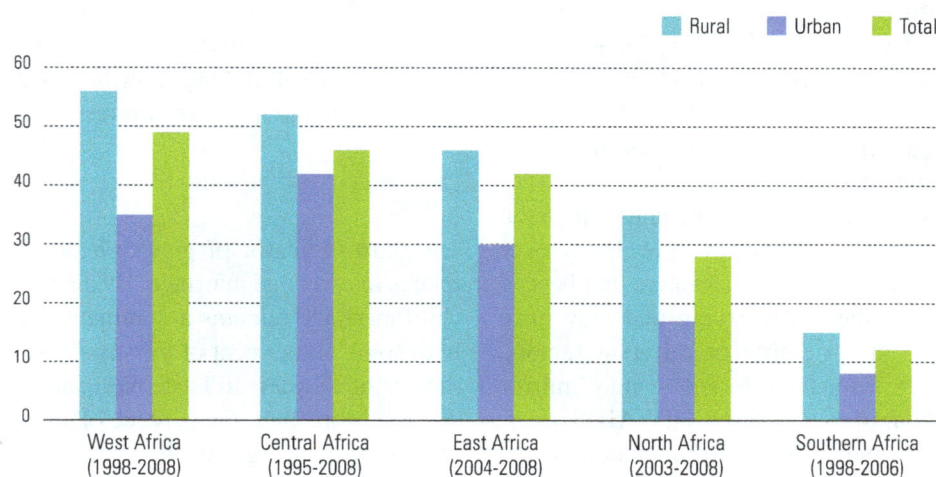

Source: Nguyen and Wodon, 2012a.

but the ratio is only 32 for women aged 20-34. Corresponding figures in Togo are 286 and 39, respectively, demonstrating that 'children delivering children' strongly increases maternal mortality (Mathur, Greene and Malhotra, 2003). On average, early age marriage affects around 50 per cent of girls under 18 years in West, Central and East Africa (figure 3.3). Figure 3.3 further shows that differences between rural and urban incidences of child marriage in all sub-regions suggest that urbanization has a positive impact in undermining the social norms and beliefs supporting child marriage. The disproportionately high prevalence of early age marriage in rural areas across the Continent calls for urgent and proactive advocacy actions on social and cultural attitudes that propagate these practices.

Child wives are also more likely to be exposed to HIV infection, contrary to the general belief according to which early marriage protects young women (UNFPA, 2010). In sub-Saharan Africa, girls aged 15-19 years are two to eight times more likely to become infected than boys of the same age group. In Kenya, married girls have a 50 per cent higher likelihood of becoming HIV-infected than unmarried girls compared to 59 per

cent in Zambia and 66 per cent in Uganda. Child marriage increases the risks of several other diseases, such as cervical cancer, as shown in Mali, Central African Republic, Malawi, Mozambique, Zambia and Zimbabwe.

Early child marriage is a serious development challenge in Africa. For instance, one percentage point increase in adolescent birth rate reduces life expectancy by nine months, increases female adult mortality by 1.1 percentage point and worsens maternal mortality by 0.2 percentage point (Annex M).

There are also psychological costs associated with early marriage, related mostly to the several health risks that child-wives face during pregnancy, delivery and even in their everyday lives. In the United Republic of Tanzania, infant mortality rates are 164 per 1,000 children born to women under 20 years old, compared with 88 for mothers aged 20-29. Globally, child mortality rates are 73 per cent higher for mothers under 20 and the correlation is also true among all the African sub-regions (Nguyen and Wodon, 2012a). Early marriage also has intergenerational consequences, including low educational attainment and weak access to economic opportunities.

FIGURE 3.4

Child marriage prevalence by sub-region (%), 2005-2013

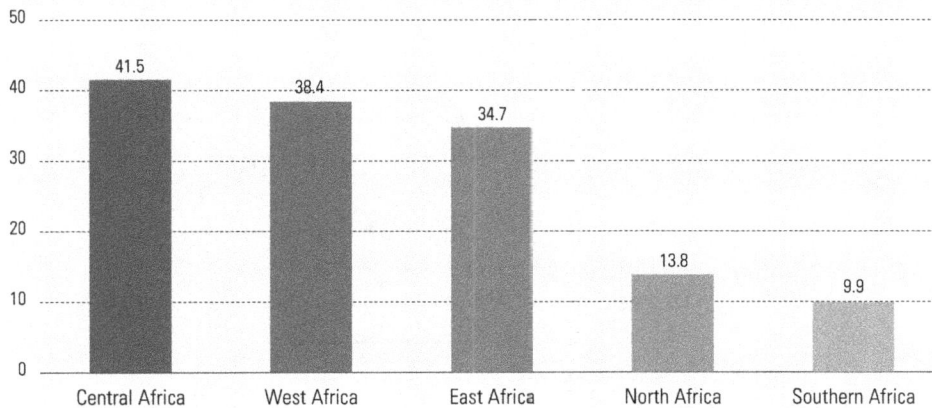

Source: Compiled by the AfHDR Team based on UNICEF Global Database, 2015.

HIV prevalence rates have remained substantially unchanged since the early 1990s. People are living longer due to improvements in treatment, but new infections are at much the same level as they were 30 years ago. With more aggressive treatment and prevention measures, there are signs that the number of new infections is beginning to diminish (UNAIDS, 2013: 1). HIV/AIDS, however, continues to be a grave concern. According to UNAIDS, in 2012, 35 million people were believed to be living with HIV/AIDS across the globe, the vast majority of whom were in sub-Saharan Africa. Globally, an estimated 55 per cent of adults living with HIV/AIDS are women, of whom 11.6 million are in sub-Saharan Africa. In Southern Africa, a staggering 22 per cent of women between the ages of 15 and 49 are believed to be living with HIV/AIDS (UNFPA and Guttmacher Institute, 2014: 24).

HIV prevention, treatment and care are crucial since women are particularly vulnerable to HIV infection due to sexual violence and other factors. These include gender-based power imbalances that inhibit women's ability to insist on the use of condoms to protect themselves and that socialize them to accept that men can have multiple partners. Some women living with HIV face the risk of mother-to-child transmission, while others have been subjected to involuntary sterilization. The different impacts of HIV/AIDS for women and men call for gender-specific health strategies.

Workplace health risks for women

At present, African women tend to be concentrated in the informal sector, mainly smallholder agriculture, with strenuous and sometimes dangerous jobs and limited access to health care and sick leave, etc. But African women are now facing a new form of health hazard in the modern formal workplace. Entering the formal work world, especially at a managerial level, has subjected African women to the same levels of stress, bad diets and lack of exercise as men, leading to a rise in the kind of diseases that were commonly associated with men. The rise of the middle-class in Africa has brought with it the rise of life-style risk factors such as obesity, diabetes and high blood pressure. These kinds of diseases are leading to an increased incidence of vascular disease. Due to high rates of economic inequality, health care systems have to deal with both the pathologies of poverty, such as diseases due to malnutrition and infectious diseases, as well as the

The spectrum of violence affecting women across Africa includes domestic violence, intimate partner violence, rape, female genital mutilation (FGM), intimidation, and additional threats to women's personal security in periods of war and conflict.

FIGURE 3.5

Percentage of women aged 15-49 experiencing sexual violence (irrespective of the perpetrator) at least once in their lifetime and in the last 12 months, 1995-2013 (latest available)

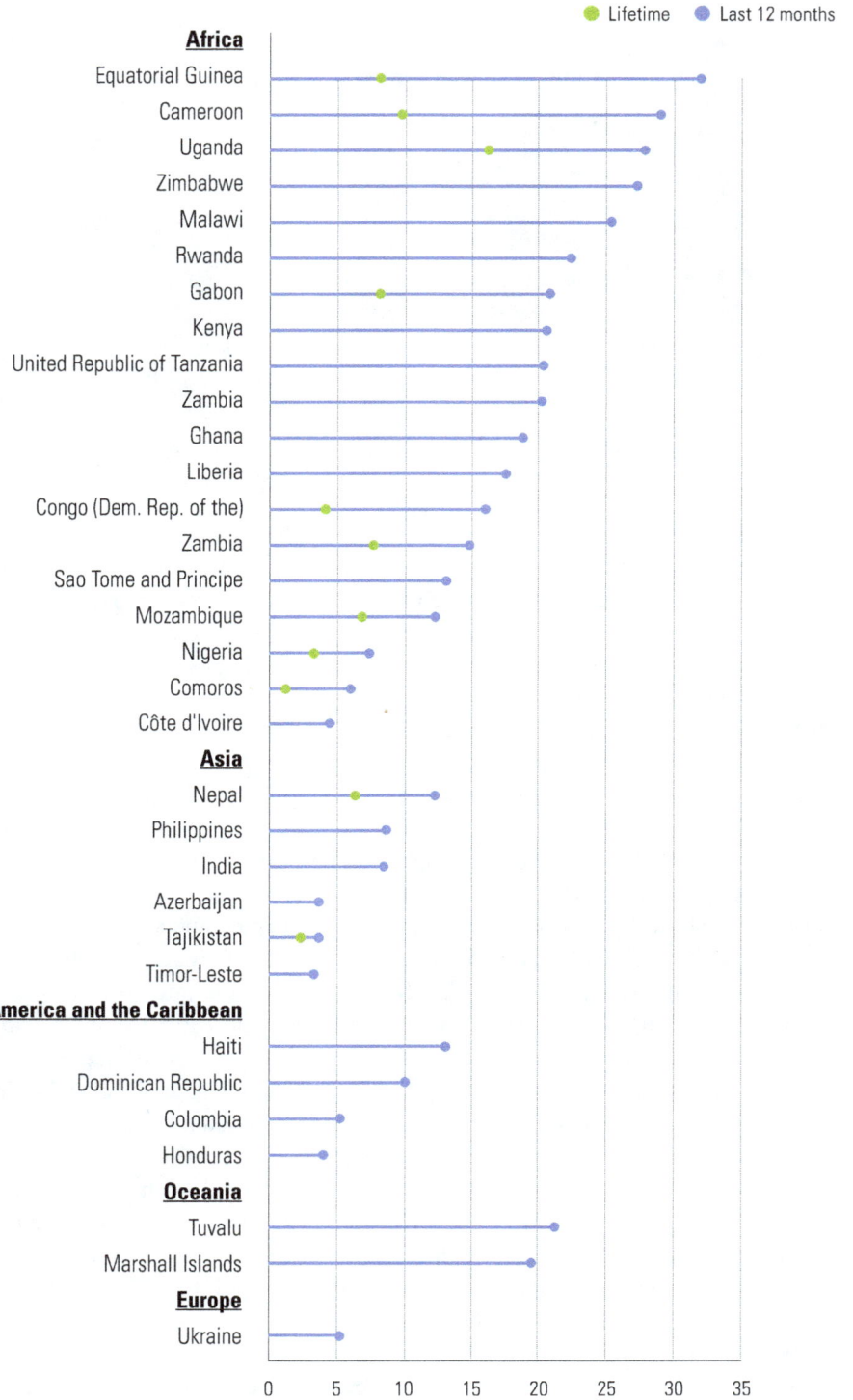

Source: Compiled by the AfHDR Team based on UNDP, 2015.

TABLE 3.2

Prevalence of physical and/or sexual gender violence by former or current partners and non-partners

Region	Prevalence (%)		Lifetime prevalence (%)
	by former or current partners	by non-partners	partner violence (physical and/or sexual) or non-partner sexual violence or both among all women (15 years and older)
Africa	36.6	11.9	45.6
Americas	29.8	10.7	36.1
Eastern Mediterranean	37	–	36.4
Europe	25.4	5.2	27.2
Southeast Asia	37.7	4.9	40.2
Western Pacific	24.6	6.8	27.9
High Income	23.2	12.6	32.7

Source: WHO, 2013b.

pathologies of wealth. Many studies would argue that the rate of non-communicable life-style diseases among African women is rising.[6]

However, currently there is no adequate system of vital registration that would allow governments to understand the full nature of the problem. There needs to be a system of standardized reporting of death certificates according to a commonly accepted medical protocol. In Africa, it is only in South Africa where it is possible to estimate the gap in data (WHO 2014a: 14); elsewhere, anecdotal evidence must be used. For instance, in Nigeria, it was found that high blood pressure was a risk factor of almost half the female heart attack patients studied (49.6 per cent) and diabetes, the second most common risk factor (at 16.9 per cent); almost a third had two or more risk factors (26.6 per cent) (Ezeala-Adikaibe et al., 2009).

Health risks from violence committed against women

Finally, an important factor challenging women's health in Africa is the high rate of violence they face. Gender-based violence is a widespread problem all over the world. As regards physical and sexual violence, WHO (2013b) has compiled data both for current or former intimate partner gender violence and for gender violence by non-partners, as well as gender violence committed against women from age 15 and older. Table 3.2 shows global comparisons of intimate partner and non-partner gender violence for women from all regions. With respect to intimate partner violence, Africa, Eastern Mediterranean and South-East Asia average around 37 per cent. All other regions sampled show gender violence rates in the 20th percentile. For non-partner violence, high-income countries have the highest prevalence rates, at 12.6 per cent, followed by Africa, at 11.9 per cent. Finally, table 3.2 shows that nearly one out of every two African women (45.6 per cent) have experienced some kind of sexual or physical violence during their lifetimes. All regions show shockingly high and totally unacceptable prevalence rates.

The spectrum of violence affecting women in the Continent includes domestic violence, intimate partner violence, rape, FGM, intimidation and additional threats to women's personal security in periods of war and conflict. As regards FGM, available data suggest that in the 29 countries where it is concentrated, more than 125 million women alive today have been subjected to the practice. Figure 3.6 shows the percentage of women and girls affected by FGM in the concerned countries.

Violence against women is discussed in more detail in chapter 6. Here, it should be noted that a high rate of violence can be likened to a completely preventable and curable disease currently burdening health care systems and preventing women and girls from enjoying full health. To the extent that gender-based violence reduces reproductive choices, it renders women susceptible to increased rates of maternal mortality and sexually transmitted diseases. There is no empirical research on what proportion of Africa's population increase is due to rape. A review of available literature for South Africa estimates that as many as 30 per cent of children born could be as a result of gender-based violence (Abrahams 2009). A simple way to reduce maternal mortality, therefore, would be to reduce gender-based violence, thus easing pressure on health care systems.

Education-related gender issues

By 2015, with a 67 per cent primary completion rate, Africa was still far from achieving primary completion rates for all. Around 20 per cent only of African countries for which data are available (i.e. Algeria, Cabo Verde, Egypt, Ghana, Morocco, Sao Tome and Principe, Seychelles and Tunisia) reached the target in 2012. In 24 out of the 44 countries (around 53 per cent) for which 2012 data are available, the primary education completion rate was at least 70 per cent, and only five countries (Central African Republic, Chad, Eritrea, Niger and South Sudan) deviated widely from the average value with a completion rate not exceeding 50 per cent. Within the Africa region, the general trend is highly diverse, with notable progress between 2000 and 2012 recorded in Ghana (net increase of 38.6 per cent), Rwanda (26.9 per cent), Morocco (25.7 per cent) and the United Republic of Tanzania (22.5 per cent); slight stagnation in others; and severe declines in Benin, Burkina Faso, Chad, Côte d'Ivoire, Eritrea, Mali and Niger. The main causes for this regression may be due to conflict, political unrest, or the impact of

FIGURE 3.6

Girls and women aged 15–19 years and 45–49 years subjected to female genital mutilation, 2002–2013 (latest available)

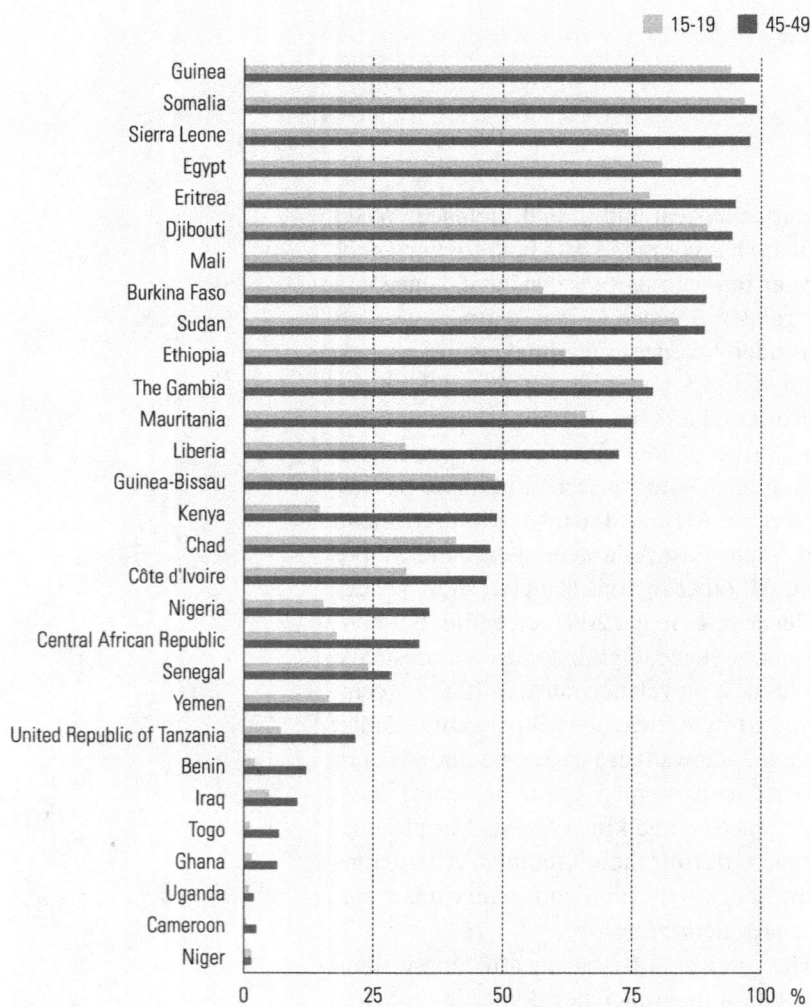

Source: Computed by the AfHDR Team from ICF, 2014; and UNICEF, 2014c; and UN Statistical Division database.

Note: In the 29 countries where FGM is concentrated, almost all girls undergoing FGM are cut before the age of 15 (UNICEF, 2013). Ranking is for presentation purposes only (see introduction to section A for further details).

the higher enrolment on education quality (UNECA et al., 2014).

These general education trends, however, mask notable education inequalities. Sub-regional differences are shown in figure 3.7, with North and Southern Africa having higher schooling rates than the other sub-regions, and Central Africa scoring significant lower for women – a dramatically low 2.5 years of schooling for girls and the widest gender gap (almost two years).

The immense benefits of investing in education have led many African countries to make huge investments in basic education. This has been a critical factor in arriving at close to universal primary education enrolment. In 2014, nearly half of all African countries had reportedly achieved gender parity in primary school enrolment (UNECA, 2015: para. 23), although concerns remain about the number of out-of-school children, the quality of education, and the learning outcomes achieved. Many countries have made huge strides towards gender parity in primary school education by legislating free and equal access to primary education, implementing policies such as free school uniforms and meals to encourage girls' attendance, and engaging in community initiatives around awareness-raising and mobilization. As a result, the gender gap in primary education has almost been closed in sub-Saharan Africa (figure 3.8).

The Continent has also shown laudable achievements in secondary education, but inequality is clearly more pervasive than in primary education. Out of 45 countries assessed, only 12 achieved parity in secondary education, most notably in North Africa (World Bank 2014a). As of 2013, an average of 22 per cent of females and 32 per cent of males aged 25 and older have at least some secondary level of education. (Figure 3.9 illustrates secondary education gender gaps by sub-region.) The most concerning situation is found in West Africa, with a gender gap of almost 50 per cent. Parity in secondary school enrolment is skewed against boys in Lesotho, Namibia, Cabo Verde, Sao Tome and Principe, Seychelles, Botswana and South Africa (UNECA et al, 2015).

FIGURE 3.7

Mean years of schooling, 25 and older, by sex and sub-region, 2014

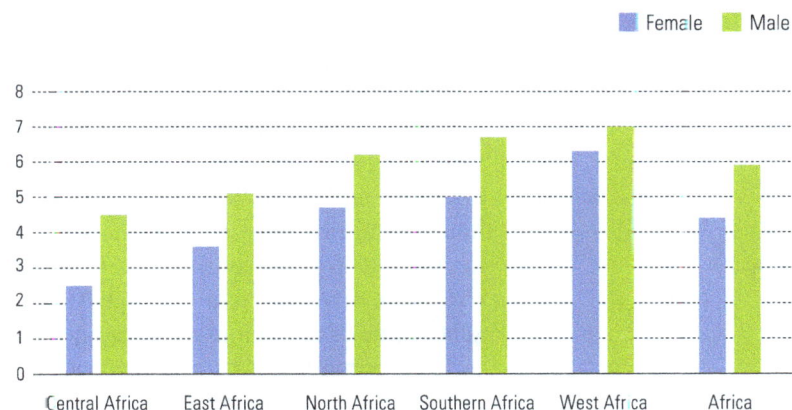

Source: UNDP 2015 Human Development Report.

FIGURE 3.8

Gender parity in primary school enrolment

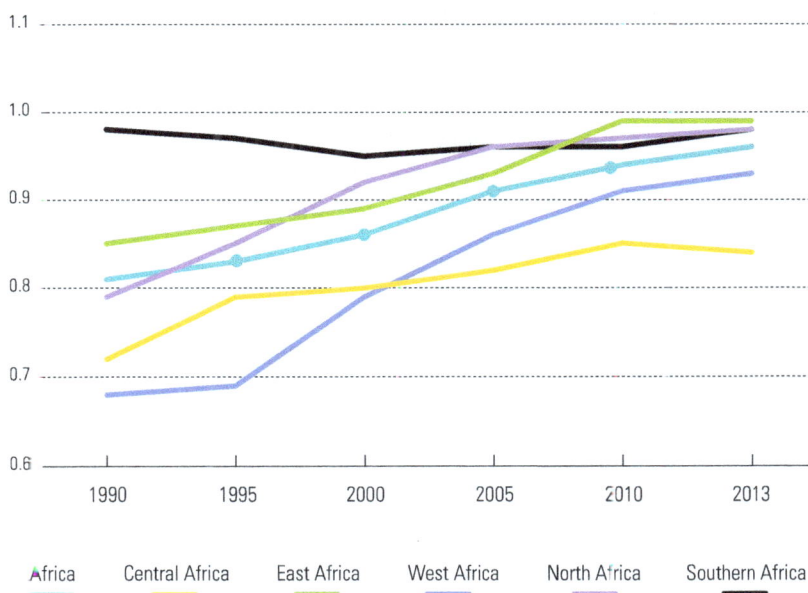

Source: UN Statistical Database, accessed 1 June 2016.

However, only a quarter of the countries in sub-Saharan Africa regularly submit data on lower secondary schooling. Any conclusions drawn from this data are therefore extremely tentative (UNESCO, 2014a:5).

With regard to out-of-school children, the global number of out-of-school children of primary school age declined for two decades, falling from about 104 million in 1990 to about 58 million in 2012 – 31 million girls and 27 million boys; sub-Saharan Africa accounted for more than half of them (51.2 per cent) and had the highest out-of-school rate of all regions. Almost one in four girls of primary school age and one in five boys in the region had either never attended school, or left school without completing primary education.

Girls comprise the majority of the world's out-of-school children. In 2012, the share of girls in the out-of-school population amounted to 53 per cent, down from 62 per cent in 1990. Gender disadvantage was most pronounced in North Africa and Western Asia, where girls accounted for over two-thirds of children out-of-school. In sub-Saharan Africa, girls accounted for 56 per cent – comprising 16.6 million for girls and 13.0 million for boys (UNESCO, 2014b).

There are various reasons for children not attending school, which are often associated with poverty, ethnicity, social exclusion, living in a rural area or slum, geographic remoteness, disasters, armed conflict, lack of basic facilities and poor-quality education. These barriers often interact with gender to create even greater disadvantages in learning opportunities (UN, 2015: 65-66).

Finally, data on tertiary education suggest very little improvement toward gender parity and very low enrolment rates for both males and females – despite government spending rates of at least ten times more at the university level than the primary level. With merely 6.8 per cent of youth enrolled in tertiary education, sub-Saharan Africa lags far behind the global average of 30 per cent. In addition, tertiary enrolments have maintained a strong male bias in total enrolments over time in some sub-regions (figure 3.10).

Broadly speaking, more qualitative data are needed to understand the situation on the ground with respect to education. As the United Nations Educational, Scientific and Cultural Organization (UNESCO) notes, many of the countries with worst performance (such as post-conflict countries) have no data at all. "Focusing only on countries with publishable data is likely to be misleading for global policy debates, particularly as many of the countries without data are likely to be the furthest from achieving Universal Primary Education" (UNESCO, 2014a: 68). The absence or dearth of empirically useful data is thus well-recognized as a problem that needs further action. In this respect, giving women a voice and encouraging them to express themselves on matters of concern, is an important approach to gaining the kind of thick data needed for carrying out additional education reforms.

Policy and programme responses for gender equality in health and education

Most African governments have made significant strides in enabling improved access for the poor to health and education, and and in ensuring that women are better able to access those services.

FIGURE 3.9

Population with at least some secondary education, by sex and sub-region, 2005-2014 (% aged 25 and above)

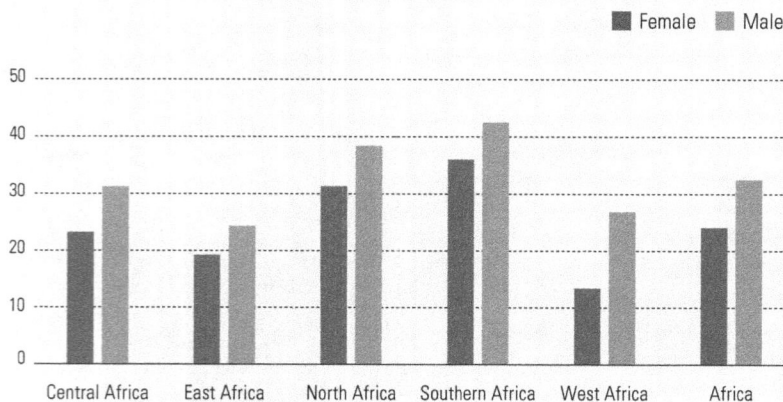

Source: Compiled by the AfHDR Team based on UNESCO, 2015.

Health

African governments are fully aware that investments in health, especially during childhood, have a huge impact on men and women in tapping their full potential to transform their society. When children are exposed to diseases or suffer low birth weights, they are at a higher risk of suffering lower cognitive development and facing difficulties in learning. This in turn, has an impact on their health outcomes in adulthood and thus a negative effect on economic outcomes for the individuals as well as for society as a whole. There is also the simple social loss of human capital investment. It should be clear that for every woman who dies, the investment that society has made into her education and training is lost. The importance of addressing current health challenges is paramount to accessing the full potential of African women and men to contribute to growth and structural transformation.

Increasing the health of African women and men requires additional efforts to better fund national health care systems. The AU Abuja Declaration encourages governments to increase health budget allocations to 15 per cent. By 2015, 27 countries have improved the proportion of total government expenditures on health. As of 2010, only Rwanda, Liberia, Malawi and Togo met the targets of the Abuja Declaration while Burundi, Democratic Republic of the Congo, Madagascar, Mali, Sierra Leone and Burkina Faso were close to achieving the target – they recorded 12.0 per cent and above (WHO, 2014b). Policies are necessary at a Continental level in order to bring countries in line with the 15 per cent benchmark set by the Abuja Declaration.

Specific legal and institutional frameworks at the Continental level have provided support in reducing maternal mortality. Africa's political commitment was expressed through the Campaign on Accelerated Reduction of Maternal Mortality in Africa (CARMMA), launched in 2004 by 44 countries and now counting 51 members. The campaign cites Zimbabwe as an innovative country in reducing maternal mortality and neonatal morbidity. The country developed and sustained a strong national family planning programme. The programme's objective was to prevent unwanted pregnancies and encourage child spacing. As a result, the percentage of married women using family planning methods has steadily increased from 48 per cent in 1994 to 60 per cent in 2006 and 65 per cent in 2009. The pill was the planning method most commonly used. Total fertility rates have also declined, from 4 in 1999 to 3.8 in 2006 (CARMMA, 2016).

Despite funding shortfalls, the Continent has seen an array of policy innovations in its health systems, which are the foundation of the last two decades of progress in improved women's and children's health. Innovations have included sector-wide approaches facilitating synergies and cost reduction between government agencies, on the one hand, and development partners, on the other. In a study by Odusola (2013), a number of innovative policy recommendations were highlighted:

Integrate the formal health system into the community. Simple models of health system delivery could help improve maternal health outcomes in Africa. Several countries have shown that this is achievable. The trans-

> Despite funding shortfalls, the Continent has seen an array of policy innovations in its health systems, which are the foundation of the last two decades of progress in improved women's and children's health.

FIGURE 3.10

Gender parity index in tertiary level enrolment by sub-region (ratio of girls to boys)

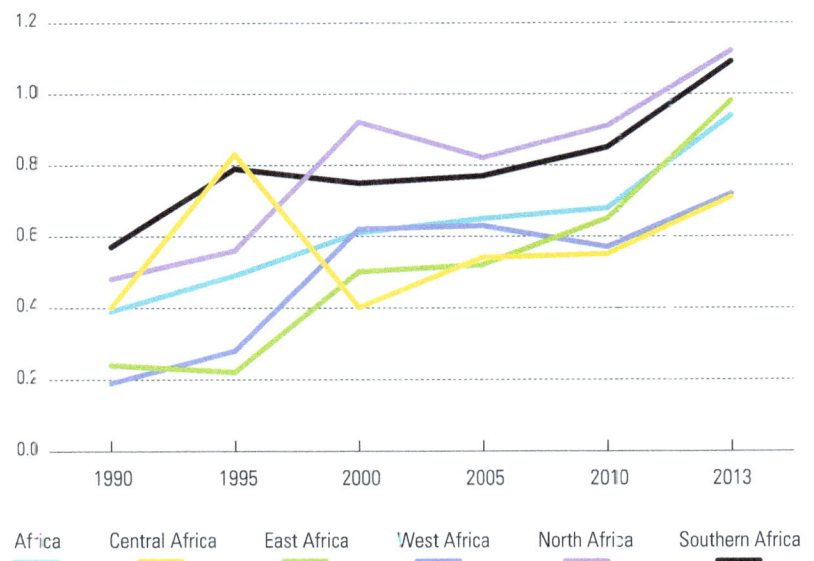

Source: Calculated by the AfHDR Team based on MDG Indicators data.

formation of traditional birth attendants (TBAs) into maternal health workers through effective training and supervision from health professionals has proved successful. A health system that leverages local knowledge (as is the case in Eritrea and Malawi regarding the complementarity of TBAs), networks and people is more likely to reach a very large segment of the poor in terms of maternal and neonatal services in Africa. Public- and private- sector providers of maternal health need to establish and maintain relationships with the local community.

Incentivize actors who may lose rent-seeking activities. It is simplistic to expect that when policy, institutional or programmatic innovations are being piloted, no problems will be encountered. At the policy and institutional levels, actors benefitting from the extant inefficiency (public and private sectors) will resist because they do not want to lose rent-seeking activities. This is also true in the case of programmatic interventions, especially when they involve transforming the role of TBAs or replacing their activities with trained birth attendants. Ethiopia, Eritrea, Mozambique and Lesotho provide positive lessons learned. It is vital to give incentives to potential losers in order to productively engage them.

Strengthen budget management and the quality of health expenditures. Increasing resource allocation without a commensurate improvement in quality public resource management is not sustainable. It is important to strengthen budget management and to improve the overall quality of expenditure in the health sector through capacity-building in budget planning and execution. In order to achieve progress, it is critical to strengthen planning, budgeting, revenue generation and financial management, and to improve the quality of expenditure. To ensure health sector governance and accountability for results, it is important for countries to institutionalize the process of tracking and reporting aggregate resource flows into the health sector. This should take the form of total health expenditures as well as reproductive, maternal,

newborn and child health expenditure per capita. Performance-based reporting that links inputs to key results (outputs and impacts) should be encouraged.

Promote strong collaboration among stakeholders. No single actor can accelerate progress towards maternal health. Effective collaboration among governments, businesses, non-governmental organizations (NGOs) and development partners has proved necessary for rapid progress. A strategy of collaboration that draws on available local context, expertise and resources to provide health care to those in greatest need should be designed and implemented. The increasing role of the private sector in delivering health services in Africa provides an opportunity to complement the public sector with a view to delivering health care in low-income settings. This underlines the need to devise a health care business model that serves the needs of the low-income group, possibly through public-private partnership and franchising.

Ensure that the public and private sectors work together to reach the poor. Health innovations driven and implemented at the national level with limited involvement of the local people tend to have limited impact and less sustainability. There is emerging evidence that, for innovations in health systems to be sustainable, close collaboration and partnership with the subnational health systems are highly crucial. Maternal health in Africa is a primary health care handled mostly at the local or provincial level. Such innovations should be fully institutionalized, operationalized and driven by local health workers and their institutions.

Take advantage of information communication and technology. Africa should take advantage of the widely spreading use of mobile phones to facilitate access to maternal health. The Balaka initiative in Malawi and the Abiye project in Nigeria have shown the value of information technology in facilitating access to health services. These initiatives should be scaled up and replicated, if possible, for better access. A sustainable solution does

BOX 3.1

Achieving dramatic reductions in Rwanda's maternal mortality rates

Rwanda is among the five top performing countries in Africa in maternal mortality reduction with a decline of 77.1 per cent between 1990 and 2013.

The Rwandan Government's approach sought first to improve the ability of health service providers to learn and adapt to change by a system of on-the-job mentorship, and second, to improve the ability of pregnant women to be active participants in their own health care by enhancing their capacity to communicate with caregivers. Third, the harnessing of the power of community caregivers, organized in their own networks to enable peer-to-peer learning, is a distinctive feature of programmes that have proven successful in recent years.

Innovative health funding and the introduction of Performance-Based Budgeting (PBF) have also contributed to this success. The main goal has been to increase accessibility of health care geographically and financially, and to strengthen the voice of the population to encourage them to demand better quality health care. The strategy is to operate within local organizations to improve the health system and empower populations.

The PBF approach consists in providing funds to health-care service providers, allowing service managers to increase their budgets based on performance. Service providers work on a competitive basis, with better performance rewarded. PBF encourages health service providers to adopt innovative strategies to improve their budgets and the quality of health services. The system also encourages transparency and accountability of health care centres. In Rwanda the system operates under three forms of contract: service providers, communities and district-level institutions. The PBF system is a key factor explaining Rwanda's success in significantly reducing maternal mortality.

Source: Compiled by the AfHDR Team based on WHO, 2013a.

not lie in technology and partnership among government, private sector, NGOs and development partners; the populations itself needs behavioural change. Education is the core driver changing behaviours in poor communities. There is no alternative to the continuous and well-targeted creation of awareness, community conversation and advocacy strategies.

Have a policy framework for scaling up innovative pilots. Africa has witnessed many successful pilot projects regarding maternal health at the government, private sector and development partner levels. These innovative projects were allowed to wither away without an appropriate framework for scale-up. While scale is very difficult to reach and could take a very long time to materialize, government and other stakeholders should not shy away from this vital responsibility.

Ensure that vital registration is an integral part of health management systems.

A critical challenge to progress in Africa remains the limited availability of timely and high-quality data. Countries should give priority to complete vital registration systems. This calls for steady investments in such systems to ensure the correct reporting of births, maternal deaths and the causes of maternal deaths, complemented with data collection through household surveys, continuous advancements in statistical modelling and analysis, and improvements in the reporting of maternal deaths from health care facilities.

Some of the most important policy innovations in Rwanda, which have led to a dramatic decrease in maternal mortality, are highlighted in box 3.1.

Education

Investing in education, especially for women and girls, has long been recognized as one of the most effective ways of promoting economic growth and sustainable development.

Education is a means for women to better access the labour market and achieve better employment outcomes. It is also an important channel through which improved human agency and participation in decision-making processes can impact long-term gender equality and social change (discussed in Chapter 6). Tight relationships between improved education and health indicators are well illustrated in the Conditional Transfer Programme in Malawi (box 3.2). Moreover, improved education for mothers has also been proven to have inter-generational impacts; it leads to better outcomes for children's nutrition and mortality. A greater share of household income for women has resulted in increased education for children.

The 2015 Africa MDG Report highlighted a number of general policy recommendations for improving the scale and quality of educational opportunities that were gleaned from best practices in several African countries (UNECA et al., 2015). These recommendations have direct bearing on expanding educational access by girls, as follows:

- **Reform policy:** Education policy reforms that reduce financial and cultural barriers to education, enforce compulsory primary education and prioritize early childhood development have yielded success in spurring enrolment. These inclusive policies were also adopted in other subsectors such as secondary education and non-formal education where access has also been expanded.

- **Empower the community:** Empowering local communities to run their own schools has boosted primary enrolment, particularly in poor communities. Prompted by fiscal constraints, there is a growing recognition that local empowerment can support schools being entirely funded by rural households, which include building classrooms and paying teachers' wages.

- **Reduce dropout rates.** Increasing access to primary schools must be complemented by improved completion rates if education is to have its intended effects. Low completion rates in primary school have been attributed to: poor health or malnutrition status of pupils; household situation (including child labour and poverty); and school factors such as teacher absenteeism, school location and poor educational provision.

- **Track attendance and enhancing the learning experience.** African governments need to address the challenge of mapping, as much as possible, all primary education facilities and identifying all school-aged children, including tracking down out-of-school children. This information is useful in gauging the scope of the nation's educational resource needs and in identifying how girls and/or marginalized children are not being adequately served by current facilities and services.

Closing the gender gap in educational attainment, especially in secondary and tertiary education, requires acknowledging the systemic discriminatory environments

BOX 3.2

Links between education and health in Malawi

After its first year of operation, Malawi's Conditional Transfer Programme led to large increases in self-reported school enrolment, as well as declines in early marriage, teenage pregnancy, sexual activity and risky sexual behaviour. The implication strongly suggests that as girls and young women returned to or stayed in school, they significantly delayed the onset of their sexual activity. In addition, girls and young women who were already sexually active reduced the frequency of their sexual activity. The programme also delayed marriage, which is the main alternative for schooling for young women in Malawi, and reduced their likelihood of becoming pregnant.

Source: Baird et al., 2011:20-21.

affecting girls. Although improvements in legal and institutional frameworks and higher political priorities can support further achievements, without tackling social norms around girls' education, success will not be complete. A number of interlocking factors obstruct school retention for girls and can diminish their learning opportunities: hostile learning environments; inadequate female teachers; discriminatory practices; sexual harassment; lack of sanitation facilities for young girls; and early pregnancies. Indeed, a lack of proper sanitation facilities tends to prevent girls from regularly attending school. When girls enter puberty, their absence from school increases if no adequate sanitation facilities are available. Reportedly, between 10-50 per cent of girls miss out on schooling for this reason.

An area of particular importance concerns the need for increased prioritization of Science, Technology, Engineering and Mathematics (STEM) education at the university level for both males, and particularly, females. Structural transformation of African economies depends on the progress of the government and private companies in being able to access STEM-based talent. The modernization of agriculture, the boost of sectors such as energy and transportation, and the development of the manufacturing sector are currently constrained by the lack of local talent (World Bank and Elsevier, 2015). The mobilization of foreign workers to fill gaps has important development costs in terms of lost job opportunities for young Africans. For example, the African Institute for Mathematical Science has graduated 960 students as of July 2015, only 31 per cent of whom were women. This shows an example of a gender gap for STEM education in line with the male bias noted above, in figure 3.8 for tertiary education. Closing the gender gap in tertiary education needs to factor in the strategic opportunity that graduating from STEM fields represents for African women and girls, as well as the overall benefits to the economy as a whole.

Obstacles to achieving equality in education also seem highly associated with governance. Some of the Continent's richest nations, such as Nigeria, appear to be making the slowest progress towards this goal:

Comparing the experiences of the two sub-Saharan African countries with the largest out-of-school populations in 1999 shows what can be achieved with strong political commitment in improving primary school completion. Ethiopia has made good progress while narrowing inequalities, and although it remains far from the target, it is advancing towards the goal. Nigeria, by contrast, has the world's largest number of children out of school. Its out-of-school population grew by 42 per cent between 1999 and 2010, and it is among the 15 countries that are likely to be off track in 2015. In addition, the high level of inequality has remained unchanged (UNESCO, 2014).

Case studies related to successful educational governance provide important lessons for broadening education. Key elements to achieve this are: empowering client communities to become active parties in decision-making instead of considering them mere subjects of consultations; incorporating information feedback loops to avoid knowledge being reserved for a selected few; and ensuring accountability at a personal, individual level so that policies, strategic plans, budgets, performance management systems and individual accountability and responsibility are all aligned. Finally, students and their families, users, affected groups, communities and taxpayers must play an integral part in defining the parameters and systems of monitoring and evaluation.

In general, more qualitative data are needed to understand the situation on the ground in terms of participation rates and the quality of education. In South Africa, although there seems to be higher educational achievement, many observers question the quality of education received in state schools, asking whether the pass rate actually reflects students' learning achievements. A recent court judgment finding the Government in contempt of court for ignoring earlier court orders to provide textbooks for schoolchildren appears to support this argument (Nkosi, 2012).

This example demonstrates that simple numerical data are not sufficient to form the basis for good policymaking. As UNESCO notes, many of the countries that show the poorest performance, such as post-conflict countries, have no data available. Focusing only on countries with publishable data is likely to be misleading for global policy debates, particularly as many of the countries without data are likely to be the furthest from achieving Universal Primary Education (UNESCO, 2014). The absence or poverty of empirical data is thus well-recognized as a problem that needs further action. In this respect, encouraging women to make their voices heard on matters of concern to them is an important approach for gaining the kind of thick data needed for carrying out additional education reforms.

Structural transformation across the African continent requires successfully leveraging the talent and intellect of African women. Significant inroads and unexpected opportunities and innovation may be irreplaceably lost when the full potential and capabilities of women's talents are squandered. As the World Economic Forum pointed out: "Because women account for one-half of a country's potential talent base, a nation's competitiveness in the long term depends significantly on whether and how it educates and utilizes its women" (World Economic Forum, 2014: 46).

Overall Policy and Implementation Issues:
Implications of the Current Status of Women's Health and Education for Promoting Gender Equality

- The status of women's health and educational attainment has greatly improved in Africa over the last two decades. Of note has been the achievement of near gender parity in primary school enrolment and major reductions in maternal mortality in most countries across the Continent.

- Gender discrimination is still significant in secondary and tertiary education, and women face severe deprivations to their health due to such factors as early age marriage, sexual and physical violence, and the continued unacceptable high incidence of maternal mortality. As a result, the number of 'missing women' is higher in Africa than any other developing region.

- African governments are generally well aware of the trends impacting on the status of women as well as the kinds of policies and programmes that could make a difference, but budget allocations to support necessary policy and programmes have fallen well short of the targets set by the AU for spending on the social sectors.

- As regards policies towards rendering health and education sectors more gender-responsive, there is room for considerable improvement through: the application of more systems-wide approaches to performance-based programming and budgeting; more gender-sensitive monitoring and evaluation; and the collection of more gender-focused data for informed decision-making.

GDP Losses due to gender gap
In labour market in sub-Saharan Africa (Billion $)

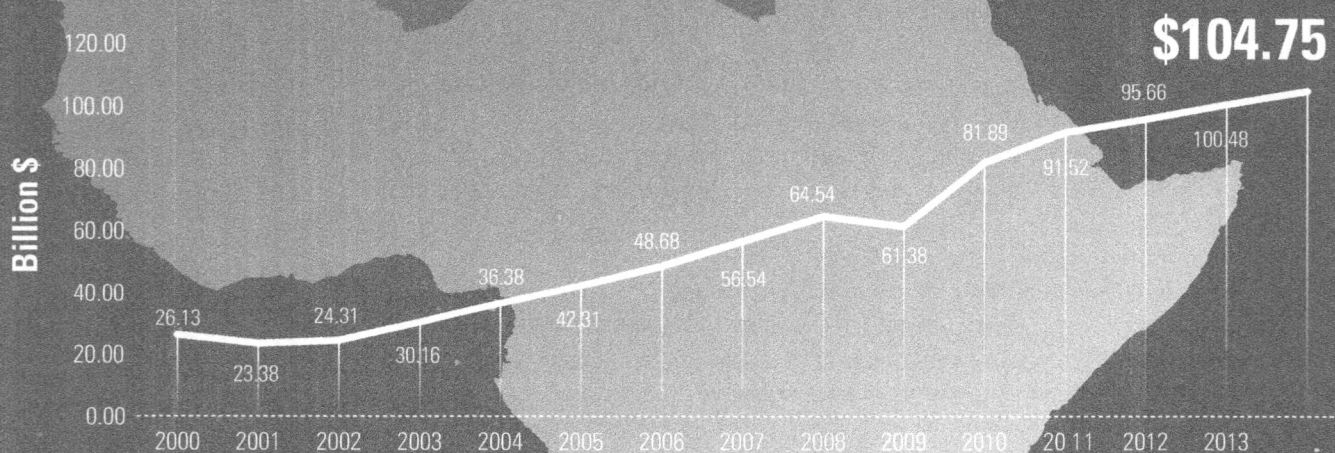

Billion $

Year	Value
2000	26.13
2001	23.38
2002	24.31
2003	30.16
2004	36.38
2005	42.31
2006	48.68
2007	56.54
2008	64.54
2009	61.38
2010	81.89
2011	91.52
2012	95.66
2013	100.48

$104.75

120.00
100.00
80.00
60.00
40.00
20.00
0.00

Source: Computed by AfHDR team.

Chapter 4

Women at Work

Chapter 4
Women at Work

This chapter explores the status of women in the 'workplace' — a term that must be understood in the African context to extend from the home to the boardroom; from unpaid labour and caregivers to owners of African companies; from market sellers and small-scale entrepreneurs in local communities to large companies engaged in cross-border and international trade; and from women with no formal training to women with advanced degrees and important positions in government, academia and the private sector.

Far too many African women are trapped at the lower end of the spectrum of economic opportunities, which often perpetuates the same socio-economic status for their own families.

As this chapter will demonstrate, however, far too many African women are trapped at the lower end of this spectrum of economic opportunities, which often perpetuates the same socio-economic status for their own families. As the economic status of women improves, so does the economic status of entire families — a major factor in reducing the blight of inter-generational poverty and low human development.

The chapter looks at women in the workplace from a number of different perspectives: (i) access to economic assets; (ii) women in labour markets; (iii) entrepreneurship; and (iv) women's work in the environment.

Access to economic assets and means of production

Economic inclusion, the universal access at a reasonable cost to a range of financial and productive assets, has proven fundamental for development. Economic inclusion has a strong positive influence on people's ability to improve their well-being and enhance their income-earning activities. It also stimulates job creation and protects people from unforeseen risks. Given women's roles in food production and household expenditure decisions, securing women's economic and financial needs can have a tremendous development impact. Securing clear land rights for women smallholder farmers is also critically linked with family nutrition, sustainable agriculture practices and higher productivity.

For the poor and near-poor, access to credit and to land are the key determinants for accelerating women's economic inclusion.

Access to financial services

The Continent has seen few improvements in the rates of access to formal financial institutions, but formal banking penetration does not generally reach the majority of the population, as in other developing regions of the world. According to the Global Findex Database, in sub-Saharan Africa, only 24 per cent of adults have bank accounts, leaving the remaining 76 per cent, more than 500 million people, outside the formal financial system. Penetration rates vary by gender, education and geographic location. The number of adults in urban or peri-urban areas who report using formal bank accounts is almost double of those in rural areas (38 versus 21 per cent) (Demirguc-Kunt and Klapper, 2012:18). With the region's history of migrant labour and rural areas predominantly inhabited by women, this urban-rural difference masks a gender divide. Thus, it is not surprising to note fewer women accessing formal bank accounts than men (22 versus 27 per cent in sub-Saharan Africa) (World Bank Global Findex Database). Education levels also play a significant role in the use of formal bank accounts; adults in sub-Saharan Africa with a tertiary or higher education are more than four times as likely to have a formal bank account as those with a primary education or less (55 versus 10 per cent).

FIGURE 4.1

Access to formal financial services, by gender and region

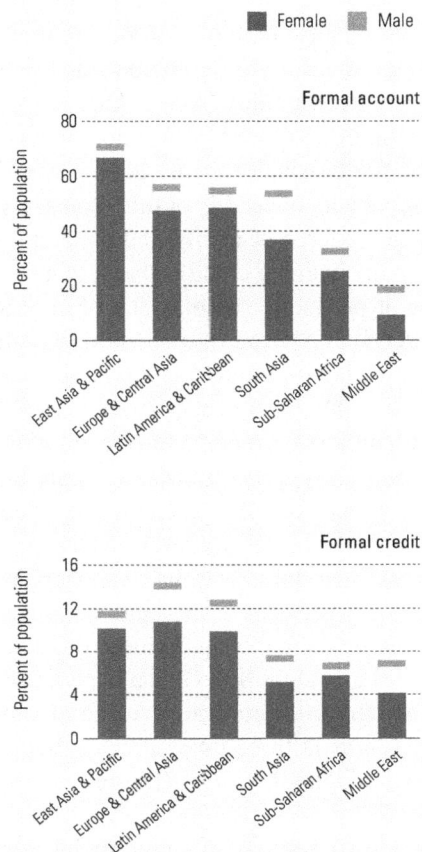

Source: Compiled by the AfHDR Team based on World Bank, 2015.

The World Bank's Global Findex Database further reveals that women are less likely than men to have formal bank accounts. In developing economies, women are 20 per cent less likely than men to have an account at a formal financial institution and 17 per cent less likely to have borrowed formally in the past year. Even if they can gain access to a loan, women often lack access to other financial services, such as savings, digital payment methods and insurance. Restrictions on opening a bank account, such as requirements for a male family member's permission, limit women's access to accounts. Lack of financial education can also limit women from gaining access to and benefitting from financial services. In addition, many women may have access to financial services in name only. The World Bank's Report on Gender at Work states: "On virtually every global measure, women are more economically excluded than men" (World Bank, 2014a). Figure 4.1 shows a comparison of men and women's access to formal financial services and credit by region.

In addition to formal institutions, community-based saving methods are partially compensating for exclusion from the formal banking sector. In the sub-Saharan African region, where they are most commonly used, 19 per cent of adults report having saved in the past year using savings groups or persons outside the family. Among those who report some savings activity in one 12-month period, 48 per cent used community-based savings methods. The practice is particularly common in West Africa. In Nigeria, for example, 44 per cent of adults (and 69 per cent of those who save) report using a savings group or person outside the family (Demirguc-Kunt and Klapper, 2012: 35).

The many positive impacts of providing even informal financial services to the poorest have been extensively documented for women, households and communities. Some of the benefits of savings groups are: they create supportive communities where there is a sense of unity and social interdependence; they support members in building assets and investing in businesses; and they create a feeling of security (CARE International, 2011). Other documented benefits include better family nutrition levels, high expenditure on healthcare and school fees, and growth in income and small businesses (CARE International, 2013). They generate a financial return on members' savings that have shown to be sustainable and robust (CARE International, 2011). It has also been shown that as savings groups mature and their funds increase, members may choose to link with banks for greater security and also to be able to access larger loans. Thus, savings group provide the opportunity to climb an entrepreneurship ladder that puts women on the first rungs of the formal economy.

BOX 4.1

Access to land

The WORTH Programme in Ethiopia

In Ethiopia, the international NGO, PACT, initiated the Women's Empowerment Programme (WORTH), which used savings groups as a starting point for supporting women to play a greater role in family decision making. The programme objectives were to increase women's incomes, and their social interaction and decision-making role in the family. With the idea that higher literacy could transform the roles of women and girls, the WORTH programme built its savings groups' training programmes around literacy, whereby members learn to read and write and do basic accounting. Material made available for reading covers self-help and basic business concepts.

WORTH reached about 9,000 individuals in 400 groups over a two-year period. It is reported that 66 per cent of group members showed an increase in their incomes, attributed to the diversification of businesses and increased investment in income-generating activities. Participating women reported that what they valued most about the programme was the increased stature they had in their communities and their increased self-confidence from both being literate and able to generate income. The programme is reported to have achieved significant levels of literacy, developed group solidarity, supported decision-making, and provided information on reproductive health.

Source: Compiled by the AfHDR Team based on PACT, 2016.

> Lack of access to land deprives African women of an important economic tool for improving their livelihoods.

Although strictly speaking the objective of the savings groups is usually to solve the financial exclusion of its members and support their economic empowerment, education is often 'piggybacked' onto savings group activities (CARE International 2011; 2013). As part of the process of setting up the savings groups, training is usually offered to members in establishing sound fund management practices and developing business skills. In some cases, organizations support savings groups with a focus on a particular subset of vulnerable people in the community, whether women or people affected by HIV/AIDS. In Mali, for example, Oxfam facilitates a group savings project, 'Saving for Change', which it has used to introduce groups to a malaria prevention and treatment curriculum (CARE International, 2011). In Ethiopia, the Women's Empowerment Programme (WORTH) empowers women in its saving groups through literacy, which has resulted in high positive impacts (box 4.1).

Worldwide, women are estimated to own less than 1 per cent of the land, but are considered to contribute between 60 and 80 per cent of their countries' food production, much of it as a free contribution to their household economies (ActionAid, 2015: 2). The situation of women's land ownership across Africa shadows this deep global inequality. Land ownership or title represents an important source of equity and collateral for women in obtaining credit and accessing other forms of productive assets; lack of access to land deprives African women of an important economic tool for improving their livelihoods. In Kenya, only 6 per cent of women hold title to land, although 96 per cent of rural women work on family farms. In Malawi, only 3 per cent of women are registered owners of commercial land, yet they represent 70 per cent of the workforce (ibid: 8-9). In Uganda, women own only 5 per cent of the land, yet account for the largest share of agricultural production (World Bank, 2008:86). Ghana is perhaps the least unequal: the monetary value of men's landholdings is three times greater than that of women's landholdings (Deere and Doss, 2006).

Both legal frameworks and social norms make it difficult for women across Africa to own assets. A survey of seven African countries (Cameroon, Ghana, Kenya, United Republic of Tanzania, Uganda, Zambia, and Zimbabwe) noted:

In many instances, when customary law applies, women's rights are excluded in areas related to adoption, marriage, divorce, and inheritance. This means that a woman's marital status may be a major factor in determining her right to inherit land. If a woman is married under church or civil law, and if she is listed as joint owner on property, she will usually inherit household land and property. But if the marriage is not registered and she is not listed on the title, the situation becomes much more complex and customary law may apply (UNDP and The Huairou Commission, 2014:7).

Recent survey data show that only one-third of women in the poorest wealth quintile households own agricultural land. Figure 4.2 shows women's share of agricultural holdings in select African countries. It is only in Cabo Verde, a service-oriented economy, that women's share of agricultural holdings is more than half.

Many factors are also threatening women's tenure rights over the land they use. The privatization of commonages, the destruction of indigenous forests, and the extension of cultivated lands as new investments and new technology redefine what is considered 'arable'. These and other factors impact negatively on women's ability to secure resources such as wood or indigenous plants. A gender-blind approach to land access shows that as men's access to land increases, women's tenure rights can become more insecure.

The exposed gender inequality in accessing land has severe developmental effects. The expansion of the economy as a whole, and the eradication of poverty in particular, are critically dependent on implementing gender equality in land ownership and agriculture. Agricultural production increases when women are given secure land tenure, as research has proven. Since land also functions as a security in accessing finance for productive investment, lack of title is a major factor holding back women's equal participation in the economy. When women's tenure rights are compromised by expanded commercial agriculture, family nutrition may be affected by a reduced variety and amount of available food, with the already well-known cascade of negative effects in diminishing family's health and education capabilities.

Women in the labour market

In 2013, the total labour force in sub-Saharan Africa was estimated at 357 million compared to 302 million in 2006, and 237 million in 1996 (ILO, 2015a). With around 13 million more young women and men seeking jobs every year, the labour market at the Continental level is growing at a rate far higher than the number of employment opportunities becoming available (table 4.1). Participation in the

With around 13 million more young women and men seeking jobs every year, the labour market in Africa is growing at a rate far higher than the number of employment opportunities becoming available.

FIGURE 4.2

African women's share of agricultural holdings, 2000-2012

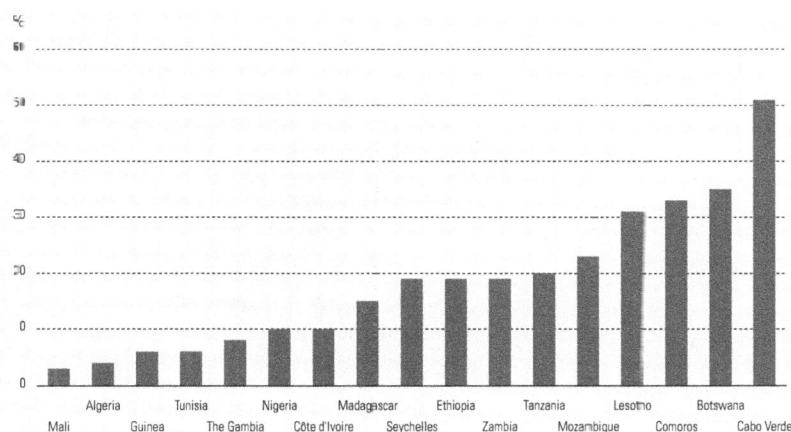

Source: Compiled by the AfHDR Team from FAO, 2016.

TABLE 4.1

Labour market trends and projections in sub-Saharan Africa, 2009-2019

Region	2009	2012	2013	2014	2015	2016	2017	2018	2019
Labour force participation rate	70.4	70.6	70.8	70.9	71	71.1	71.2	71.1	71.3
Unemployment rate (total)	7.9	7.9	7.7	7.7	7.7	7.7	7.7	7.7	7.6
Youth unemployment rate	12.5	12.3	11.8	11.8	11.8	11.8	11.8	11.8	11.8
Employment growth	2.8	3.1	3.3	3.1	3.1	3.1	3.1	3	3
Youth employment growth	2.2	2.7	3.3	2.7	2.7	2.7	2.7	2.7	2.6
Real wage growth	3.2	2.5	0.4	0.3	0.7	1.1	1.4	1.4	1.4
Productivity growth	-1.9	0.8	0.4	1.0	1.3	1.7	1.6	1.5	1.5

Source: Compiled by the AfHDR Team based on ILO, 2015c.

FIGURE 4.3

Labour force participation rates of adults and youth, by sex, 1991-2020

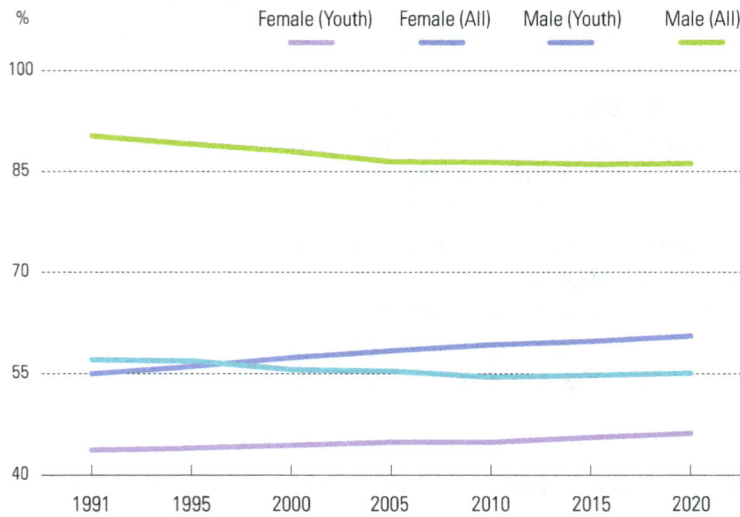

Source: Compiled by the AfHDR Team from ILO, 2015a.

labour force symbolizes a nation's potential for fostering economic growth by utilizing its most strategic asset – its human capital. In 2013, 77 per cent of males over 15 years of age were part of the labour market, compared with 65 per cent of women (ibid.).

Inequality in relation to the different participation rates of women and men in labour markets in Africa impedes the Continent's ability to fully use women's labour capabilities. Historical trends are positive, nonetheless, and evidence shows that Africa's labour gender gap is being narrowed but not closed (figure 4.3). The narrowing of the gap may be related to rising female education and falling fertility rates, although a full explanation is country-specific. Globally, progress in economic development has been accompanied by new employment opportunities for women in wholesale and retail trade, and the manufacturing sector. Economic integration has also led to growth in the export-oriented sectors employing women (UNDP 2013 HDR).

There are wide variations in labour participation by gender across sub-regions and different age groups. In North Africa, for example, gender gaps in labour force participation are wider across all age groups. The male participation rate is more than 50 percentage points higher than the female rate, compared to an average gap of 12 percentage points for sub-Saharan Africa. This situation can partly be explained by traditional value systems, which constrain women's work outside the home. In fact, between 1991 and 2013, the gap increased by 11 percentage points for the age group 35-54 years. The gap is lower for youth (aged 15-24) due to attitudinal change and less adherence to traditional beliefs in this age group. By contrast, gaps in participation are relatively low in East and Central Africa. Compared to 1991, the female participation rate in Central Africa was only two percentage points higher. In Western Africa, the gender gap in participation increased by only three percentage points for people aged 65 years and older.

Progress in participation has also been uneven across countries. For example, between 1991 and 2013, the female labour force participation rate in Zimbabwe increased by over 16 percentage points in contrast to a 10 percentage point increase for males. In Benin, the participation rate for males declined by 10 percentage points, while it increased by about the same magnitude for females (AfDB, 2014a). In Niger, the gender gap reduced from 65 percentage points in 1991 to 49 percentage points in 2013, a gap that is still unacceptably high. The uranium and telecommunications segments, as well as the discovery of oil have attracted foreign private investment, with spillover effects in sectors that employ women (AfDB, 2014c). While it is difficult to pinpoint the exact causes of increasing participation for women, global economic development and economic integration are opening up opportunities for them. Generally, higher prices for commodity exports, reductions in debt burdens, greater inflows of private capital, new discoveries of mineral and oil resources, and improved macroeconomic management are among the positive trends contributing to increased economic opportunities for women.

Figure 4.4 shows that the gender gap for labour force participation rates are lower for the age group of 15-24 years in all sub-regions. This can be related to the fact that young people may be in school or are less likely to participate in the labour market, although not always by choice. Figure 4.3 further shows that North Africa has the highest labour gap, which may be due to cultural and religious reasons that women are less likely to be in the labour market. Africa has the fastest growing and most youthful population in the world; over 40 per cent of the Continent's population is under 15. This poses challenges, but also brings opportunities for the region as a whole. A lack of adequate education and skill mismatches between skills supply and demand are the main obstacles to labour market participation. With the right policies, Africa could reap a demographic dividend.

The gender wage gap

The gender pay gap is defined as the relative difference in the average earnings of women and men. It is pervasive across all labour markets, and Africa is no exception. The gap manifests itself in two forms – direct discrimination where females with the same level of educational attainment and work experience are treated differently based on their sex and indirect, such as sex segregation of occupation, which is more subtle. Two main factors are responsible for gender pay gaps: (i) unequal access to opportunities such as education, due to traditional norms and value systems that ascribe different roles to women and men, and linked to the resources that women and men could access; and (ii) women's primary responsibility for home-care work, which channels them towards similar work areas in the labour market, called the 'selection effect'.

A majority of 'feminized' occupations such as clerks, teachers and nurses are poorly paid. Even in jobs such as teaching, the higher the level of education, the lower the proportion of female teachers. This indicates that although women's educational attainment has improved, it still trails behind that of males. (See figure 4.5 for the Malawian example.) There are also two ways to understand the selection effect – women deliberately

FIGURE 4.4

Gender gap in labour force participation rate by sex, broad age groups and sub-region

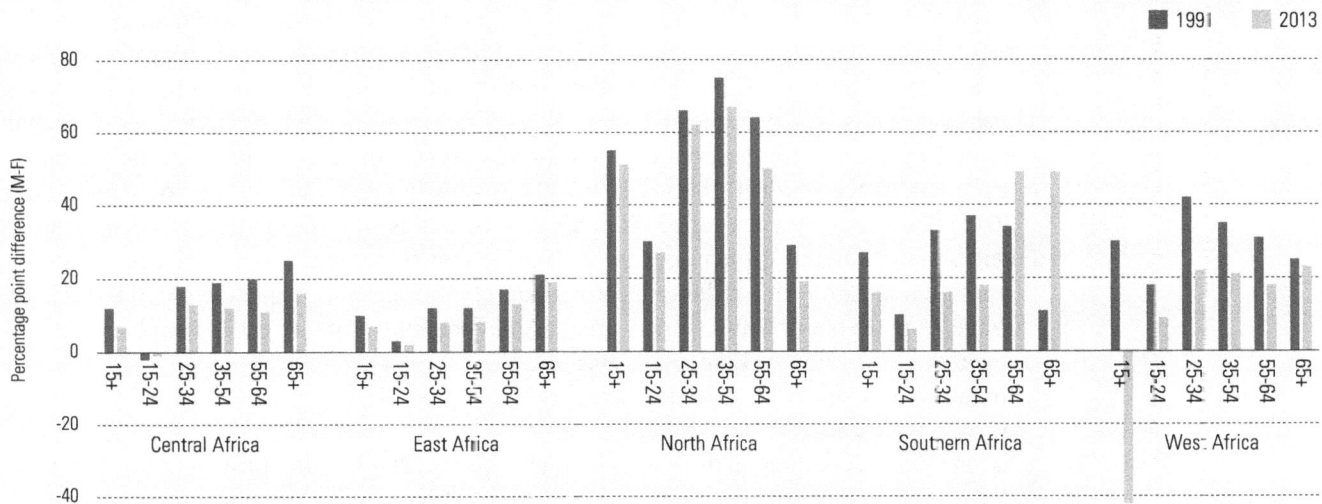

Source: Compiled by the AfHDR Team from ILO, 2015a.

FIGURE 4.5

Comparison of paid and unpaid labour in Malawi, by sex

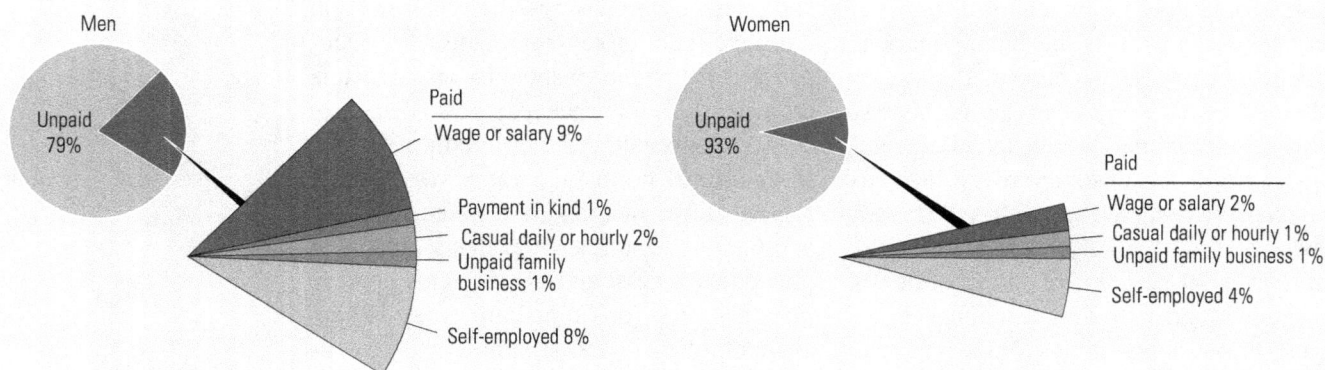

Men

Unpaid 79%

Paid
Wage or salary 9%

Payment in kind 1%
Casual daily or hourly 2%
Unpaid family business 1%

Self-employed 8%

Women

Unpaid 93%

Paid
Wage or salary 2%
Casual daily or hourly 1%
Unpaid family business 1%

Self-employed 4%

Source: UNDP 2015 Human Development Report.

> In terms of occupation type, women are heavily clustered in low paid occupations such as clerical work and manual labour.

choosing low-paid jobs or employers indirectly favouring men over women by failing to adapt the labour market to suit them. Other factors include the perception of women as economic dependents and the overall wage structure in a country, which are often shaped by wage-setting mechanisms designed with a focus on workers in male-dominated sectors (ILO, 2015c). For example, in some countries, the wage gap is wider at the top of the wage distribution ('glass ceilings') and in others, at the bottom of wage distribution ('sticky floors').

A gender wage gap outside agriculture is pervasive across all labour markets in sub-Saharan Africa, where, on average, the unadjusted gender pay gap is estimated at 30 per cent. Thus, for every US$1 equivalent earned by men in manufacturing, services and trade, women earn 70 cents (UN Women, 2016). The country gaps range from 17 per cent in Botswana to 39 per cent in Malawi, among countries with available information. Wage gaps explain why women are over-represented in the working poor. Based on findings from seven West African countries, women were found to have a high representation (70 per cent) among the lowest earnings decile, while only representing one-fifth of the highest decile, with cross-country variation. This gap in remuneration interferes with women's enjoyment of just and favourable conditions of work and equal remuneration for

work of equal value. It also results in women not being able to fully enjoy their rights to education and to participate in community activities and decision-making. The Integrated Local Development Programme in Morocco is helping to address some of these challenges (box 4.2).

Gaps in earnings between women and men are influenced by parameters such as age, occupation type, education, parenthood and marriage. One study found that the presence of children in a household is associated with gender pay gaps of 31 per cent compared to 4 per cent for those without children (Ñopo, Daza and Ramos, 2011). In terms of occupation type, women are heavily clustered in low paid occupations such as clerical work or manual labour. Increased female participation in the labour market has not led to increased opportunities in high paying jobs. The data show that the magnitude of the gender wage gap varies across occupation and the sector of the economy, among other variables (table 4.2).

Unemployment and informal employment

In 2013, unemployment in sub-Saharan Africa was 7.4 per cent, compared to 12.4 per cent in the North Africa sub-region, which is only slightly above the world average of 6 per cent (table 4.3). Unemployment statistics for Africa may seem encouraging compared to

TABLE 4.2

The gender wage gap in sub-Saharan Africa, by occupation and sector

Gender wage gap (%)	Occupation
39	Professionals and technicians
28	Elementary occupation
26	Skilled agricultural
24	Service workers
16	Administrative personnel and intermediary level
16	Machine operators
6	Directors and upper management

Gender wage gap (%)	Economic sector
58	Communal services
43	Mining and quarrying
35	Wholesale and retail trade, hotels and restaurants
27	Finance and business services
26	Agriculture, hunting, forestry and fisheries
19	Construction

Source: Ñopo, Daza and Ramos, 2011.

TABLE 4.3

Unemployment rates among the labour force, by developing region, 2013, 15 years and older

Region	Total %	Female%	Male %
Latin America & Caribbean	6.2	7.6	5.2
South Asia	4.3	4.4	4.1
North Africa	12.4	21.5	9.3
Sub-Saharan Africa	7.4	8.3	6.7
World	6	6.4	5.7

Source: Compiled by the AfHDR Team from ILO, 2015c.

BOX 4.2

The Integrated Local Development Programme, Oriental Region, Morocco

In the oriental territories of Morocco, women are significantly affected by economic difficulties and face challenges in accessing even basic social services. While young men have more opportunities to migrate to cities, young women face cultural and societal constraints that prevent them from accessing education and participating effectively in their communities. In addition to their traditional roles relating to the education of children, maintaining the household and manufacturing handicrafts, rural women are actively involved in the family economy through production activities related to farming and agriculture.

The Integrated Local Development Programme (DéLIO) was therefore designed in order to:

* promote good governance, enhance local knowledge, and strengthen capacity building within local structures;
* develop income-generating activities and job creation; and
* preserve natural resources.

After conducting an upstream analysis of rural girls' and women's lives, DéLIO proposed concrete, constructive measures. The programme encourages equal participation of men and women in the project's activities, such as ensuring gender equality during stakeholder consultations and specifically inviting women to participate in activities.

The DéLIO's partnership approach to decentralization has been well received by local stakeholders, including provinces, municipalities and civil society women's organizations. It also complements concurrent programmes and projects in the area, such as the National Initiative for Human, the Moulouya River Basin Agency, the agricultural development fund and the education programme.

DéLIO has built on complementarities with actions initiated by other partners. For example, the women's unit of the honey production operations in the Tafoughalt region was established through a project funded by the European Union. This unit is now fully operational because DéLIO provided additional facilities, including transportation. Another example is the olive-grinding unit in the same region, which was established by a partnership between a Moroccan association and Spain. DéLIO provided the modern equipment and helped to launch the activities. The municipalities' development plans were summarized, edited and printed through a partnership between United Nations Children's Fund (UNICEF), DéLIO and the General Directorate of Local Communities.

Source: PACT, 2016.

some developed economies where the rates are often in the double digits. But results should be analysed in line with the significant size of the informal economy of African economies and underemployment. Young people between 15 and 24 years of age bear a disproportionate burden of unemployment. Across sub-Saharan Africa, the ratios of youth to adult unemployment are close to or above two, while in 2013, the same ratio was nearly four in North Africa. There are almost twice as many female youth as males who are at risk of labour market and social exclusion.

On average, women spend twice as much time as men on domestic work, which includes child and elderly care, domestic work, and fetching water and wood. In Ghana and Zambia, time spent on transportation activities is three times greater for men than women, which suggests an area where there may be infrastructure gaps. In fact, improvements to access to water and wood were found to lead to approximately 900 hours/year work reductions in Uganda (Arbache, Kolev and Filipiak, 2010). In United Republic of Tanzania, women spend more than five times more than men doing domestic work (Budlender, 2008).

Social norms and beliefs assign African women the primary responsibility for care and domestic work. Studies show that in sub-Saharan Africa, 71 per cent of the burden of collecting water for households falls on women and girls. It is estimated that they spend 40 billion hours each year collecting water, an amount equivalent to a year's worth of labour by the entire workforce in France (UNDP, 2009).

The very high percentage of women in the informal sector has major implications for gender equality. Women as informal workers are less likely to have formal working arrangements, be covered by social protection, such as pensions and health care, or have regular earnings. The informal sector provides women with greater flexibility to meet family care obligations. Thus, their participation in the labour force has not been consistent with improved formal work opportunities. As such, women run the high risk of being trapped in a vicious circle of poor remuneration and

> Social norms and beliefs assign African women the primary responsibility for care and domestic work. In sub-Saharan Africa, about 71 per cent of the burden of collecting water for households fall on women and girls. This translates to about 40 billion hours per annum.

TABLE 4.4

Female share in non-agricultural, informal sector employment

Country	Survey year	% Female employment in non-agricultural informal sector
Mauritius	2009	6.7
South Africa	2010	16.8
Lesotho	2008	48.1
Ethiopia (urban)	2004	47.9
Zimbabwe	2004	53.1
Liberia	2010	65.4
Côte d'Ivoire	2008	82.8
Zambia	2008	70.3
Madagascar	2009	63.8
Uganda	2010	62.2
Tanzania (United Republic of)	2005/06	49.8
Mali	2004	79.6

Source: Compiled by AfHDR Team from ILO, 2013.

limited ability to invest in their families' healthcare and education, which in turn affects the overall development and growth prospects – not only for themselves, but also for future generations.

Using survey data for the 2004-2010 period, it is estimated, that the share of non-agricultural informal employment in sub-Saharan Africa is about 66 per cent of all female employment (Vanek et al., 2013). The proportion of women in non-agricultural informal employment ranges from 6.7 per cent in Mauritius to 82.8 per cent in Côte d'Ivoire (table 4.4). Limited access to education and the mismatch between women's skills and those demanded by the labour market contributed to the high share of women's employment in the informal economy.

Understandably, there is a significant although incomplete overlap between working informally and being poor. And improving the economic outcomes of female and male informal workers and supporting the informal sector are key components of Africa's development strategy. This has often included the determination of priority sectors and a greater concern for productivity, skills development, entrepreneurship and social protection.

In South Africa, for example, the Government launched one of the most extensive efforts anywhere in the world to formalize and regulate paid domestic work, a sphere widely dominated by women workers. To protect domestic workers, South Africa gave them, for the first time in the country's history, a political status and the right to organize into trade unions. In addition to trade union rights, key labour legislation was extended to give domestic workers access to the same rights as all other workers. This included a much-publicized national minimum wage, mandatory contracts of employment, state-legislated annual increases as well as an inclusion into unemployment insurance benefits, and even state-sponsored training (Ally, 2008).

The proportion of 'youth not in employment, education or training' (NEET) is a broad measure of untapped potential of youth. Because the youth NEET group is neither improving their future employability through investment in skills, nor gaining experience through employment, this group is particularly at risk of both labour market and social exclusion. In Africa, the NEET rate is 20 per cent for males and 35 per cent for females, with variations between North Africa and sub-Saharan Africa. In North Africa, the NEET rate is 22 per cent and 42 per cent for males and females, respectively, compared to 19 per cent and 33 per cent, respectively, in sub-Saharan Africa. At a country level, in 2012, the NEET rate in Benin was over 25 per cent; 29 per cent in Egypt and Liberia; 18 per cent in Malawi; 14 per cent in Mali; 16 per cent in Togo; and 28 per cent in Zambia (ILO, 2015a).

Unequal access to education and skills training, early marriage rates among female youth, and responsibilities for unpaid care and domestic work are some of the factors contributing to the high NEET rate among female youth.

Paid and unpaid work, care work and discretionary time

In terms of paid and unpaid work, men's and women's roles are generally very different, reflecting societal contexts, norms and values,

as well as perceptions, attitudes and historical gender roles. These different roles lead to markedly different opportunities and outcomes for human development. For example, the total time spent on work by women tends to exceed that by men. An analysis of time use surveys representing 69 per cent of the world's adult population shows that women account for 52 per cent of total hours worked, and men, 48 per cent (figure 4.6). Of the 59 per cent of work that is paid, mostly outside the home, the men's share is nearly double that of women – 38 versus 21 per cent. The picture is reversed for unpaid work, mostly within the home and encompassing a range of care responsibilities; of the 41 per cent of unpaid work, women perform three times more than men – 31 against 10 per cent.

According to time use surveys conducted in some 60 developing countries, women are typically responsible for more than 75 per cent of the time that their households spend on unpaid care. In low-income households, this adds up to many more hours than spent in middle- or high-income households, which generally have better access to basic services and can afford to hire help or buy labour-saving technology. In Africa alone, women average 200 million hours a day collecting

FIGURE 4.6

Comparison of hours spent on paid and unpaid works in developing countries, by sex

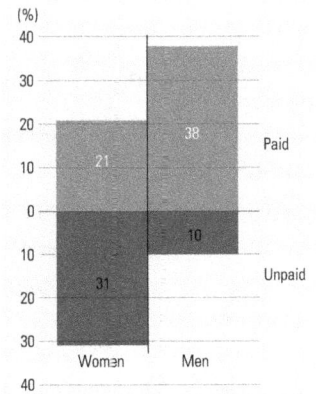

Note: Data represent the female and male population-weighted average of 63 countries representing 69 per cent of the world's adult (ages 15 and older) population.

Source: UNDP 2015 Human Development Report.

FIGURE 4.7

Comparison of leisure time for men and women, by human development group

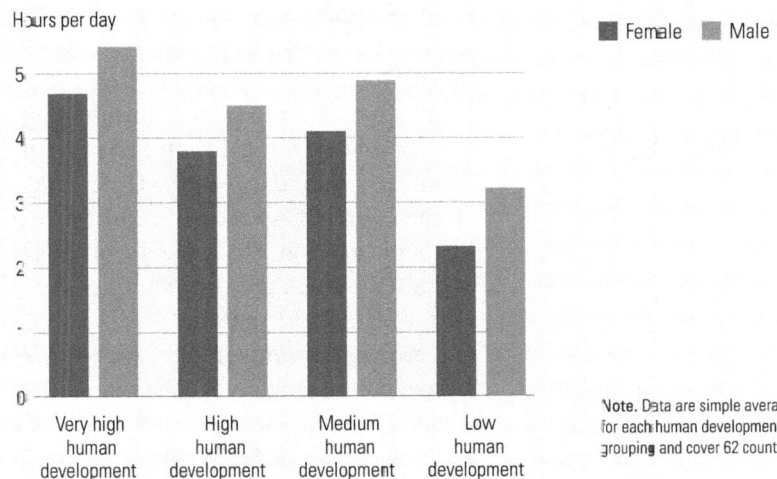

Note. Data are simple averages for each human development grouping and cover 62 countries.

Source: UNDP 2015 Human Development Report.

water. Even when the burden of this work is lessened, it remains labour-intensive and is an obstacle to pursuing other activities such as education, paid work and leisure.

The large percentage of women's time spent in unpaid work is reflected in women's discretionary free time. As women generally work longer hours than men, often involving unpaid care activities, women have less discretionary free time than men. In a sample of 62 countries, men average 4.5 hours a day of leisure and social activities, compared with women's 3.9 hours. The gap is wider at lower levels of human development: a 29 per cent gap in low human development countries, compared with 12 per cent in very high human development countries (figure 4.7). In sub-Saharan Africa, women tend to show both a high labour force participation rate and a high burden in care work, heavily restricting their free time. In United Republic of Tanzania, for example, women have less than two hours of leisure time per day (UNDP, 2015b).

Paid maternity leave and childcare

The absence or presence of paid maternity leave and the availability of childcare are other important barometers of gender equality in the economy, in addition to their social implications. The ILO Maternity Protection Convention, 2000 (No. 183) provides that mothers, regardless of the type of work, are entitled to maternity leave of not less than 14 weeks, which should be paid for collectively by employers and social insurance, at a rate of at least two-thirds the normal wage of the employee. Of the 44 sub-Saharan African countries with data, only 18, a majority of them French-speaking, conform to ILO Recommendation 191. Republic of the Congo and South Africa are two countries that provide longer paid maternity leave than the recommended number of weeks – 15 and 17 weeks, respectively; the remaining 24 countries provide less than 14 weeks of paid maternity leave (ILO, 2014).

Paid maternity leave provides a measure of job security guaranteeing that women of childbearing age have access to jobs and maintain their wages and benefits during the maternity period. Government-funded paid maternity leave has proven to have a positive effect on female employment in countries with higher levels of discriminatory social practices such as in Africa and South Asia. In one analysis, the predicted values of female labour force participation increase by 20 per cent in such countries if governments provide paid maternity leave.

With respect to childcare, only 18 countries have been identified across the African continent in which governments provide child support services for children below primary school-going age. The countries are spread across four sub-regions: Cameroon, Chad, Democratic Republic of the Congo, Gabon and Madagascar in Central Africa; Egypt and Tunisia in North Africa; Mozambique and Zambia in Southern Africa; and Benin, Burkina Faso, Liberia, Mali, Niger, Senegal and Sierra Leone in West Africa (World Bank, 2015a). In the public provision of childcare, the government funds childcare facilities and services, or subsidizes the use of private childcare facilities and services as well as the hiring of child-minders. Childcare takes several forms – kindergartens or crèches, day-care centres, after-school centres, in-home care and child-minding arrangements.

In the absence of public facilities and workplace childcare programmes, the concern is that women from poor households will opt out of the labour market or continue in the informal sector where they can combine work and childcare, or rely on informal networks for support. For example, in response to the question, "Who takes care of your child while you are working", 51 per cent of women from the poorest wealth quintile households in sub-Saharan Africa (with DHS data) said that they relied on their partners, other relatives, older children and neighbours, while 43 per cent combined work with childcare (ICF International, 2015). In Central Africa Republic, Côte d'Ivoire and Democratic Republic of the Congo, more than half of children under five are left in inadequate care – i.e. they are left alone or in the care of another child under ten years of age for more than one hour. Women are also more likely than men to cite

BOX 4.3

Childcare services in Kenya

The Ruiru Rose Farm

In Kenya, very few social security and workplace laws favour workers with family responsibilities. The Ruiru Rose Farm (greenhouses and factory) employs 360 permanent workers, of whom 60 per cent are women and 80 seasonal workers during peak seasons. The company provides childcare services for children between two months and four years in its day-care centre, in partnership with Pollen Ltd., German Development Bank (DEG) and the Max Havelaar Foundation.

The day-care centre is open all year, six days per week, and has a capacity for 100 children aged two months to four years. As of June 2008, it enrolled 60 children. Parents drop their children off at the crèche before walking or riding to work. The services provided at the centre include full nutrition and health-care services. In addition to the on-site nurse, the local family physician conducts regular visits together with a paediatrician to advise on the adequacy of the facilities and to carry out medical check-ups. The centre also has its own water well and grows its own vegetables and fruits.

The above has led to a reduction in women's absenteeism (unpaid leave for urgent matters) and unplanned annual leave to care for sick children), resulting in increases in productivity and the company's output delivery. In addition to the reduced absenteeism, from the employer's perspective, some other benefits of childcare include an increase in employee loyalty and commitment. In addition, most parents have seen an improvement in their families' living standards and their children's health and social skills. The day-care centre seems to benefit single mothers even more, as some reported that with the affordable childcare, they could now afford both lunch and transportation to work, instead of walking for almost an hour per day. Overall, childcare improved educational outcomes, not only for the children who attend, but also for older siblings who might otherwise be kept at home to look after younger siblings.

Source: Hein and Cassirer, 2010.

childcare responsibilities as the reason for not being in the labour force.

Workplace provision of childcare services is inexpensive and has been found to have high returns. Experience from Kenya and South Africa shows that workplace provision of childcare services provides a triple win – for employers, employees and communities. BMW Automobile Company in South Africa, First National Bank, Johannesburg and Old Mutual Cape Town are among large companies in South Africa providing workplace childcare services for employees. The programmes have been found to reduce family-related absenteeism, increase productivity and worker welfare, and help attract and retain workers.

Workplace childcare programmes are even more critical when companies with large numbers of workers are located in relatively isolated rural areas where there are few childcare services. On-site crèches and kindergartens for agricultural workers in Kenya are good examples (box 4.3).

Entrepreneurship

Among the business indicators used in many African countries, small- and medium-sized enterprises (SMEs) constitute the majority of African private enterprises; they represent more than 90 per cent of Ghana's total firms and 90 per cent of South African's total

BOX 4.4

Togo's INNOV'UP Programme

In Togo, women are important economic actors and contribute 46 per cent of GDP. However, women's enterprises are mainly informal, with over 70 per cent representation in this sector through small craft and trade activities. Although 54 per cent of the workforce is made up of women, there are only 30 per cent women in manufacturing and 40 per cent in agribusiness.

The Togolese leadership has reiterated its commitment to the economic empowerment of women, with the adoption of various gender mainstreaming policies and measures since 2006 and the ratification of the 2011 National Policy for Equity and Gender Equality. Despite these efforts, the implementation of gender mainstreaming policies have yet to reach their full potential and a great deal of work remains to be done to promote women entrepreneurship in the formal sector. Some of the major obstacles that women entrepreneurs are confronted with include lack of access to credit and productive resources (bookkeeping and computing skills, modern equipment, land, etc.), family constraints, poverty as well as social, cultural and economic biases.

To support the significant potential and contribution of women to Togo's economy, the Government of Togo and its development partners launched new initiatives to further empower women economically by helping them identify and exploit niche markets and by increasing their engagement across value chains. This is expected to help female entrepreneurs and women in the workforce take full advantage of business and job creation opportunities in the formal sector. In this context, the Federation of Women Entrepreneurs and Businesswomen of Togo, in collaboration with UNDP and the National Employment Agency, created the first business incubator support system for current and prospective women entrepreneurs, under the INNOV'UP programme.

The INNOV'UP incubator programme promotes women-owned or -operated businesses in the informal sector through active support and integrated economic initiatives in high potential areas for wealth and sustainable employment creation. The services offered through INNOV'UP include providing women entrepreneurs with work areas that are equipped with high-speed Internet connection broadband, top-notch IT services and group workspace. The centre also supports women entrepreneurs with business plan writing, networking, as well as bookkeeping and finance to provide them with critical business skill and opportunities. Several women's start-ups from various industries have benefitted from special services, training and other resources that have been instrumental to their success including:

Bouff Express – a newcomer in Togo's fast food industry

IBA – a rising star in mobile money and solar energy products in rural areas

Ets Genial Wok – a specialist in transforming fruits into juices and other beverages

Bioric Oil – a highly specialist in beauty products including castor oil.

The INNOV'UP incubation programme will serve at least 50 companies every two years and provide them with high quality services and technical support. In return, these recipients of the programme will create much-needed jobs and wealth creation opportunities for Togo's women and increasingly young population.

Source: Case study provided by UNDP Togo Country Office.

FIGURE 4.8

Percentage of firms with female participation in ownership in selected countries, 2006-2013 (%)

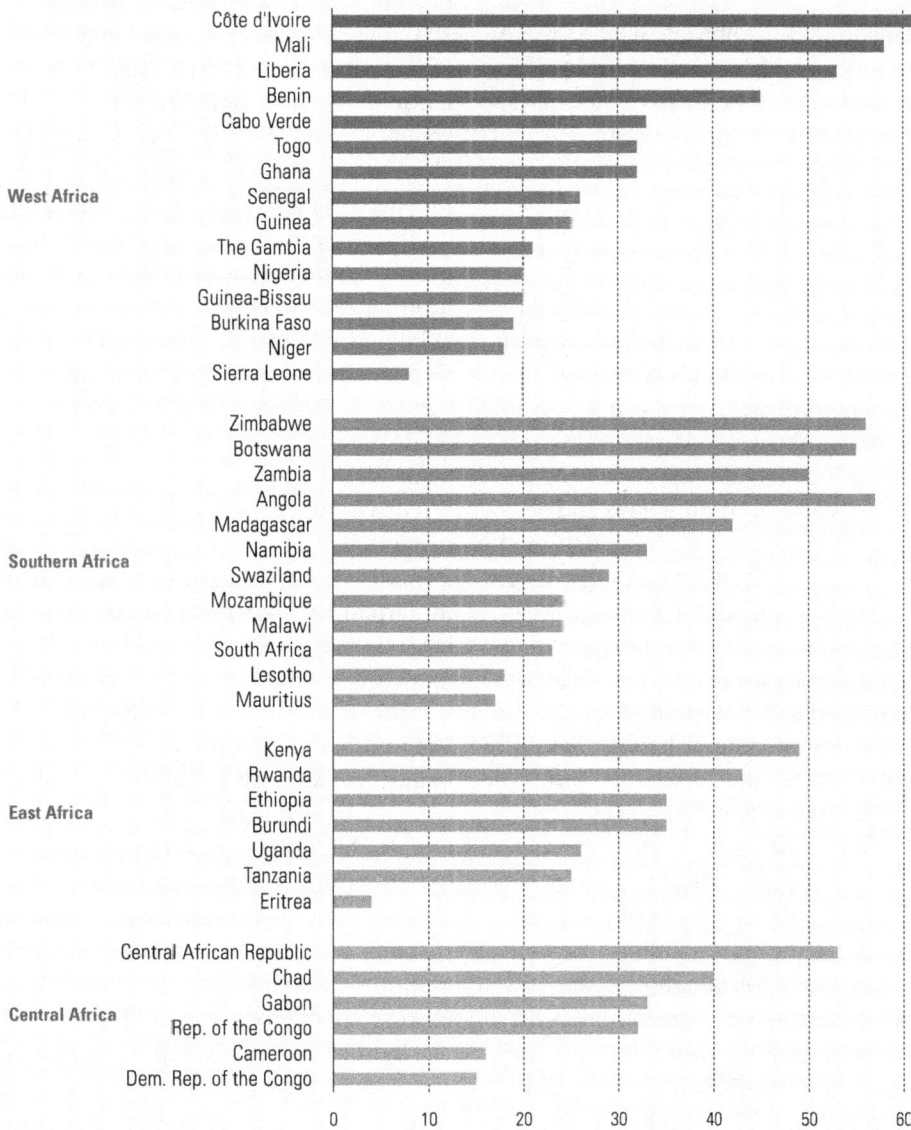

Source: Compiled by the AfHDR Team from World Bank, 2015b.

formal businesses. In Nigeria, SMEs account for a 70 per cent share of the entire manufacturing sector. Due to the small size of the formal sector, SMEs in the informal sector are crucial drivers for job generation. In countries such as Cameroon, Ghana, South Africa, Botswana, Ethiopia and Nigeria, SMEs are responsible for the creation of more than half of total employment opportunities. They have become the engines of growth in the region

and have served as an impetus for economic diversification in the past. (See box 4.4 for an example from Togo.) Nevertheless, in most African countries, SMEs contribute less than 20 per cent to GDP compared to up to 60 per cent in high-income countries (Tadesse, 2009).

The level of gender equality in SME ownership is often associated with constraining employment opportunities and slowing the integration of small-sized enterprises into the formal economy. A World Bank study (2015b) found that among 40 sub-Saharan countries, only eight showed a gender balance in SME ownership or a situation favourable to women. In the remaining 32 countries, women represent a minority of SME ownership; in many countries, less than 20 per cent of their SMEs have some level of female ownership.

Women's work and the environment

The natural environment is the obvious foundation for the livelihoods of people living in rural areas, representing the majority of people across almost all African countries. Environment-based livelihoods can be related directly to agricultural commodities and products, aquaculture, water sources, firewood, indigenous plants and other forestry-related resources such as handcrafts and tourism. Across the diverse environmental-based livelihood types, gender inequality arises and may put women at a disadvantage in accessing and benefitting from the natural habitat. Specific factors such as gender-based divisions of labour, income and power differences between men and women, the nature of their particular cultural roles and gender disparities in access to ownership of and benefits from productive resources are at the base of those inequalities. Environmental sustainability cannot be separated from the issue of gender inequality. Environmental degradation, deforestation and resource depletion intensify inequalities in livelihoods through their adverse impacts on already disadvantaged women.

For example, gender-based roles and gender job delineation make women and girls in Africa disproportionately responsible for water collection. They are expected to walk daily in search of clean water in order to perform their household chores. Depletion of water sources due to droughts or pollution increases inequalities by aggregating walking distance and time to the chore. This has an impact on educational advancement for girls, since they are more likely to combine water collection and schooling. Therefore, access to

clean water is important for girls' education, affording them health gains, time savings and more privacy. Women's involvement in water collection has also been shown to prevent them from engaging in higher return activities. One study in the United Republic of Tanzania, for example, indicates that the amount of time females spend collecting water is up to 250 hours per person per year, close to a month and a half of full-time work. Freeing women's time from water collection needs to be prioritized by policymakers for its positive implications in women's educational, health and economic spheres.

The 2012 Africa Human Development Report emphasized the importance of agriculture livelihoods for Africa's food security. GDP growth generated by agriculture has been also recognized as at least twice as effective in reducing poverty as growth generated by other sectors (UNDP, 2012a: 29). In Africa, women play a critical role in agriculture because they account for the largest share of farm workers. They are involved in cultivating for household consumption as well as in supplying markets. Discrimination against women in accessing land, together with prevailing social norms, are at the base of gender inequalities in agriculture. By far, the major part of women's labour in agriculture is non-wage-based, performed at home and within small-scale agricultural systems where marriage laws and customs assign ownership of land and decision-making about crops to men. Evidence shows that agricultural yields improve when women are granted land rights and the same access as male farmers to agricultural inputs such as fertilizers. Supporting women in increasing agricultural productivity through more inputs and technology, and through wider access to land ownership is a necessary action to reduce gender inequalities in agriculture.

Agricultural and other rural-based livelihoods are under threat from the looming impacts of climate change. There are expected threats to water availability, droughts and other severe weather patterns, such as flooding and changes in the patterns of seasonal rains. Increased exposure to droughts, more intense storms and floods will affect women's

> Environmental sustainability cannot be separated from the issue of gender inequality. Environmental degradation, deforestation and resource depletion intensify inequalities in livelihoods through their adverse impacts on already disadvantaged women.

livelihoods by damaging crops, reducing opportunities for employment, pushing up food prices, and affecting food security and health. Household insecurity resulting from low agricultural productivity and declining incomes will threaten advances in gender equality while threatening the nutritional status of children and their future human development prospects.

African forests have important economic, environmental and socio-cultural values through the provision of timber and non-timber products. Natural forests host a rich biodiversity and serve as the mainstay of the tourism industry for many countries. They support invaluable ecological functions such as water and soil protection. In Africa, handcrafted products made primarily of wood and other forest products are the source of livelihoods for millions of women and men. The majority of the population rely on wood energy for cooking, heating and food preservation. Forests are also one of the sources for the wild plants that women gather as part of the family sustenance in Africa.

At the same time, however, deforestation poses a major challenge as a diminishing source of livelihoods. Forests currently cover only about 23 per cent of Africa's land (FAO, 2012:184). Deforestation is often caused by pressures on the need for forest-clearing for new agricultural land and for firewood – tasks linked to women's work activities. Commercial timber trade is also one of the main sources of deforestation in a number of African countries. Weak enforcement and implementation of forestry legislation are contributing to rampant illegal logging, a significant loss of local and national revenue, as well as serious environmental impacts, which reinforce women's disadvantages.

Thus, women face a number of obstacles that hinder their full participation in forestry activities. They often have restricted access to productive resources, particularly tenure rights to land and trees. In one area of Kenya, the women were discouraged from growing trees because tree planting traditionally establishes tenure rights to land, and the men were afraid of losing control (FAO Corporate Document Repository).

BOX 4.5

The pilot village of Rubaya Cell, Rwanda

The village of Rubaya Cell, in Rwanda's northern district of Gicumbi, is located among the most environmentally fragile parts of Rwanda. Overexploitation of agricultural lands, inadequate soil and water conservation, and the destruction of wetlands are among the environmental challenges faced by the population. The pervasive effects of the environmental degradation in the area lead to lower and declining productivity, diminishing size of arable and pasture lands, and low income opportunities.

Rubaba Cell was launched in 2011 as a pilot village focused on addressing the current environmental challenges while concentrating on the goal of reducing poverty. It was an initiative of the Rwanda Environment Management Authority (REMA) with financial support from UNDP and United Nations Environment Programme (UNEP) under the Poverty and Environment Initiative. By 2012, the demonstration village was home to almost 200 people.

A combination of new technologies and sustainable management practices were successfully launched in Rubaya. Water management was improved due to the construction of water reservoirs and water harvesting tanks. The recover running water from heavy rain seasons is applied to irrigation, while tanks collect clean water to supply households. The village produces biogas and fertilizers from their cows as a result of training and the use of biogas digesters. New practices of terraces prevent further erosion of the soils, and solar energy provides more hours of light within the house, thus allowing family members to engage in education.

In the own words of a woman from Ruyaba Cell:
Before I came to live in the village, I was distressed by the fact of not being able to afford a solid shelter to house my six siblings and I was lonely with no close people to confide in...today, I not only have a nice house to come to, but I have neighbours to talk to; I have clean water at close distance; I have biogas to cook, milk and lighting for my siblings to be able to study in the evenings, and I go to university.

Source: UNDP, 2012b.

As forestry resources become scarce due to deforestation, agriculture expansion or logging, women's access becomes more limited. In Burkina Faso, for example, women lost a valuable source of shea nuts, traditionally collected for food and as a source of income, when village lands were cleared of shrubs in order to establish fast-growing pole plantations. Firewood collection fuels additional inequalities since, like water fetching, it is a task traditionally carried out by women. It has been estimated that wood collection can take 700 hours per person per year since distances to fuel wood sources can be up to five kilometres (Modi et al., 2005).

Due to the differentiated impact of climate-related events and environmental degradation on women and men, environmental sustainability is interconnected to gender equality aspirations. Interventions that would prevent wider gender inequalities are: actions to protect, restore and promote the sustainable use of terrestrial and marine ecosystems, water resources, biodiversity and forests; and actions to combat desertification and reverse land degradation. New approaches to adaptation are still needed to ensure the availability of social protection programmes aimed at building the resilience of vulnerable groups, such as women, and empowering them to manage climate risks. The pilot village of Rubaya in Rwanda is a good example (box 4.5). The impact of climate change reinforces the argument for economic diversification as an important adaptation strategy for African countries, and for especially the women who rely on narrow ranges of climate-sensitive economic activities.

Similarly, policy measures and regulations such as environmental impact and risk assessment procedures should be gender-sensitive. Economic initiatives with environmental risks, such as large-scale mining operations, logging and the expansion of large-scale agribusiness, require an assessment of the potential impacts on women and girls in terms of their health, their access to arable land and safe water, and changes to their traditional livelihoods.

The economic costs of lower participation rates of women in African economies

An important policy question arises for African governments in terms of the economic costs of lower participation rates by women in productive and remunerative economic activities. Economists have been exploring the degree of correlation between the fostering of gender equality, women's empowerment (defined as the ability of women to access the components of development – health, education, earning opportunities, rights and political participation) and overall economic development. Because country circumstances differ significantly, the directions of these correlations are not fully understood. Some

have argued that there is the potential bidirectional relationship between gender equality and women's empowerment, on the one hand, and economic development, on the other hand. The proponents of this bidirectional relationship argue that women's empowerment can substantially improve overall economic outcomes. It has already been shown that access to the components of development can play a crucial role in driving down inequality between men and women.

A study by Bandara (2015) analysed the 'impact of the gender gap in effective labour in Africa' (defined as the combined effect of the gender gaps in labour force participation and education) on economic output per worker. The analysis indicated that the gender gap in effective labour has a negative impact on the economic output of workers in African countries. A 1 per cent increase in the gender gap in effective labour leads to a reduction in output per worker by 0.43-0.49 per cent in Africa overall – 0.29-0.50 per cent in sub-Saharan Africa, and 0.26-0.32 per cent in a

TABLE 4.5

Economic cost of gender disparity in labour market in sub-Saharan Africa

Year	Cost of Gender Gap	Percentage share in GDP
2000	26.13	7.11
2001	23.38	6.83
2002	24.31	6.63
2003	30.16	6.44
2004	36.38	6.24
2005	42.31	6.18
2006	48.68	6.09
2007	56.54	6.09
2008	64.54	6.09
2009	61.38	6.06
2010	81.89	6.04
2011	91.52	5.99
2012	95.66	5.99
2013	100.48	5.99
2014	104.75	5.97
Average: 2010-2014	94.86	6.00

Source: Computed by the AfHDR Team.

wider group of countries from Africa and Asia. The estimated total annual economic losses due to gender gaps in effective labour could exceed $60 billion in sub-Saharan Africa. Results confirm that Africa is failing to achieve its full growth potential because a sizeable portion of its growth reserve – women – is not fully utilized.

This report calculates the economic costs of gender disparity in labour market in Sub-Saharan Africa and finds that women and African economies will benefit immensely if women's pay and their access to paid works were equal to those of men. The region has been losing billions of dollars over the years (Table 4.5) – peaking at about $105 billion in 2014. On average, between 2010 and 2014, the region lost about $95 billion annually - equivalent of about 6.0 percent of GDP. The magnitude of the loss indicates that low pay is an important factor perpetuating discrimination and exploitation. The loss is not only limited to the direct cost but also indirect costs associated with limited life choices like sexual and reproductive rights, sending their children to best schools and ensuring their families have access to quality health services.

Thus, in practice, persistent discrimination against women can substantially hinder development and could slow the pace of economic growth. It is clear that having high per capita GDP growth does not necessarily imply having a more gender-equal society. Indeed, even though the growth rate in Africa over the last decade has been substantial, mainly due to a sharp increase in the demand for natural resources and raw materials, the socio-economic structures of most African countries have not changed in tandem with GDP growth, nor has the status of women. From a policy perspective, then, macro-economic policies that fail to fully incorporate women's potential as a substantive component of any growth-oriented strategy risks diminishing potential economic growth outcomes. Empowering women is not only an ethical duty in its own right, but is also a rational economic decision. The position that women's empowerment is desirable for efficiency shapes both the policy debate and the resultant economic policies.

Overall Policy and Implementation Issues:
Implications of the Current Economic Status of Women in Promoting Gender Equality

Significant economic and workplace disparities between African men and women continue to be the norm rather than the exception.

- These disparities are found across the region in terms of access to economic assets, participation in the workplace, entrepreneurship opportunities, and use of and benefits from natural resources and the environment. There are sub-regional variations in economic disparities.

- The economic disparities identified reinforce the view that the absence or weakness of legal norms promoting women's empowerment and equal access to economic assets represents an ongoing and major obstacle.

- For many countries, the lack of programmes and entitlements in areas such as paid maternal leave and childcare services block or limit women's advancement in the workplace.

- Gender-defined economic roles, especially for the rural poor in such tasks as fetching firewood and water for the family, continue to hamper women's economic opportunities due to the significant time burdens.

- The pervasive gender gap in economic activities is constraining the continent's achievement of its full economic potential – averaging a loss of about $95 billion annually since 2010 in sub-Saharan Africa.

Women representation
in lower houses of parliament in Africa (%)

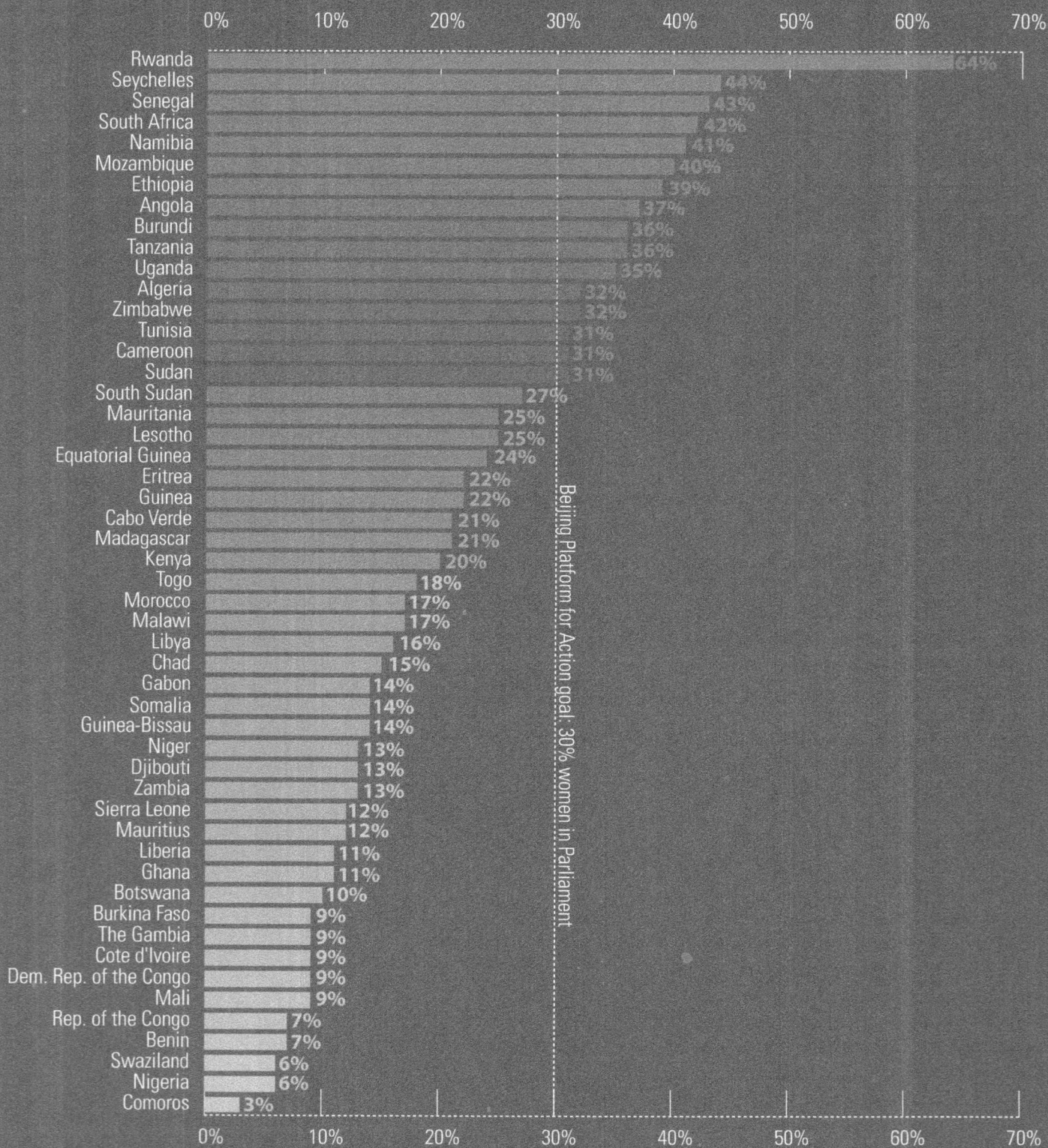

Country	Percentage
Rwanda	64%
Seychelles	44%
Senegal	43%
South Africa	42%
Namibia	41%
Mozambique	40%
Ethiopia	39%
Angola	37%
Burundi	36%
Tanzania	36%
Uganda	35%
Algeria	32%
Zimbabwe	32%
Tunisia	31%
Cameroon	31%
Sudan	31%
South Sudan	27%
Mauritania	25%
Lesotho	25%
Equatorial Guinea	24%
Eritrea	22%
Guinea	22%
Cabo Verde	21%
Madagascar	21%
Kenya	20%
Togo	18%
Morocco	17%
Malawi	17%
Libya	16%
Chad	15%
Gabon	14%
Somalia	14%
Guinea-Bissau	14%
Niger	13%
Djibouti	13%
Zambia	13%
Sierra Leone	12%
Mauritius	12%
Liberia	11%
Ghana	11%
Botswana	10%
Burkina Faso	9%
The Gambia	9%
Cote d'Ivoire	9%
Dem. Rep. of the Congo	9%
Mali	9%
Rep. of the Congo	7%
Benin	7%
Swaziland	6%
Nigeria	6%
Comoros	3%

Beijing Platform for Action goal: 30% women in Parliament

Chapter 5

Women, Politics and Leadership

Chapter 5
Women, Politics and Leadership

Many of the international and regional conventions and declarations have stressed the importance of increasing women's participation in political, economic and social decision-making. This chapter thus explores the progress and status of women in politics and other ways in which women in leadership positions are helping to shape the national dialogue. It reviews women in politics, government, trade unions and the private sector. The chapter concludes by focusing on the role of women in peacebuilding, a critical role in light of the devastating civil wars and conflicts that have long plagued the continent.

Women in politics

Women have become much more visible in African politics, where they are beginning to change the political agenda in their respective countries. The period since the 1995 Beijing Plan of Action has seen the ascension of African women to key decision-making positions, including the election and re-election of Africa's first female presidents. H.E. Ellen Sirleaf Johnson, the first elected female head of State in Africa, became President of Liberia as it emerged from conflict in 2005 and is currently serving her second term after re-election in 2011. Joyce Banda became President of Malawi in 2012, and H.E. Catherine Samba-Panza took over the Presidency of the Central African Republic in 2014. In 2015, H.E. Ameenah Gufrib-Fakium became President of Mauritius. Other women who were not elected nevertheless have also assumed top leadership positions in African states. Moreover, the election of H.E. Dr. Nkosazana Dlamini Zuma as the Chairperson of the African Union Commission in 2012 was a milestone in its 50-year existence since no woman had previously led the organization.

This emerging trend in women's political participation in Africa has been reflected by the increase in the number of women in parliament. At present, among lower or single house elective bodies, Rwanda is the global leader at 64 per cent, followed by Seychelles (44 per cent), Senegal (43 per cent) and South Africa (42 per cent); Namibia and Mozambique are close behind, at 41 per cent and 40 per cent, respectively. As table 5.1 shows, 14 countries surpassed the critical mass of 30 per cent representation that was promoted in the Beijing Platform for Action. Women are similarly visible in regional bodies, holding 50 per cent of the African Union parliamentary seats. Four African countries rank in the top ten globally, and another eight countries rank among the top 30 countries.

Even though some countries have made impressive strides in representation in their national assemblies, the role of women in African political parties still reveals the need for considerable improvement. Table 5.2 presents 2007 data in selected countries, showing the percentage of women in senior positons in political parties. The data reveal that while political parties are no longer a male-exclusive institution, there is still considerable room for more female participation.

At the local political level, there have been remarkable achievements in women's representation. Women make up almost 60 per cent of local government positions in Lesotho and Seychelles, 43 per cent of the members of local councils or municipal assemblies in Namibia, and over one-third of local government seats in Mauritania, Mozambique, United Republic of Tanzania and Uganda. In Sierra Leone, the level rose from 10 per cent in 2012 to 16 per cent in 2013 (IPU, 2015; UN Women, 2015).

> Women's political participation in Africa has been reflected by the increase in the number of women in parliament.

TABLE 5.1

Percentage of women in African upper and lower houses of parliament

Country	% Women in lower or single house	% Women in upper house or Senate
Rwanda	64	39
Seychelles	44	–
Senegal	43	–
South Africa	42	35
Namibia	41	23
Mozambique	40	–
Ethiopia	39	32
Angola	37	–
Burundi	36	42
Tanzania (United Republic of)	36	–
Uganda	35	–
Algeria	32	7
Zimbabwe	32	48
Tunisia	31	–
Cameroon	31	20
Sudan	31	35
South Sudan	27	10
Mauritania	25	14
Lesotho	25	24
Equatorial Guinea	24	14
Eritrea	22	–
Guinea	22	–
Cabo Verde	21	–
Madagascar	21	–
Kenya	20	27
Togo	18	–
Morocco	17	12
Malawi	17	–
Libya	16	–
Chad	15	–
Gabon	14	18
Somalia	14	–
Guinea-Bissau	14	–
Niger	13	–
Djibouti	13	–
Zambia	13	–
Sierra Leone	12	–
Mauritius	12	–
Liberia	11	10
Ghana	11	–
Botswana	10	–
Burkina Faso	9	–
The Gambia	9	–
Côte d'Ivoire	9	–
Democratic Republic of the Congo	9	5
Mali	9	–
Congo (Rep. of the)	7	19
Benin	7	–
Swaziland	6	33
Nigeria	6	7
Comoros	3	–

Source: IPU, 2016.

TABLE 5.2

Senior positions in political parties in selected African countries, by sex, 2007

Country	Percentage of women out of total (%)	Total number of women	Total number of men	Total number
South Africa	25	24	71	95
Benin	18	86	386	472
Madagascar	18	86	386	472
Uganda	15	9	50	59
Tunisia	14	119	728	847
Burkina Faso	12	119	850	969
Ghana	12	8	60	68
Ethiopia	5	31	637	668
Tanzania (United Republic of)	4	1	22	23
Egypt	4	226	5,414	5,640
Mozambique	0	0	31	31

Source: Based on UNECA, 2007.

The increase in participation by women in elections can be measured not just in terms of female elected candidates, but also by the percentage of female voters. More women than men vote in Botswana, Cabo Verde, Lesotho, South Africa and Senegal, although overall rates for men seem to be about 5 per cent higher in all countries surveyed by Afrobarometer (Tripp, 2013).

The engendering of democracy in African states is not in question. The increased presence of women in politics is contributing towards addressing deeply historical inequalities in the political systems of the Continent. Women's political participation and representation in governance have long been taken as key indicators of the general level of democracy in a country. To the extent that more women are involved in politics, women's rights, priorities, needs and interests are less likely to be ignored or silenced. Historically, women's involvement has been minimized even though they account for at least half of the populations in most countries. For this very reason, their level of involvement and engagement in public and political life is key. Engendering African democracies

BOX 5.1

Training women for political candidacy in Tunisia

During the revolution of 2011, woman as well as men demonstrated in the streets of Tunisia. More women's organizations sprung up in response to the greater participation of women in public life, and despite the political polarization that emerged, these groups managed to stay united to press for the preservation and advancement of women's rights. The Constitution of January 2014 ensures equality of opportunity to achieve parity between women and men in elected posi-tions, and highlights the role of the state in eliminating violence against women.

Women now make up 31.3 per cent of the elected national representatives in Tunisia, a significant change from the 11.5 per cent in 1999. This progress is due in large part to the efforts that women's organizations have made, pushing for a more representative parliament that would understand women's specific needs and challenges. In particular, the use of alternating gender lists for elections has been instrumental in achieving this increase in women's political participation.

However, important challenges remain, including attitudes that a large proportion of Tunisians hold about women in political life. A UNDP survey from 2013 found that 28 per cent of Tunisians were hostile to women's political participation, of whom 24 per cent felt that women's place was in the home.

In January 2014, **Association Tounissiet**, *Tounissiet Gabès, Association Tunisienne des Femmes Juriste*s and *La Justice Fondement de la Cité* jointly launched a project to encourage women from *Grand Tunis* and *Gabès* to take part in elections later that year. One hundred women with leadership potential were selected to take part in a series of trainings to help develop their skills as political candidates, including political theory, communication and media relations.

Of these 100 women trained, 12 stood as candidates in the electoral lists, and three were elected to the *Assemblée des représentants du peuple* (ARP, Assembly of the Representatives of the People). In addition to the tangible effects of three newly elected women as a result of the programme, the larger cohort of women has gained confidence, and will be a remarkable resource for the future, both as political candidates and as role models for Tunisian women more broadly.

Key to the success of this intervention was the process of selection for the training participants. This selection was made by the collaborating organizations whose strong background in working with women on the ground made it possible to identify women whose aptitude for leadership might otherwise have been overlooked.

Source: Case Study prepared by UNDP Tunisia Country Office, 2016.

BOX 5.2

Inter-African collaboration to support women's political effectiveness

The collaboration of Cabo Verde women parliamentarians in building the capacity of their counterparts of Guinea-Bissau represents a good example of inter-African South-South Cooperation. These efforts led to the formation of a nucleus of eight women parliamentarians capable of conducting critical analysis of public budget gender sensitivity and producing sound policy recommendations. In addition, the training of the Court of Auditor's judges by Cabo Verdean experts on how to analyse and express their opinion on the State General Account has permitted, for the first time, the audit exercise of 2009 and 2010 public accounts and the production of two reports used by the National Parliament. The exchange through study tours to Mozambique, Cabo Verde, Togo and Mali by the Guinea-Bissau Ministry of Public Service and Parliament members contributed to enhancing the Government of Guinea-Bissau's efforts to implement public administration reform and modernization.

Source: UNDP Country Office Case Studies.

through greater women's participation is part of the structural transformation necessary for achieving social equality and higher human development.

The most relevant drivers of the progress being achieved in different African states in engendering their democracies are illustrated in figure 5.1. It is essential to further strengthen these drivers to continue the structural transformation in the political arena, which in many countries still remains largely male-dominated. African activists and women's movements – e.g. Action for Development in Uganda, the National Women's Lobby Group in Zambia, the National Committee on the Status of Women in Kenya, and the Women of Zimbabwe Arise as well as Forum Mulher in Mozambique – have played key roles in the local, national and international networks promoting a collective voice. The influence of women's movements has been a factor in the transformation of national constitutions in several countries. This has resulted in more gender-equitable access to civil law (generally understood as a better vehicle for women's political participation), the protection of women's rights and the realization of their citizenship.

However, it is still necessary to broaden grassroots support for feminist and women's associations and increase their efforts in advocating for women's political representation and participation. The expansion and strengthening of a multi-generational network and pool of women leaders across the Continent would multiply achievements in engendering democracy.

Holding political office per se has been insufficient in effectively addressing gender inequality. Occupying a seat in parliament is an important achievement, but gender dynamics pervading the political sphere impose additional obstacles. Elected women are still subject to existing structures and manipulations that constantly subvert commitments to gender equality and complicate the pursuit of gender-balanced policies.

Prevailing social norms will continuously challenge any past progress and future actions to fully leverage women's potential for participating in political decision-making

FIGURE 5.1

Drivers for increasing women's participation in politics in Africa

and governance. Although there has been increasing representation of women in parliaments and cabinets, all national reviews on the implementation of the Beijing Platform for Action indicate that there is still a low representation of women in decision-making processes.

Leadership in the public and private sectors

Women's leadership in the public administration

As in the sphere of politics, women's leadership in public administration has been on the ascent in recent decades. Yet, many African states have fallen behind on the target of a minimum of 30 per cent of women in leadership positions, as originally endorsed by the United Nations Economic and Social Council in 1990 and reaffirmed in the Beijing Platform for Action in 1995.

Table 5.3 shows the percentage of women holding senior leadership positions in the administration of 11 African countries, as compiled by the UNDP's report on Gender Equality in Public Administration (UNDP, 2014). While in several countries, more than one third of civil servants are women, only

Although some countries have been highly successful in electing women to their parliaments and other elected offices, existing social and political structures still proscribe women's full potential in helping to equally shape the national and local political and policy agenda.

Botswana and South Africa have surpassed the milestone of 30 per cent of women in senior decision-making positions. While the country figures in this table are dated to some extent, they suggest that the gap in women's leadership in the public sector may be closing but needs urgent attention. At a global level, achievements are not much better. According to a recent study developed in the G20 major economies, women still represent less than 20 per cent of public sector leadership even though they account for almost half of the overall public sector workforce (UNDP, 2014).

A fundamental argument for increased representation of women in the public service is that when the composition of the public sector reflects the composition of the society it serves, the government will be more responsive and effective. Thus, closing gender gaps in public administration is important for ensuring truly inclusive development and democratic governance, and helps to restore trust and confidence in public institutions as well as enhance the sustainability and responsiveness of public policies. This is a critical policy issue in both developing and developed countries.

Women's equal participation in public administration and decision-making is a necessary condition for women's interests to be taken fully into account and properly addressed. According to UNDP's 2011 Human Development Report on Sustainability and Equity, analysis shows how power imbalances and gender inequalities at the national level are linked to unequal access to clean water and better sanitation, impacts on land degradation, and other environmental concerns (UNDP, 2011:45-46). Without a critical mass of women in public administration, who generally represent more than half of the population, African countries may not be able to tap into the full potential of their national workforce, capacity and creativity.

Since the civil service is an important employer in many countries, equal participation in the public service can have a significant impact on women's economic empowerment. Anti-discrimination policies and legislation partially explain the progress made by women in achieving leadership positions. The affirmative action on women's participation in leadership and governance in Kenya is a good example (box 5.3). The lack of enforcement of these instruments and weak accountability for their implementation are also part of the root cause of the leadership gap still prevailing in the Africa region.

Female leadership in trade unions

Women in Africa have played a critical role in advancing and protecting workers' rights. For more than a decade, they have been advocating for workers' rights and have supported initiatives in the mobilization of workers and the organization of trade unions within various workplaces. Women in trade unions have made links between struggles in the factory, the community, the country, and at home. They have pushed for a range of reforms by opening the debate on the links between realms usually conceived as separate: the personal and the political; the home and the workplace; and child-bearing and work-related labour. Some activities promoted by women leaders have involved community education programmes on domestic violence

> Closing gender gaps in public administration helps to ensure democratic governance, restore trust and confidence in public institutions, and accelerate the responsiveness of government policies and programmes.

TABLE 5.3

Women's participation in public administration and managerial positions

Country	Overall (%)	Decision-making levels (%)
Benin (2011, 2012)	19	22
Botswana (2012, 2009)	52	45
Burundi	–	12
Cameroon (2010)	25	–
Gambia (2007)	25	20
Mali (2009)	28	15
Morocco (2009)	34	15
Nigeria (2006)	24	22
South Africa (2011)	56	35
Tunisia (2011)	41	27
Uganda (2011)	33	22

Source: UNDP, 2014.

and workplace harassment against women; others include awareness campaigns that explicitly link sexual violence/exploitation at the workplace and the home.

In South Africa, for example, women workers called for "equal pay for work of equal value" and challenged discriminatory practices in wages. In 1981, after pressure from women who raised the issue with the National Union of Textile Workers, an agreement was reached with the company South African Fabrics to close the wage gap between women and men workers in the industry and pay women the minimum rates, equivalent to those of male workers. The gains that women were making in some workplaces were vital in mobilizing them to be proactive in protecting their rights to employment. Moreover, several studies on women and trade unions have shown how African women workers in textile industries have organized against inhumane working and living conditions (e.g. low wages, workplace harassment, substandard housing, state/corporate restrictions on unionization). In some cases, women have used part of their own meagre wages and allied themselves with local women's and community organizations to set up several activities. This includes setting up of legal aid centres that assist in fighting workplace sexual harassment, the publication and distribution of newspapers, and the establishment of a women's centre that provides legal education, medical assistance, small credit and skills training. This challenges the traditional definitions of labour issues or workplace politics (Baskin, 1991).

In recent years, women's membership in trade unions has increased, but has not resulted in a corresponding expansion of women's presence in union decision-making bodies (table 5.4). When achieving leadership positions, women's participation in trade unions tends to be limited to 'women's issues' and women are excluded from participating in 'hard core issues' that require collective bargaining agreements with employers and governments.

Women's collective action, therefore, has focused on the expansion of women's organizations, which engage in advocacy, lobbying,

BOX 5.3

Kenyan affirmative action on women's participation in leadership and governance

In Kenya, women's participation in leadership, governance and decision-making has increased from 20.5 per cent in 2008 to 38.6 per cent in 2012 due to affirmative action measures provided in the Constitution.

The implementation of the Constitution led to more than 600 women being nominated in county assemblies since only 88 women (6 per cent) had been elected out of the 1,450 county assembly members. The National Assembly constitutes 19.8 per cent women (47 women representatives, 16 elected and six nominated members of Parliament). Women comprise 23.35 per cent in both the National Assembly (19.8 per cent) and the Senate (26.9 per cent) combined, for a total of 87 women compared to 331 men. This is the highest number of women legislators ever recorded in Kenya. In the last Parliament, there were only 9.9 per cent women under the old Constitution. In addition, for the first time in history, the country has a female Deputy Speaker of the National Assembly and a female Chief Whip in the Senate.

Within the judiciary, women constitute 28.6 per cent of the total number of Supreme Court judges, and the number of women magistrates rose from 182 in 2013 to 219 in 2014. Women also hold 33.3 per cent and 26.9 per cent in the positions of Cabinet Secretary and Principal Secretary, respectively. In all other constitutional offices, women comprise 41.7 per cent of chairpersons of constitutional commissions, compared to 50 per cent in the independent offices. Overall, there was an increase in women representation in public institutions from 32.4 per cent in 2008 to 38 per cent in 2012.

Source: Case Study prepared by UNDP Kenya Country Office, 2015.

TABLE 5.4

Involvement in trade union leadership positions in selected countries, by sex, 2007

Country	Percentage of women out of the total (%)	Total number of women	Total number of men	Total number of leaders
Uganda	34	30	59	89
Mozambique	27	102	270	372
South Africa	26	6	17	23
Benin	20	69	269	338
Burkina Faso	19	41	180	221
Ethiopia	17	622	3,010	3,632
Tanzania (United Republic of)	17	2	10	12
Madagascar	1	20	104	124
Ghana	12	25	180	205
Egypt	4	1	22	23
Tunisia	1	1	99	100

Source: UNECA, 2007.

and coalition-building with trade unions, human rights groups and government agencies. One example is the National Union of Eritrean Women (NUEW), founded in 1979, which, under a broad gender equality mission, advocates for equal pay for equal work, equal rights to skills development and promotion, and improved access to paid maternal leave and childcare services. The association manages skills training, literacy and self-improvement programmes, as well as rural credit schemes and other development projects. It also routinely monitors and advises other bodies on legislation, trade union contracts, and policies that affect women. Each of these projects was accompanied by consciousness-raising seminars. NUEW had a positive effect on the lives of tens of thousands of women and helped give them access to areas of the country's economic, social and political life previously denied to them (Thurshen, 2010).

The potential of trade unions to bring about the much-needed structural change in labour markets may be lost if the gender gap in leadership is not resolved. The traditional masculine culture of trade unions and the male bias of the union agendas are structural inequalities to confront and question. It is necessary for a more inclusive and equity-based trade union agenda to transform trade unions and thus influence economic and social agendas.

Women's leadership in the private sector

Figure 5.2 provides a regional comparison of women in senior leadership positions in private companies and the percentage of companies with no women in senior management positions across different regional groups. From this perspective, Africa performs fairly well in comparison to other regions, outperforming Developed Asia and the Pacific, Latin America and North America in the number of senior positons held by women. Developed Asia and the Pacific, and Latin America also have higher percentages of companies with no women senior managers.

Turning specifically to Africa, just as in the public sector, gaps in women's leadership also persist in the formal private sector. Although the trend is improving, the percentage of firms with a female top manager still ranges between 7 and 30 per cent, as presented in figure 5.3.

In addition, data do not support the general perception that male enterprises outperform female ones, nor do they justify the gap in leadership. Information on enterprise performance disaggregated by the gender of the top manager is available for a limited number of countries. As shown in table 5.5, results are mixed. For example, capacity utilization is higher among enterprises with female top managers in a number of countries, especially those in West Africa. Employment growth follows a similar pattern.

The proportion of women in boardrooms is unacceptably low but the trend is positive. In South Africa, during the eight-year period from 2004 to 2013, this proportion increased from 7 to 17 per cent in publically traded company boards, and from 7 to 34 per cent in state-owned enterprise boards. Data from other African countries show that achievements are highly insufficient and that gender inequality in boardrooms is the standard across the continent.

FIGURE 5.2

Women in senior management positons in the private sector, by regional group

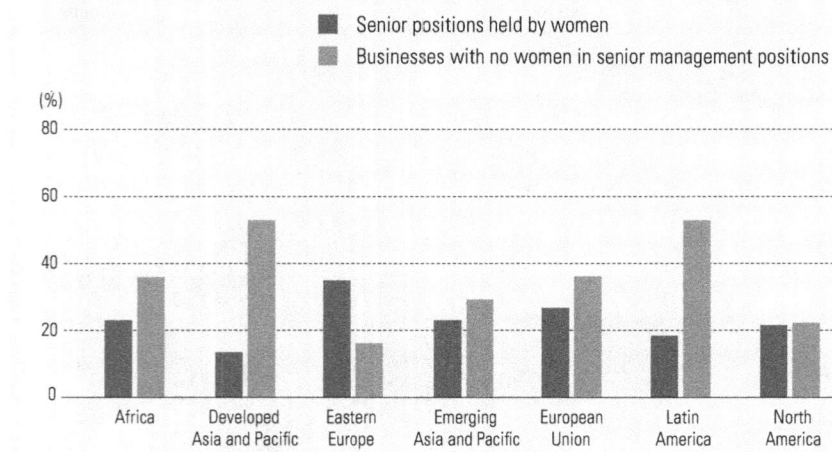

Source: Compiled by the AfHDR Team from UNDP, 2015.

FIGURE 5.3

Percentage of firms with female top managers

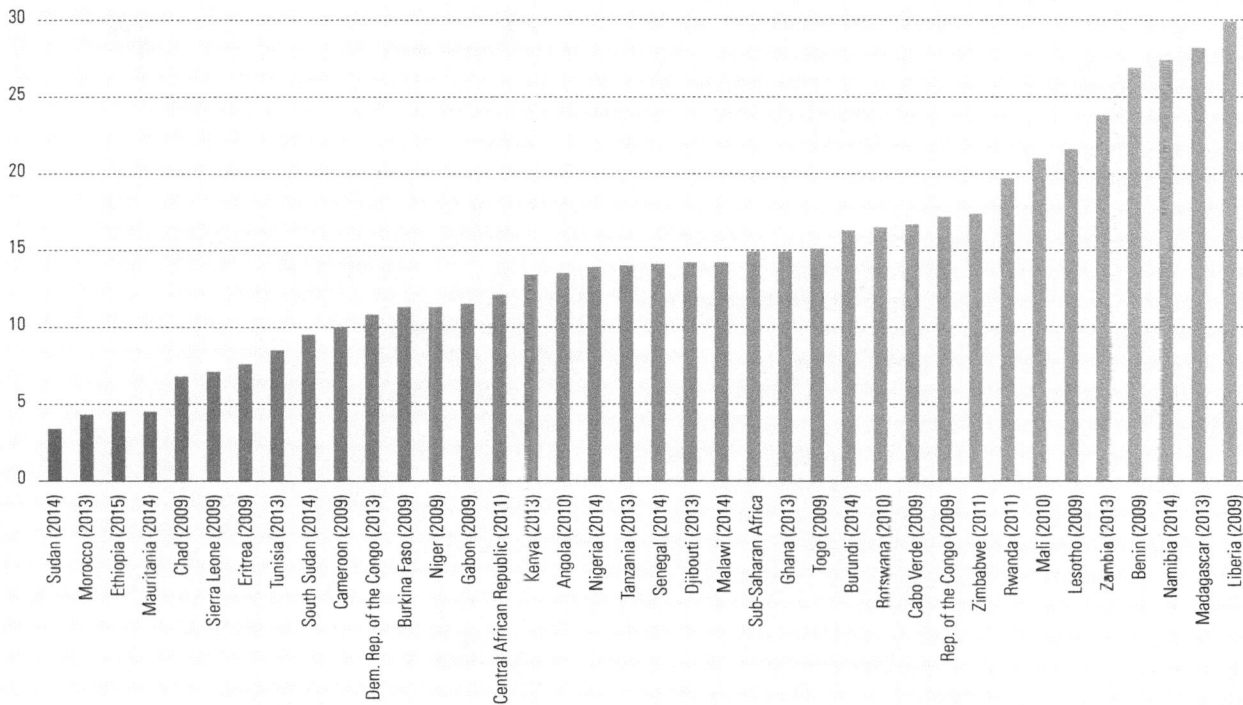

Source: Compiled by the AfHDR Team from World Bank, 2015b.

TABLE 5.5

Enterprise performance of top managers, by sex (%)

Numbers in **bold** signify best performance.	Capacity utilization		Real annual sales growth		Annual employment growth (%)		Annual labour productivity growth (%)	
	Female	Male	Female	Male	Female	Male	Female	Male
Angola	**69.2**	61.3	**76.3**	64.8	**16.4**	14	**66.1**	57.8
Burkina Faso	**74.8**	71.5	12	**13.7**	**9.1**	6	5.6	**8.9**
Botswana	**79.2**	75.6	–	11.4	**9.3**	6.6	–	3.5
Cameroon	67.3	**72**	14.7	**16.4**	3.5	**3.9**	9.8	**13.7**
Ethiopia	72.9	**73**	**0.4**	-3.6	-4.4	**14.7**	**-11.2**	-16.8
Ghana	**70.8**	66.1	7.3	**10**	**8.2**	5.2	1.8	**5.8**
Kenya	62.4	**73.5**	-9.5	**19.8**	-0.7	**2.9**	-10.1	-21.7
Madagascar	61.1	**63.5**	-3.4	**1.1**	-1	**-0.5**	**4.1**	3.4
Mali	**79.1**	73.8	–	**45.9**	**5.3**	4.2	–	**43.6**
Tanzania (United Republic of)	62.8	**83.2**	-21.9	**-19.6**	**14**	10.1	–	-26.6
Uganda	**77**	74	**-20**	-37.3	-4	**3.7**	**-13.9**	-38.4
Dem. Rep. of the Congo	72	**77.6**	9	**12.3**	5.1	**5.2**	3.4	**6.6**
Zambia	66.5	**67.5**	7.4	**12.3**	**3.3**	0.6	4.8	**12.3**

Source: Compiled by the AfHDR Team from World Bank, 2015b.

BOX 5.4

SECURICO: Women's leadership in Zimbabwe's security industry

Rolling up her sleeves back in 1998, Divine Ndhlukula converted her cottage into an office with four employees before walking confidently "through the door" into a male-dominated and openly prejudicial security industry. Armed with just a small budget, limited knowledge of security and a passionate belief that service quality, professionalism and good old-fashioned organizational skills would win the day, Divine's company, SECURICO, gradually started to make inroads into the industry.

In 2002, the company became the first Zimbabwean security firm to offer an asset/cash-in-transit service. In 2005, it expanded into dog services establishing a subsidiary company, CANINE Dog Services, which breeds, trains and leases guard dogs. In 2008, the company acquired an electronic security systems company, Multi-Link (Pvt) Ltd., and integrated it into SECURICO as its Electronic Division. The company has partnerships in South Africa, China and India, and is the second largest electronic security systems provider in Zimbabwe.

The firm has grown into a reputable company with an annual revenue of US$13 million and 3,400 employees, of whom 900 are women. There can be no doubt that SECURICO has developed into a world-class security services organization recognized for its ISO certifications and industry awards, more than 20 in over a decade. In 2013, Divine was voted African Woman of the Year and also won the 1st Runner-Up UNCTAD Empretec Women in Business Award.

As the awards publically recognized, Divine has proven to be an exceptional entrepreneur, overcoming social barriers to lead a trendsetter and industry-changing firm.

Source: BBC News. The woman who took on Zimbabwe's security men and won, 6 July 2012.

Almost 60 per cent of all the companies listed on the Nairobi Securities Exchange in Kenya have exclusively male board members. The remaining 40 per cent of companies are majority-owned by multinationals, and women's presence represents around 22 per cent of the boards. In Mauritius, a 2004 study conducted by UNDP reported that 23 per cent of women participated in public boards and 19 per cent in the private sector. For Rwanda, 2011 data suggest that women occupy slightly over 12 per cent of the seats on company boards, well below Rwanda's performance in women's involvement in the national legislature (ILO, 2015).

A key long-term issue in narrowing the gap in leadership relates to addressing the current gender education gaps. Educational gaps overlap with the leadership gap in part because the pool of women in science and technical fields is limited and not growing. A significant number of girls and women in secondary and tertiary education do not specialize in engineering and agricultural sciences, which tend to be male-dominated sectors. Gender disparities are particularly marked in the agricultural sciences, for instance. At the post-graduate level in East, Central and Southern Africa, only about 16 per cent of graduate students are women (INNOVATE 2013). Efforts in closing the educational gap in tertiary education will amplify opportunities for women in leadership positions.

Boxes 5.4 and 5.5 provide two examples of women who have succeeded both as entrepreneurs and chief executive officers (CEOs), one from Zimbabwe, in the security industry, and one from Kenya, in the telecom sector.

Quotas and women's leadership

Unequal access to top decision positions denies capable women the opportunity to contribute to society's well-being and denies society the opportunity to benefit from their leadership. The under-representation of women in decision-making positions undermines the economic and other potentials of African states.

To respond to the problems of under-representation, the use of mandatory quotas in the private sector is increasingly being considered but has yet to be routinely applied. A few countries already have legislation requiring corporations and businesses owned by government to have quotas for women at middle management and senior executive levels. Quotas in some countries are imposed on private sector employers by local or national laws, and there are also cases where employers have introduced quotas on their own initiative to foster a culture of inclusion and increase the number or percentage of employees from a certain demographic, ethnic group or sex. Box 5.6 summarizes the positive experience in South Africa in establishing quotas and becoming the leading African country for women on corporate boards. South Africa's experience offers a valuable lesson on the benefits of extending affirmative action beyond the electoral process. It can be extremely difficult and politically sensitive to amend a constitution to include a quota provision, but its effects are proven to trigger dramatic increases in women participation in the organizations targeted by them (Fridell, 2009).

Quotas should also be considered within the public administration. Women's representation in local governments has proven to make a difference. Indeed, the civil service is an important employer in many countries and equal participation in public administration can have a significant impact on women's economic empowerment. Women's participation in the public sector is a goal in itself that has positive impacts on human development.

Conflict resolution and peacebuilding

Discussion of men's and women's participation in public life cannot overlook their engagement with peace and security institutions and frameworks for addressing conflict resolution. Based on the threats that the high prevalence of conflicts pose, regional and international organizations have prioritized multiple efforts in the last decades on conflict prevention, conflict resolution and peacebuilding. The result has been a collection of legal frameworks, peace and security institutions addressing conflict in Africa.

BOX 5.5

Wananchi Group Holdings: Women's leadership in the East Africa telecom sector

In East African business circles, few entrepreneurs shine brighter than Njeri Rionge. One of Kenya's more successful and revered entrepreneurs, Rionge has co-founded multi-million dollar companies in quick succession. She co-founded Wananchi Online, a leading Internet provider, today transformed into Wananchi Group, East Africa's leading cable, broadband TV and phone company. She also founded Ignite Consulting, a thriving business consultancy; Business Lounge, Kenya's leading startup incubator; Ignite Lifestyle, a health care consultancy; and Insite, one of Kenya's most successful digital marketing outfits.

Rionge ventured into business at the age of 19, selling yogurt at schools in Kenya's capital of Nairobi, while travelling to London to purchase and resell luxury merchandise not available in Kenya. Since then, she has focused on creating African firms that support the growth of the continent, which she sees as the 'next economic frontier'. She has used her knowledge of global market trends, services and products to bring innovation to the Kenyan market and create companies that later transfer to new managers that can boost the growth and bring firms to the next level. Rionge is another exceptional woman making a difference in a male-dominated sector and proving the long-term, positive transformation that women in business can foster based on their individual talent and courage. As stated by Ms Rionge, resilience or *"having a strong backbone that can handle challenges is the key to successful entrepreneurship"*.

Source: Forbes, 2011. Africa's Most Successful Women: Njeri Rionge, 3 August 2011.

BOX 5.6

South Africa's experience with quotas in the mining sector

Women are increasingly represented in leadership positons in the extractives sector. In South Africa, up until the 1990s, legislation prohibited women from working underground. This changed in 2002 when the South African Mining Charter introduced quotas urging mining companies to employ a 10 per cent female staff quota (Mining.com 2014). The adoption of quotas in South Africa was part of broader measures intended by the Government to rectify injustices in the past by helping those who have historically been at a disadvantage, including coloured (mixed-race) South Africans and women.

Since legislators and mining companies started applying quotas to bring in more women technicians and executives, there have been an increasing number of women board members. According to a 2013 PwC report on women in mining, a South Africa firm leads the way in the number of female senior executives (21 per cent) in the top 100 listed mining companies worldwide; by comparison, the senior executive percentages for the five companies immediately following the South African leader were between 4 and 12 per cent (PwC, 2013-2015).

Building on this progress through quotas, women's rights groups and their allies in South Africa introduced the 2014 Women Empowerment and Gender Equality Bill (WEGEB), which aims to broaden employment, education and health opportunities for women. Proponents of WEGEB claim that, unlike provisions under Mining Charters, which allow extractive industry companies to renew their licences when they did not meet gender quotas, the new Bill will mandate a 50 per cent quota for women and stiff penalties for organizations that fail to comply. Beyond differences between mining and other industries, South Africa, among emerging economies in Africa, has the highest overall percentage of women on corporate boards (17.9 per cent) (Gladman and Lamb, 2013:19).

The use of boardroom quotas, as witnessed in South Africa since the early 2000s, has been a major success. Not only are gender-based quotas empowering qualified women who are ready for leadership in major corporations, but they are also enabling women to progress in the extractive industries at a significant pace.

Source: CNBC Africa, 2013.

As will be noted in Chapter 6, United Nations Security Council Resolution 1325, adopted in 2000, formally acknowledged the changing nature of warfare, in which civilians are increasingly targeted, and women continue to be excluded from participation in peace processes. It not only addresses the inordinate impact of war on women, but also the pivotal role that women should and do play in conflict management, conflict resolution and sustainable peace.

A second United Nations Security Council Resolution 2242, adopted in 2015, called on members states as well as all United Nations bodies to move much more aggressively in incorporating women's perspectives into all operations. With regard to peacekeeping operations, the Resolution called for gender analyses and technical gender expertise to be included throughout all stages of mission planning, mandate development, implementation, review and mission drawdown. It called on the Secretary-General to initiate a revised strategy, within available resources, to double the numbers of women in peacekeeping operations over the next five years.

Peace processes have been a principal ground for decision-making and for the exercise of power and influence. The profusion of peace agreements across the Continent calls for a gender analysis of the different levels of participation of women and men in the different agreements. Yet, women's formal participation has been limited, as suggested by table 5.6.

Historically, despite the appalling situation they endured, women from all classes and ethnic groups and across borders have mobilized extensively to facilitate the cessation of war and support peacebuilding. The various strategies that they have used include behind-the-scenes lobbying of warlords and political leaders, organizing public rallies and demonstrations, and providing peace-making-related services, such as civilian electoral education and training. Some of these successful strategies are discussed in the Liberia and Burundi experiences mentioned below.

Women's peace activism has crossed national borders in many cases. The experiences of women from conflict-affected countries are compelling evidence of women's choices in confronting difficult situations and in becoming significant players in conflict resolution and sustainable peacemaking. Such is the potency of this moral authority that women in post-colonial Africa have utilized them to wage peace in the Democratic Republic of the Congo, Central African Republic, Sierra Leone, Liberia, Guinea and South Africa. Here, women have continually drawn on the moral authority granted to them by virtue of their being mothers, as creators of life, to call and create strategies for peace throughout Africa (Mazurana and McKay, 1999).

While there has been considerable progress toward the development of a peace and security architecture that responds both to women's and men's needs, they nonetheless play a different role in formal peace-making processes. In general terms, there has been a lack of or insignificant women's representation and participation in most of the formal mediation, negotiation and signing of peace agreements. Moreover, even small achievements in representation such as women's active participation in peace promotion and peace negotiations in Burundi's 2000 Reconciliation Agreement was the result of using informal channels and mechanisms such as intense pressure and advocacy from women's movements and civil society.

The trend in Africa has been that women tend to influence the peace process not as participants at the negotiating tables or mediators, but as advocates from outside. Despite their exclusion, African women's associations have continuously found creative ways of expressing their concerns in peace processes. When excluded from the peace table, women have often used parallel processes on their own. When locked out of the rooms where decisions are being made, women have presented their positions and recommendations through the 'gaps under the doors', spoken to delegates outside meetings, or demonstrated in the street, as occurred in Liberia in 2003 (box 5.7).

Thus, women in Africa have played an active role in conflict and post-conflict situations as peace advocates. Various studies have examined how women in several African countries such as Burundi, Liberia, Rwanda, Uganda, Nigeria, Sierra Leone and South Africa have been involved in conflict resolution. They suggest that the debate has moved beyond victimhood and towards women becoming agents for social change, despite challenging, complex and conflicting circumstances.

TABLE 5.6

Percentage of women's participation in peace processes in Africa, 1992-2011

Country	Women signatories (%)	Female lead mediators (%)	Women witnesses (%)	Women in negotiating teams (%)
Sierra Leone (1999) The Lomé Peace Agreement	0	0	20	0
Burundi (2000) Peace and Reconciliation Agreement for Burundi	0	0	–	2
Somalia (2002) Eldoret Declaration on Cessation of Hostilities and the Structures and Principles. Principles of the Somalia National Reconciliation Process	0	0	0	–
Côte d'Ivoire (2003) Linas-Marcoussis Peace Accords	0	0	0	–
Democratic Republic of the Congo (2003) The Sun City Agreement ("The Final Act")	5	0	0	12
Liberia (2003) Accra Peace Agreement between the Government of Liberia, the Liberians United for Reconciliation and Democracy, the Movement for Democracy in Liberia and the political parties	0	0	17	–
Sudan (2005) The comprehensive peace agreement between the Government of the Republic of Sudan and the Sudan People's Liberation Movement/Sudan People's Liberation Army	0	0	9	–
Sudan (2006) Abuja Darfur Peace Agreement	0	0	7	8
Democratic Republic of the Congo (2008) Goma - North Kivu Acte D'Engagement	5	20	0	–
Democratic Republic of the Congo (2008) Goma - South Kivu Acte D'Engagement	0	20	0	–
Uganda (2008) Juba Peace Agreement	0	0	20	9
Kenya (2008) Nairobi Agreement on the Principles of Partnership of the Coalition Government	0	33	0	25
Central African Republic (2008) Accord de Paix Global	0	0	0	–
Zimbabwe (2008) Agreement between the Zimbabwe African National Union-Patriotic Front (ZANUPF) and the Two Movement for Democratic Change (MDC) Formations, on Resolving the Challenges Facing Zimbabwe	0	0	0	–
Somalia (2008) Agreement between the Transitional Federal Government of Somalia (TFG) and the Alliance for the Re-Liberation of Somalia (ARS) (The Djibouti Agreement)	0	0	10	–
Central African Republic (2011) Accord de cessez-le-feu entre l'UFDR et le CPJP [Agreement outlining provisions for a ceasefire between the 'Union des Forces Démocratiques pour le Rassemblement' (UFDR) and the 'Convention des Patriotes Pour la Justice et la Paix' CPJP)]	0	0	0	–

Source: Castillo Diaz and Tordjman, 2012.

BOX 5.7

Empowered women can build a peaceful, secure and resilient Africa.

Reflections by Leymah Gbowee, Nobel Laureate

Over the course of my journey as an activist, I have come to believe without a doubt that engaging women in more formal socio-economic, political and peace processes is an important step to ensure that Africa continues to move toward a more inclusive and sustainable human development.

Prolonged and even sudden conflict can set back years of development because it destroys women's and men's capabilities, choices and livelihoods, and transfers poverty across generations. It is no accident that countries in conflict or recovering from conflicts remain at the bottom of UNDP's Human Development Index.

The reality is that women in countries experiencing conflict play important roles that often go unnoticed. African women are not only affected by conflict, but are also actively engaged as conflict preventers, combatants and peacebuilders, and take part in rebuilding in the aftermath. They provide for their families and maintain the social fabric before, during and after the conflict. Women in many countries have moved from victimhood to become agents of social change despite complex social and economic challenges. Women are playing important roles in the Democratic Republic of the Congo, Liberia, Rwanda, Sierra Leone, Sudan and Uganda, including participating in dialogues for peace, contributing to post-conflict governments and mobilizing a critical mass of women to advocate for women's rights.

We know that engaging women in peacemaking and peacekeeping leads to better development outcomes for society and that enhancing women's effective participation is vital for sustainable peace and security. This statement re-echoes and reaffirms what women activists have been saying over the last decades, "If given the space, women can change the dynamics of war and peace."

There are many examples to date of women's involvement in peace processes that led to positive results. In my own country, Liberia, we, the women, showed that there is "power for peace" through collective action by women. The devastation of the Liberian conflict on the lives of thousands of women provoked us to organize and agitate for an end to the war. A diverse group of women through the Liberian Women's Initiative prevailed upon warlords and political leaders in concerted actions all over Liberia, as well as in Nigeria and Ghana during the peace negotiation processes (African Women and Peace Support Group, 2004). Through the Women of Liberia Mass Action for Peace under the banner of the Women in Peacebuilding Network, which I co-ordinated, Liberian women mobilized aggressively for peace between 2000 and 2003, using advocacy, mass protests and sit-ins as well as the presentation of petitions to the former Liberian President Charles Taylor and other international actors. Our activism combined with international action on war crimes and military action resulted in the signing of the peace agreement, officially ending the war.

Our experience in Liberia and in countries where I have been involved in peace efforts confirms that actively engaging women in peace and security contributes to human development by addressing the root causes of conflict. While these causes are diverse, social, political and economic inequality plays a significant role together with state collapse, economic decline, and historical patterns of conflict and battles for control of natural resources (DFID, 2001).

Geographic disparities, gender inequality and social exclusion interact to keep women out of peace processes. In the last decade, many of the peace processes on the African Continent between 1991 and 2012 had no women as lead mediators. Maximizing the benefits of women's engagement in conflict prevention and peacebuilding calls for moving from inclusion to partnership for social change.

Source: Mamma, 2008.

There are many negative implications of the gender gap in peace processes on the potential for structural transformation and increased human development; the more evident implication is likely to be the impossibility of reaching sustainable peace agreements if based on exclusively male participation in negotiation. Only inclusive engagement of both women and men is likely to lead to sustainable peace, as wide representation will better ensure that the emerging peace is owned by both females and males, and their needs and perspectives are included.

As observed when analysing unequal gender representation in politics as well as public and private leadership positions, gender disparities in peace agreements carry the same fundamental consequences of ignoring the talent and creativity of half the population. Women's absence from peace processes cannot be explained by their alleged lack of experience in conflict resolution or negotiations.

There is sufficient first-hand expertise within the women's movement across Africa in the fields of gender, children's rights, women's rights and conflict transformation (Castillo Diaz and Tordjman, 2012). Gender equality at the highest decision-making structures of local, national, regional and international institutions charged with managing peace and security across Africa would indubitably support more effective and more sustainable conflict resolution across the Continent.

Efforts to strengthen women's participation in conflict resolution and post-conflict reconstruction should identify, recognize and strengthen the non-violent forms of political action in which females engage. This would necessitate careful context-specific research into women's formal and informal non-violent political activities before and during conflict in order to include their practices, experiences and voices in any conflict resolution and post-conflict reconstruction efforts. Thus, the challenge is to go beyond the mere inclusion of women in peace processes and open up possibilities to identify, recognize and strengthen different non-violent forms of female political agency and include voices that are representative of different groups of women.

Overall Policy and Implementation Issues:
Implications of Women's Political Voice and Leadership in Promoting Gender Equality

Significant progress has been made in advancing women's participation in holding elective office and in positions of leadership in the public and private sectors. However, overall progress at the political and leadership level is still well below what is needed to have a demonstrable impact on attaining full gender equality in African countries.

- Some countries have successfully elected women to their parliaments and other elected offices, but existing social and political structures still proscribe women's full potential in helping to equally shape the national and local political and policy agenda.

- In addition to women in politics, women have made advances in leadership positions in such areas as public service, trade unions and the private sector, but here again, progress in achieving gender equity is still lagging due to a combination of political, economic and social resistance to change.

- In order to accelerate the pace of women in politics and leadership, some African governments have begun experimenting with the use of gender quotas in different sectors and levels of government, and the private sector. A quota system may represent a useful policy tool if used with care and sensitivity.

- Women's roles in conflict resolution and peacebuilding have expanded considerably from only a decade ago when women could only informally influence negotiations for the cessation of hostilities or peace agreements. There is a growing recognition that women should be an integral and formal part of any peace negotiations process, given their role in securing and maintaining peace.

Discrimination against women

Very low

Low

Morocco .11	Madagascar .10	South Africa .05	Namibia .12	Lesotho .09			

Tunisia .20	Guinea-Bissau .21	Congo (Rep. of the) .20	Kenya .22	Uganda .22	Rwanda .13	Swaziland .21	Zimbabwe .14

Togo .19	Senegal .20	Angola .17	Rwanda .13	Burundi .17	Malawi .21	Mozambique .14

Medium

Guinea .32	Ghana .30	CAR .33	Ethiopia .24

Côte d'Ivoire .25	Benin .28	Burkina Faso .28	Cameroon .28	Tanzania .25

High

Mauritania .39	Liberia .38	Nigeria .39	Niger .44	Sierra Leone .37	Congo (Dem. Rep. of the) .43	Somalia .46

Egypt .43	Sudan .52	The Gambia .52	Mali .52	Chad .47	Gabon .40	Zambia .45

Very high

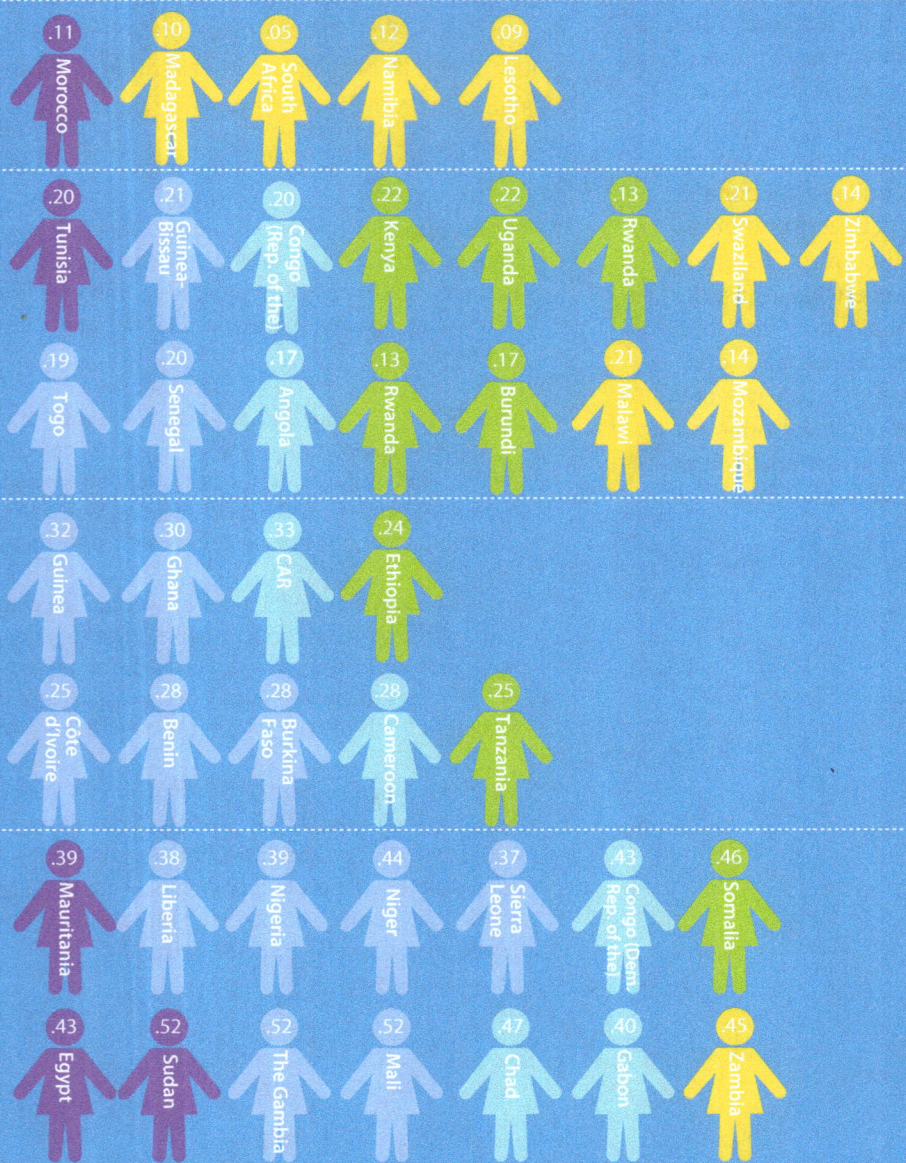

Northern **Western** **Central** **Eastern** **Southern**

Source: Designed by the AfHDR Team from Social Institutions and Gender Index (2014).
Note: Discriminatory family code · restricted physical integrity · son bias restricted resources and assets · restricted civil liberties

Chapter 6

Legal and Social Norms Impacting Gender Equality

Chapter 6
Legal and Social Norms Impacting Gender Equality

This chapter reviews the role of legal and social norms in terms of influencing progress in gender equality. While most African countries have ratified or approved a wide range of international and regional norms and conventions, their application is often proscribed by social norms at the local level that impede advances in gender equality and women's empowerment.

Since 1945, the international community, together with African regional bodies and African states, have put in place a wide array of legal norms, precedents and legislation promoting gender equality. In addition, international declarations from various international and regional conferences have been promulgated that have addressed women's issues, such as the 1995 Beijing Declaration and Platform of Action at the Fourth World Conference on Women. In many ways, these various legal standards are the pillar on which all women's rights are premised. Yet the continuing disparities in gender equality, as highlighted in Chapter 2, underscore the fact that legal norms and declarations on their own are insufficient to achieve full gender equality in Africa (or anywhere else). Legal standards are certainly an important and necessary condition, but are insufficient for accelerating the pace toward gender equality.

In contradistinction to legal norms, there are interlocking social norms and cultural barriers that permeate every society and that often underpin the basis for gender inequality. It is the gap between legal rights and expectations, on the one hand, and prevailing practices and behaviours embodied in social and cultural norms, on the other hand, that pose a fundamental challenge for accelerating gender equality and women's empowerment.

The first section of this chapter therefore reviews the legal norms and standards that set the bar by which all countries measure their progress and shortfalls. The section looks at international standards, followed by a second section on Africa-wide standards. In turn, an overview of some sub-regional standards is presented, as well as a review of specific national standards and laws. The second section of the chapter then turns to social norms and standards as a challenge to more quickly achieving gender equality.

Legal norms and standards

International legal instruments

The **Universal Declaration of Human Rights** (UDHR), adopted by the United Nations General Assembly in 1948, is the first international standard and remains the cornerstone of the international framework of human and civil rights. Its purpose was to articulate some of the key principles found in the original 1945 United Nations Charter, such as:

[t]o achieve international co-operation in solving international problems of an economic, social, cultural, or humanitarian character, and in promoting and encouraging respect for human rights and for fundamental freedoms for all without distinction as to race, sex, language, or religion ... (Article 1.4).

Further, Article 55c states that:

... the Nations shall promote universal respect for, and observance of, human rights and fundamental freedoms for all without distinction as to race, sex, language, or religion... .

> Legal norms and declarations on their own are insufficient to achieve full gender equality. The gap between legal rights and socio-cultural norms poses a fundamental challenge.

It is important to keep in mind the context in which the UDHR was written. In 1948, the United Nations consisted of only 48 member states compared to 193 today. Only three African countries were member states at the time: Egypt, Ethiopia and South Africa. The tragedy and suffering of the Second World War were still fresh on the minds of the international community, and the growing divisions between the 'East' and 'West' were already apparent. Due to the divide between East and West, the negotiations for the UDHR were protracted and difficult.

Clearly, the UDHR was not drafted specifically to address women's issues, but is still considered the cornerstone of the entire international human rights system. Together with its two key international covenants, it forms the International Bill of Human Rights. And it is the legal baseline when approaching the international framework on women's rights.

Because the UDHR was adopted in the United Nations General Assembly, it was not legally binding on member states, but was important in terms of establishing clear legal international norms and benchmarks. To address this shortcoming, the UDHR was followed by two legally binding covenants that were developed through the United Nations Commission on Human Rights: the **International Covenant on Economic, Social and Cultural Rights** (ICESCR) and the **International Covenant on Civil and Political Rights** (ICCPR).

Adding to the UDHR and its Covenants, another key element of the international framework on women's rights is the **Convention on the Elimination of All Forms of Discrimination against Women** (CEDAW), adopted by the United Nations General Assembly in 1979. The CEDAW consists of a preamble and 30 articles, and defines what constitutes discrimination against women:

... any distinction, exclusion or restriction made on the basis of sex which has the effect or purpose of impairing or nullifying the recognition, enjoyment or exercise by women, irrespective of their marital status, on a basis of equality of men and women, of human rights and fundamental freedoms in the political, economic, social, cultural, civil or any other field.

By accepting the Convention, member states commit themselves to undertake a series of measures to end discrimination against women in all forms, including:

- to incorporate the principle of equality of men and women in their legal system, abolish all discriminatory laws, and adopt appropriate ones prohibiting discrimination against women;

- to establish tribunals and other public institutions to ensure the effective protection of women against discrimination; and

- to ensure elimination of all acts of discrimination against women by persons, organizations or enterprises.

The Convention's implementation is monitored by the **United Nations Committee for the Elimination of Discrimination against Women** ("the CEDAW Committee"). Other gender-related global institutional monitoring mechanisms include the **United Nations Working Group on Discrimination Against Women** and the **United Nations Special Rapporteur on Violence Against Women and Special Rapporteur on Trafficking in Persons**.

Figure 6.1 provides an overview of the key international frameworks, conferences and mechanisms supporting women's rights.

In broad terms, international legal instruments are commonly accepted in Africa; only a small number of African states have not yet embraced all the fundamental ones providing the legal foundation for human and women's rights.

In addition to the above legal instruments, there has been progress in efforts to comply with some key international standards related to women's rights and violence. The UN Security Council Resolution 1325: Women as Active Agents in Peace and Security, adopted in 2000, formally acknowledged the changing nature of warfare, in which civilians are

FIGURE 6.1

Key international frameworks, conferences and mechanisms supporting women's rights

1945-1969	Universal Declaration of Human Rights (1945)
	International Covenant on Economic, Social and Cultural Rights (1966)
	International Covenant on Civil and Political Rights (1966)
1970-1979	Convention on the Elimination of All Forms of Discrimination Against Women (1979)
1980-1989	UN Committee on the Elimination of Discrimination Against Women (1982)
1990-1999	Bejing Declaration and Platform for Action (1995)
	UN Conference on the Environment, Rio de Janeiro (1992)
	UN Conference on Human Rights, Vienna (1993)
	International Conference on Population and Development, Cairo (1994)
	World Summit for Social Development, Copenhagen (1995)
	Habitat II, Istanbul (1995)
	UN Special Rapporteur on Violence Against Women and Trafficking in Persons (1994/5)
2000-2010	Millennium Development Goals (2000)
	Security Council Resolution 1325 on Women, Peace and Security (2000)
2011-2016	Sendai Framework for Disaster Risk Reduction 2015-2030 (2015)
	Addis Ababa Action Agenda (2015)
	Agenda 2030: Sustainable Development Goals (2015)
	Security Council Resolution 2242 on Women, Peace and Security Agenda (2015)
	Paris Climate Agreement (2015)

Source: Compiled by the AfHDR Team.

increasingly targeted, and women continue to be excluded from participation in peace processes. Resolution 1325 addresses not only the inordinate impact of war on women, but also the pivotal role women should and do play in conflict management, conflict resolution and sustainable peace. Only 11 African countries are in compliance with all the provisions of the binding United Nations Security Council Resolution 1325 on Women, Peace and Security.[12]

International conferences

Various international conferences have also played an important role in drawing attention to women's equality and empowerment, highlighting current trends and conditions, and developing specific agendas and resolutions for action. The Beijing Declaration and Platform of Action was endorsed in 1995 at the Fourth World Conference on Women, one of the largest United Nations Conferences of the last several decades, and included numerous heads of state and government and foreign ministers in attendance. As is the case of most international conferences, the Beijing Declaration and Platform were adopted by consensus of the plenary following long and protracted negotiations. The Beijing Declaration and Platform are not, however, legally binding.

Nonetheless, the Declaration was forthright in calling attention to unfulfilled obligations by United Nations member states. Specifically, the Platform of Action stated:

… While the significance of national and regional particularities and various historical, cultural and religious backgrounds must be borne in mind, it is the duty of States, regardless of their political, economic and cultural systems, to promote and protect all human rights and fundamental freedoms … .

The implementation of this Platform, including through national laws and the formulation of strategies, policies, programmes and development priorities, is the sovereign responsibility of each State, in conformity with all human rights and fundamental freedoms, and the significance of and full respect for various religious and ethical values, cultural backgrounds and philosophical convictions of individuals and their communities should contribute to the full enjoyment by women of their human rights in order to achieve equality, development and peace… .

Africa-wide legal norms

Africa, like other regions of the world, has complemented the international framework on human and women's rights with its own legal and institutional structures that respond to African priorities. The Organization of African Unity (OAU) and its successor, the African Union (AU), have adopted three key instruments that govern Africa's resolve to promote human rights, gender equality and women's empowerment: the African Charter on Human and Peoples' Rights, the Protocol to the African Charter on Human and Peoples' Rights on the Rights of Women in Africa (the "Maputo Protocol") and the Solemn Declaration on Gender Equality in Africa (the Solemn Declaration, or SDGEA).

The first human rights legal instrument adopted by the OAU was the African Charter. It was approved in 1981 and came into force in 1986 upon ratification by an absolute majority of member states. The African Charter states that all rights must be made effective under national legal systems by the states; thus, in the event of violations, affected individuals and peoples are entitled to effective domestic remedies, whether judicial or administrative, as well as redress.

The African Charter is a legally binding document. To date, 53 African states – all of the AU member states with the exception South Sudan – have ratified the Charter, whose key principles include non-discrimination and the elimination of discrimination against women as well as the protection of their rights. It covers the range of civil and political rights, from respect for life and integrity to fundamental freedoms, to fair trial guarantees and the right to participate in government. The Charter's economic, social and cultural rights are also extensive.

Figure 6.2 shows a chronology of the major legal instruments affecting women's rights. The rights of women in Africa are specifcally addressed in another legal instrument: the 2003 Maputo Protocol. It has been signed, ratified and/or deposited by all but three States Parties to the African Charter. The Maputo Protocol confers specific obligations on States, including to: guarantee equality between men and women in their constitutions and laws; integrate a gender perspective into all laws, policies, plans and activities; and take positive and corrective action in areas where discrimination against women still exists.

FIGURE 6.2

Timeline of international and regional legal declarations and instruments

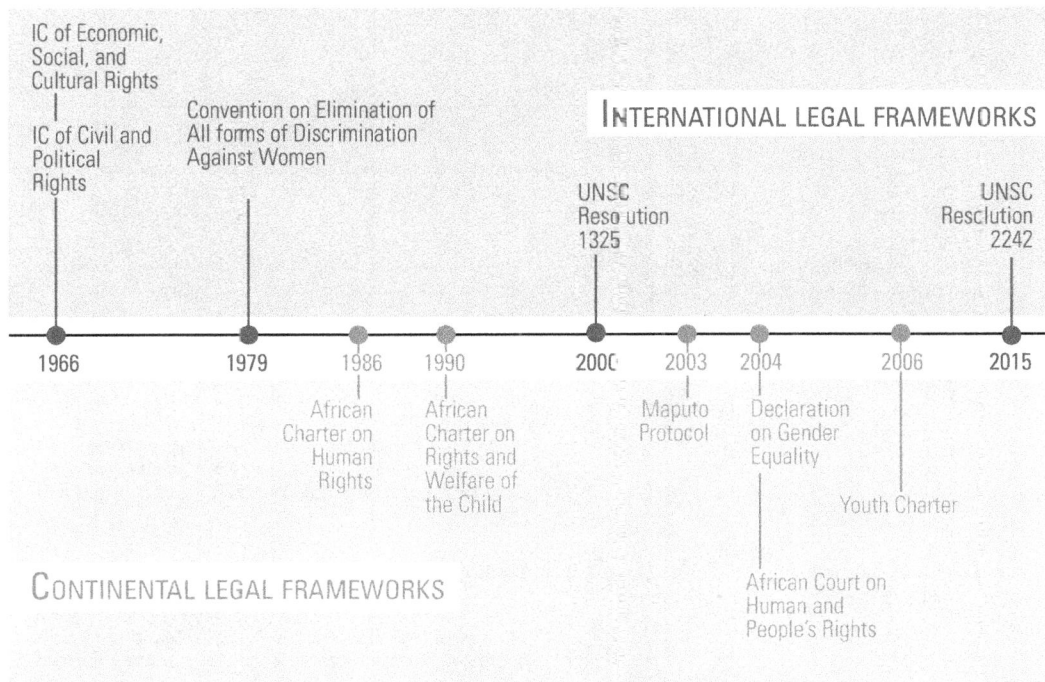

Source: Compiled by the AfHDR Team

The Maputo Protocol covers basically the same range of civil, political, economic, social and cultural rights outlined in various international covenants. In some areas, it goes even further, for instance, in explicitly addressing violence against women, female genital mutilation (FGM) and the situation of women in polygamous marriages.

The Protocol further recognizes additional rights of women, such as the right to peace and to protection in situations of armed conflict, putting into practice the Continental equivalent of United Nations Security Council Resolution 1325. It confers special protection for particular situations, such as the rights of widows.

The heads of state and government of AU member states also issued the 2004 Solemn Declaration on Gender Equality in Africa (SDGEA). This legal instrument commits all bodies of the AU, the regional economic communities, and all levels of government to the principle of gender equality, including by setting up and supporting gender-promoting institutions. It also addresses issues such as gender-based violence, gender-specific measures against the HIV/AIDS pandemic, the gender gap in primary school education, and recruitment of child soldiers, including girls.

In addition to these protocols, the growing awareness in Africa of gender equality is also evidenced by the 2007 **African Charter on Democracy, Elections and Governance**, a binding treaty signed by 38 countries to date. It covers the African legal framework for democracy and governance, and addresses issues such as gender parity in electoral processes and legislatures.

TABLE 6.1

Country ratification status of African legal instruments related to women's rights

Treaty	Date of Adoption	Ratification Pending
African Charter on Human and People's Rights	1981 Signed: 45 Ratified: 53	South Sudan
African Charter on Rights and Welfare of the Child	1990 Signed: 44 Ratified: 47	Central African Republic, Democratic Republic of the Congo, Somalia, South Sudan, Sao Tome and Principe, Tunisia
African Charter on the Establishment of an African Court of Human and People's Rights	1998 Signed: 52 Ratified: 30	Angola, Botswana, Central African Republic, Cabo Verde, Djibouti, Democratic Republic of the Congo, Egypt, Equatorial Guinea, Eritrea, Ethiopia, Guinea Bissau, Guinea, Liberia, Madagascar, Namibia, Seychelles, Sierra Leone, Somalia, South Sudan, Sao Tome and Principe, Sudan, Swaziland, Zambia, Zimbabwe
Protocol to the African Charter on Human and People's Rights on the Rights of Women in Africa	2003 Signed: 49 Ratified: 37	Algeria, Botswana, Burundi, Chad, Egypt, Eritrea, Ethiopia, Madagascar, Mauritius, Niger, Somalia, South Sudan, Sao Tome and Principe, Sudan, Tunisia
African Youth Charter	2006 Signed: 36 Ratified: 14	Angola, Benin, Botswana, Burkina Faso, Central African Republic, Cabo Verde, Chad, Comoros, Djibouti, Democratic Republic of the Congo, Egypt, Equatorial Guinea, Eritrea, Ethiopia, Gabon, The Gambia, Ghana, Guinea Bissau, Guinea, Libya, Lesotho, Liberia, Madagascar, Mauritania, Nigeria, Niger, Rwanda, Senegal, Seychelles, Sierra Leone, Somalia, South Sudan, Sao Tome and Principe, Sudan, Swaziland, Togo, Tunisia, Uganda, Zimbabwe
African Charter on Democracy, Elections and Governance	2007 Signed: 46 Ratifed: 24	Algeria, Angola, Botswana, Burundi, Central African Republic, Cabo Verde, Comoros, Congo, Democratic Republic of the Congo, Egypt, Equatorial Guinea, Eritrea, Gabon, The Gambia, Kenya, Libya, Liberia, Madagascar, Mozambique, Mauritius, Namibia, Senegal, Seychelles, Somalia, Sao Tome and Principe, Swaziland, Tanzania, Tunisia, Uganda, Zimbabwe

Source: Compiled by the AfHDR Team from AU, 2016.

With regard specifically to girls, a key binding instrument of the African legal system is the 1990 **African Charter on the Rights and Welfare of the Child** ("Charter on the Child"). All but four AU member states are parties. Its fundamental principles include non-discrimination and ensuring the best interests of the child. It also provides for special protection from harmful social and cultural practices, including armed conflict, sexual exploitation and trafficking, among others.

When reviewing the ratification status of the Africa-wide instruments created under the framework of the African Union, the gap is notably wide. Table 6.1 shows that many countries have yet to sign and/or ratify key legal instruments. These include the Maputo Protocol (18 pending countries), the African Court of Human and People's Rights (27 pending countries) and the Charter on Democracy, Elections and Governance (32 pending countries). Thus, despite the Africa-wide progress made, there is need for a more concerted effort to bring many more countries into alignment.

Sub-regional legal and institutional frameworks

Five of the eight sub-regional economic communities created in Africa have developed many substantial normative or institutional frameworks relating to gender; table 6.2 provides a summary of these instruments.

Available sub-regional instruments have been positive in bridging continental and national legal instruments. They have supported member states in implementing global and continental agreements by providing operational guidance in a number of areas. These include establishing gender targets and goals, compliance mechanisms, gender indicators for monitoring, as well as specific gender manuals to guide gender mainstreaming in thematic areas as diverse as HIV/AIDS and health, peace and conflict resolution, information technology, investment promotion and private sector development.

TABLE 6.2

Women's rights supported by declarations and policies in African Economic Commissions

Sub-regional body	Policies, declarations and plans
Southern African Development Community (SADC)	1997 Declaration on Gender and Development
	2008 Protocol on Gender and Development
	2009 Annual Barometer to monitor Protocol compliance
	SADC Gender Unit
	SADC Workplace Gender Policy
	SADC Women's Economic Empowerment Framework
Common Market for Eastern and Southern Africa (COMESA)	2014 Social Charter
	COMESA's Gender and Social Affairs Division
	COMESA Gender Manuals
	COMESA Gender Mainstreaming Strategic Action Plan
Intergovernmental Authority on Development (IGAD)	2000 Regional Action Plan for Implementation of United Nations Security Council Resolution 1325 on Women, Peace and Security
	2008 Regional Action Plan for the Implementation of United Nations Security Council Resolutions 1820 on Sexual Violence in Armed Conflicts and Post-Conflict Situations
	2009 Addis Ababa Declaration on the Enhancement of Women's Participation and Representation in Decision Making Positions
	2013 Regional Action Plan for the Implementation of United Nations Security Council Resolutions on Women and Security
	2014 Regional Strategy for Higher Representation of Women in Decision Making Positions
East African Community (EAC)	EAC Sectoral Council on Gender and Community Development
Economic Community of West African States (ECOWAS)	Revised ECOWAS Treaty
	1999 Protocol Relating to the Mechanism for Conflict Prevention, Management, Resolution, Peace-keeping and Security
	2001 Declaration on the Fight against Trafficking in Persons
	ECOWAS Gender Policy
	2003 ECOWAS established a Gender Development Centre
	2010 ECOWAS Regional Action Plan for the Implementation of United Nations Security Council Resolutions 1325 and 1820
	Dakar Declaration
International Conference on the Great Lakes Region (ICGLR)	2006 Protocol on the Prevention and Suppression of Sexual Violence against Women and Children
	2011 Kampala Declaration on Sexual and Gender-Based Violence
	Sexual and Gender based Violence Checklist

Source: Compiled by the AfHDR research team.

The sub-regional community with the strongest framework on gender is SADC. Its annual Barometer on compliance with its Protocol on Gender and Development could be a model for other sub-regions in terms of reporting, monitoring and evaluation of gender equality and women's empowerment. Similar to UNECA's African Gender and Development Index, the SADC Index and the perception-based Citizen Score Card are used to measure SADC members' performance in 28 target areas. Results are reported in the annual Afrobarometer and are used to inform policy, planning and programming. Other sub-regions may wish to consider developing their own variations of the SADC's Gender and Development Index, Citizen Score Card and annual Barometer to help monitor and assess national progress and to inform strategies, planning and programming.

National legal frameworks

National legal systems in African countries have moved in many ways to incorporate gender-related international, continental and sub-regional legal instruments. In recent years, countries have undertaken legislative reforms, including new constitutions, constitutional amendments, changes to existing legislation, and new laws to address gender issues.

By 2009, for instance, Tunisia had raised the minimum age of marriage to 18, while Lesotho, Namibia, Seychelles, South Africa, United Republic of Tanzania and Zimbabwe had criminalized marital rape. A total of 17 countries had passed laws criminalizing gender-based violence, and Ethiopia and Uganda had passed laws on FGM and other harmful traditional practices (UNECA, 2015: 3-4, 11, 32). The penal codes of Burkina Faso, Ethiopia, Egypt, Ghana and Senegal have been updated to explicitly prohibit FGM. In Burkina Faso alone, over 900 people have been convicted of the offence since 1997 (UNFPA, 2014a:37). Box 6.1 outlines the legal and policy reforms in Burkina Faso that made it possible. Since 2009, other gender-related positive legal developments included Cabo Verde's 2011 Gender-based Violence (GBV) Law, Botswana's Domestic Violence Act – including legal remedies for victims of marital rape and Angola's 2011 Law against Domestic Violence, the implementing document for which was passed in 2013. The setting up of a Working Group that provides a periodic review of the implementation of human rights instruments in Mozambique is novel (box 6.2).

Finally, when examining national legal norms and standards, and the challenges of promoting legal reforms, we must recognize the significant role that traditional law plays in weakening reform efforts. In many African countries, strong parallel systems of customary

BOX 6.1

Case study: Reducing female genital mutilation in Burkina Faso

Burkina Faso has made serious efforts to combat female genital mutilation (FGM) for over more than a decade. Its Penal Code has been updated to explicitly prohibit the practice and its provisions have been enforced, with more than 900 convictions since 1997. Burkina Faso set up a National Action Plan (2009-2013) to combat female circumcision, with oversight by a National Council.

Accompanying this overarching legal effort, Burkina Faso has tackled specific aspects of the problem, for example, through a joint United Nations Population Fund/United Nations Children's Fund programme to eliminate cross-border female circumcision. In its *Ecole des maris* (School for Husbands) outreach project, influential men in the community are encouraged to promote education for girls and prevention of gender-based violence.

In its Beijing +20 report, Burkina Faso reported that the percentage of 15 to 19 year olds estimated to have been excised dropped from 65 to 58 per cent between 2003 and 2010. For 20 to 24 year olds over the same period of time, the decrease was from 76 to 70 per cent.

Source: UNFPA, 2014a.

BOX 6.2

Mozambique and reporting on implementation of human rights instruments

In 2011, Mozambique set up a multi-sector Working Group on Human Rights under the coordination of its Ministry of Justice. The Working Group has, in conjunction with civil society organizations, developed an Action Plan for Universal Periodic Review (UPR) Implementation for Mozambique. The aim is to analyse the recommendations and related human rights instruments so as to determine how to incorporate them into national development plans. Attention is paid to clearly identifying the expected results, indicators of progress, the means of verification and time-frame for action. The cost and source of funding are also addressed.

In addition, a Monitoring Committee has been set up, following the detailed monitoring mechanisms established in the Action Plan. Furthermore, the Ministry of Justice has made plans to commission independent reviews to assess implementation of UPR recommendations and to inform the next cycle. United Nations Population Fund (UNFPA) supported the authorities in incorporating into the Action Plan recommendations addressing early pregnancy, early marriage, obstetric fistula, sexual abuse and violence against women during Mozambique's mid-term review in June 2013.

Source: UNFPA, 2014b.

law clearly conflict with the progress states have undertaken to provide for enabling legal frameworks in favour of gender equality. The SADC Barometer has reported that one of the most significant challenges faced by their member states is the tensions between traditional and formal laws (SADC 2014: 41), which need to be more fully understood and resolved at the country level. In-depth debate is needed on the social norms, traditions and beliefs that form the basis of customary laws and that may build walls or barriers to gender equality.

Social norms and gender equality

To some extent, all societies – whether in developed or developing countries – have created gender stereotypes that influence and inform the daily interaction of men and women in the home, community and workplace. Africa is no different. Social norms are part of the 'DNA' of human societies whose basic nature they codify. Although they are often unwritten, they shape laws and governance structures. They determine the specific mindset underlying customary principles, values and socially accepted behaviours

shared by individuals belonging to the same culture. They dictate what is normal and what is not, what is right and wrong, and what is appropriate and unacceptable in most aspects of life.

Consciously or unconsciously, social norms are the underlying factor affecting how information is processed, decisions made and actions taken. From one generation to the next, members of a society transmit the intangible assets that social norms represent. Social norms represent the ethical and moral basis of a society. Social norms are reflected in African laws, institutions and policies. They are also at the root of some of Africa's most important achievements and its greatest challenges.

Over the past several decades, social norms and gender stereotyping of all societies have been undergoing constant change as a result of economic and social pressures, the availability and speed of global mass communication, the massive rural-to-urban migration that is shifting the world's demographics, and all the other myriad ways in which change takes place at the interpersonal level. Such changes in social norms that impact gender stereotyping may occur, from one generation to the next, at a very slow pace or not at all. They may occur in only a few short years. Similarly, changes in social norms and gender stereotyping are occurring rapidly within countries as more and better educated men and women enter the workforce, establish new patterns of family life, notably smaller families, and have even higher expectations for their own children.

Africa's adherence to the universal human rights framework validates positive social traditions when they are consistent with accepted human rights, such as in the case of charity, assistance to pilgrims or persons in need found in the traditions of many societies. Here, the social norm favours and nurtures the human right of persons in need or those associated with granting asylum for political refugees. The contrary is also true; a myriad of destructive social norms undermine rather than foster the full realization of agreed human rights. This includes multiple norms and traditions confronting the very foundation of the concept of human rights – their universal application to all human beings without exception. Any social norm – regardless of whether it concerns race, age, gender, religious affiliation, sexual preferences or ethnic background – that endorses discrimination is, automatically, antagonistic to human rights.

African governments face a dilemma in trying to tackle the various social and cultural norms that hinder women's empowerment. Elected leaders and government officials often feel apprehensive about moving too quickly for fear of alienating different political constituencies and socio-economic groups. Understandably, they recognize the risks of expecting individuals or community leaders to easily and quickly reverse or abandon long-held beliefs. Yet, the arguments for promoting and encouraging changes in social norms that negatively impact women are equally if not more compelling, as amply demonstrated in the previous chapters.

Social norms and agency

Gender inequalities in the home, the workplace and society reflect both a cause and a consequence of these outcomes. Many social norms have very important and positive roles in creating strong family and community bonds, and establishing conditions for trust and support in times of crisis and hardship. Other social norms, however, condone or ignore high levels of violence against women and girls, including early marriage, and male-determined definitions that lead to discrimination against women and girls.

From both an international and African perspective, the resulting deprivations and constraints sometimes reflect persistent violations of the most basic human rights. Also, in many instances, constraints are magnified and multiplied by poverty and lack of education. Together these challenges have implications for women's lives, but also hold back progress for their families and countries as a whole. Freedom from these kinds of deprivations whose root cause can be traced back to social norms is a fundamental aspect of achieving women's equality, reducing extreme poverty, and boosting shared prosperity.

Drawing on the founding ideas of Amartya Sen and early Human Development Reports, 'agency' is defined as the ability to make decisions about one's own life and act on them to achieve a desired outcome, free of violence, retribution or fear (World Bank, 2014a). The ability to make those choices is often called 'empowerment'. Women are often at a systematic disadvantage in their ability to make effective choices, including decisions at home, on employment, on whether or when to get married, on how many children to have and on whether to become politically active.

In this sense, agency deprivation is commonly linked to three key sources of disadvantage: lack of control over household resources, attitudes that expose them to increased risk of gender-based violence, and early-age marriage. Research carried out by the World Bank (Klugman et al., 2014) shows how almost one in five (18 per cent) rural women with no more than a primary education experience three major deprivations, compared with one in 50 urban women with a higher education. Second, almost half of all women report agency-related deprivations in more than one area of their lives. And third, nearly one in eight women experiences such deprivations in all three areas. In Niger,

> African governments face a dilemma in trying to tackle the various social and cultural norms that hinder women's empowerment. Elected leaders and government officials often feel apprehensive about moving too quickly for fear of alienating different political constituencies and socio-economic groups.

for example, almost all women experience at least one constraint, and almost half (45 per cent) experience all three.

Further analysis shows that deprivation of agency is linked to other sources of disadvantage, especially lack of education. About 90 per cent of women with no more than a primary education experience at least one of the disadvantages, compared with 65 per cent of women with a secondary education and higher. Nearly one in five women with no more than a primary education experiences all three deprivations, compared to one in 20 with secondary schooling and higher.

Another agency deprivation, lack of control over household resources, varies according to whether women work and the type of work women do. On average, women who work in wage employment have more control over household resources than those who are paid in kind and those who do not work outside the home. For example, in Mozambique, fewer than 20 per cent of women wage earners lack control over household resources, compared with 21 to 40 per cent of women who worked but were paid in kind or who did not work in the past year.

In the same World Bank study, education levels were also highly correlated with a woman's degree of sexual autonomy—measured by whether a woman says that she is able to refuse sex, to ask her partner to use a condom, or both. In 10 countries surveyed, women with higher education have greater agency, and secondary education often has major benefits. In Cameroon, Côte d'Ivoire and Mozambique, for example, 61 to 80 per cent of women with no education lack sexual autonomy, compared with fewer than 20 percent of women with higher education.

Social norms and gender equality in the African context

General patterns

According to the 2015 Afrobarometer survey, one quarter of Africans do not embrace the concept of gender equality, i.e. they disagreed or strongly disagreed with the fundamental notion of equal rights between men and women. This reflects prevailing social norms assigning different standings, roles and privileges for women and men. Changing these social norms lies at the heart of the challenge for gender equality and women's empowerment.

Gender stereotyping, while not a norm in itself, is nonetheless a habit that fuels destructive social norms. It has been broadly identified as impeding the achievement of gender equality and the advancement of women. Simplified assumptions about what it is to be a 'woman', 'a poor woman', 'a young woman' and 'an African woman' are all gender stereotypes that pose barriers to women and have the power to spread violence and the use of coercion against them.

Gender stereotypes assign specific qualities to masculinity and femininity, thus defining the expected roles for men and women in society. Male virtues include risk taking, aggressiveness, an unemotional attitude and virility. Men are expected to be providers, heads of households and benevolent decision-makers. Common stereotypes of women are that they are "obedient, caring, good mates, responsible for all housework and care of all family members" (World Bank, 2014a). Women are, in summary, appreciated as "wives, mothers and homemakers" (ILO, 2015c). Gender norms and stereotypes, for example, underpin Nigeria's self-perception of being a country "producing good wives and mothers to build the nation" (Odejide, 2014). Gender stereotyping is common across the African continent. In 2014, all 51 national reviews on the implementation of the Beijing Platform for Action submitted to United Nations Economic Commission for Africa (UNECA) were consistent in their recognition that conservative gender norms, based on long-standing stereotypes, continue to prevent the full realization of women rights on the continent.

Customary and religious leaders play a prominent role in impeding changes to social norms. Beyond many other social expressions and actors that reproduce such traditions, these leaders are powerful stakeholders in many African countries. Figure 6.3 illustrates how discrimination is embedded in traditional

Social and institutional silence on violence against women combine to perpetuate systemic and normalized violence in Africa.

FIGURE 6.3

Discrimination of women by traditional leaders in selected African countries

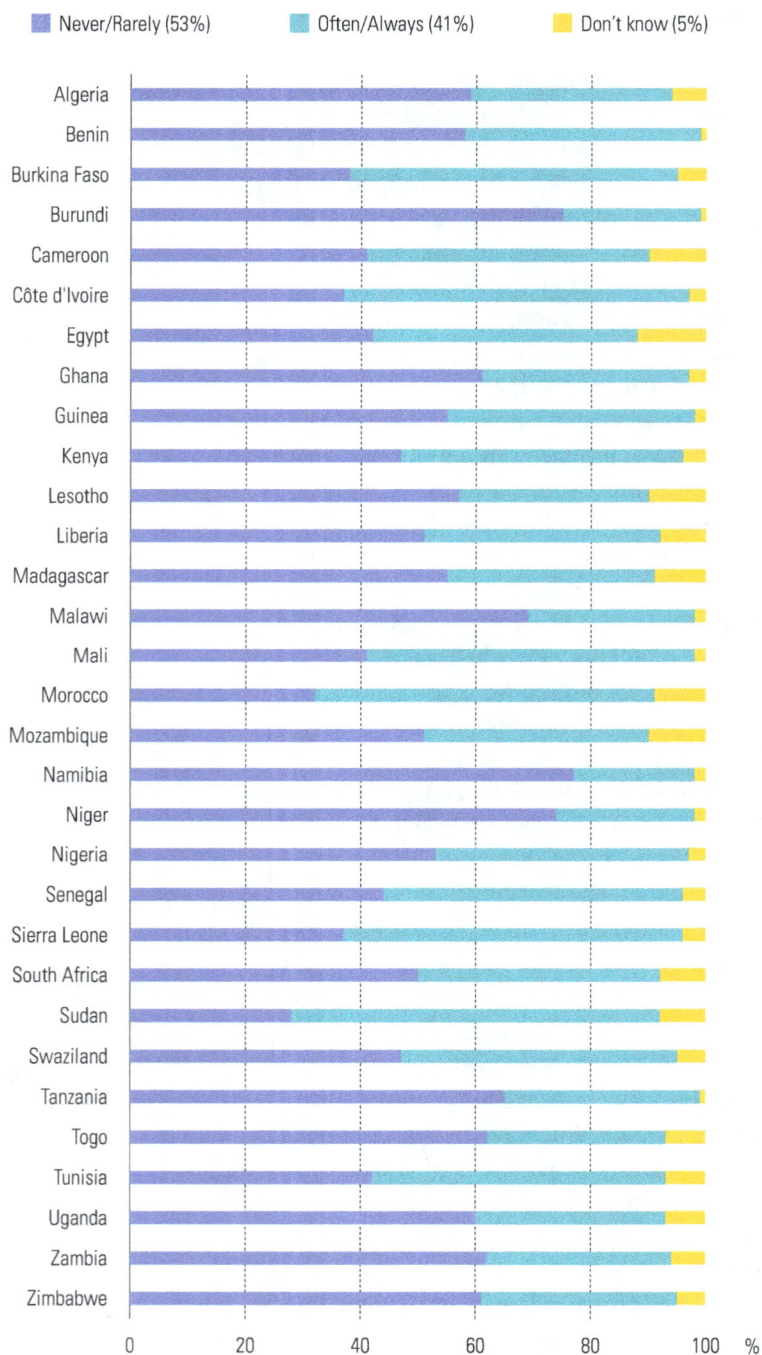

■ Never/Rarely (53%)   ■ Often/Always (41%)   ■ Don't know (5%)

Algeria
Benin
Burkina Faso
Burundi
Cameroon
Côte d'Ivoire
Egypt
Ghana
Guinea
Kenya
Lesotho
Liberia
Madagascar
Malawi
Mali
Morocco
Mozambique
Namibia
Niger
Nigeria
Senegal
Sierra Leone
South Africa
Sudan
Swaziland
Tanzania
Togo
Tunisia
Uganda
Zambia
Zimbabwe

0   20   40   60   80   100   %

Source: Compiled by the AfHDR Team from Afrobarometer 2011/2013 (n = 47,997).

leadership in Africa. A high proportion of citizens believe that their traditional leaders always or often treat women unequally, which is 40 per cent on average for the continent, reaching as high as 60 per cent in countries such as Morocco, Côte d'Ivoire and Sierra Leone. While stereotypes are not norms, they must be discussed as part of the reconstruction of social norms affecting gender relationships.

Finally, it must be understood that women often uphold the system of social norms that limits their own empowerment. It is the community as a whole, including women and men, that shapes and replicates the concept of what is normal. Women therefore contribute to reinforcing the same social norms that discriminate against them. Episodes of domestic violence towards daughters-in-law perpetrated by mothers-in-law and the role of mothers in organizing the mutilation of their daughters' genitals have both been well-documented. Deconstructing these norms is closely associated with awareness because it is necessary for women to first gain consciousness of the negative effects on themselves caused by the traditions they perpetuate.

Gender-based violence, physical harm and early marriage

Violence against women has become socially accepted across the Continent. Most of the violence is not perpetrated by strangers in dark alleys, but by partners, close relatives and men living next door. Men who sexually violate women are not rare and unknown aggressors. They are mostly part of a woman's circle of family and associates; they are men considered 'normal' in a society where violence is deeply embedded. In school, girls' early dropout rate has been associated with teenage pregnancy and sexual harassment by teachers and fellow pupils. Violence against women takes multiple expressions including domestic violence, intimate partner violence, rape, intimidation, sexual harassment and FGM. Africa has an alarming incidence of violence against women, fuelled mostly by social norms around women's inferiority (see figure 6.4 for impacts on women's well-being).

FIGURE 6.4

Impacts of intimate partner violence on women's well-being

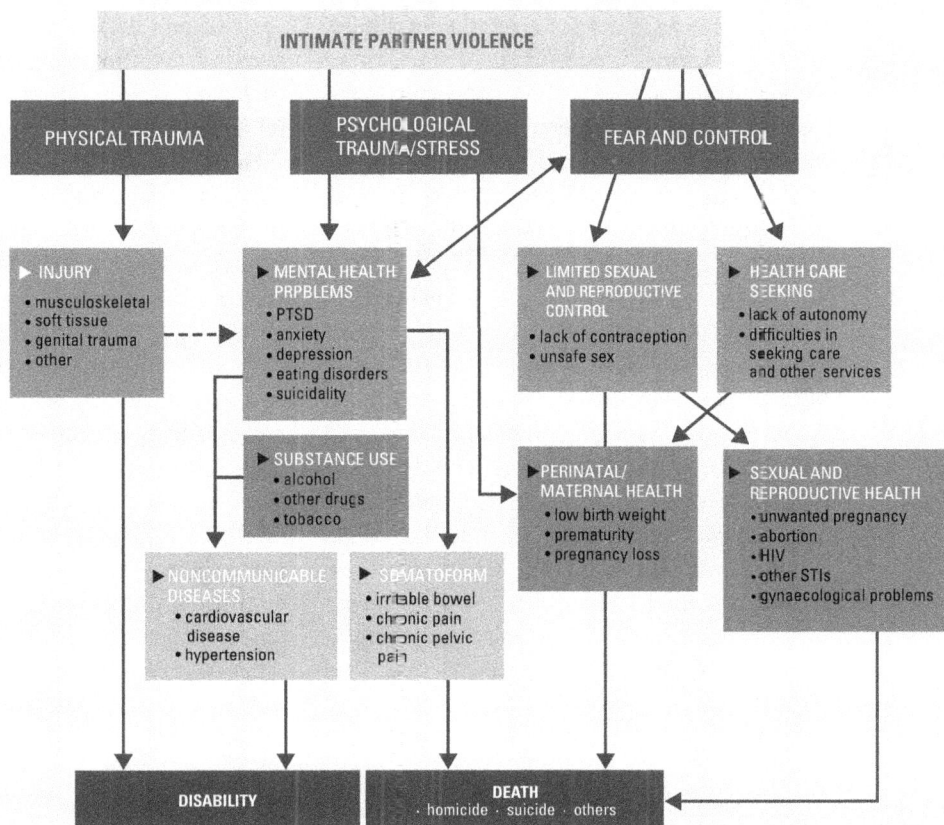

INTIMATE PARTNER VIOLENCE

PHYSICAL TRAUMA

PSYCHOLOGICAL TRAUMA/STRESS

FEAR AND CONTROL

▶ INJURY
- musculoskeletal
- soft tissue
- genital trauma
- other

▶ MENTAL HEALTH PROBLEMS
- PTSD
- anxiety
- depression
- eating disorders
- suicidality

▶ LIMITED SEXUAL AND REPRODUCTIVE CONTROL
- lack of contraception
- unsafe sex

▶ HEALTH CARE SEEKING
- lack of autonomy
- difficulties in seeking care and other services

▶ SUBSTANCE USE
- alcohol
- other drugs
- tobacco

▶ PERINATAL/ MATERNAL HEALTH
- low birth weight
- prematurity
- pregnancy loss

▶ SEXUAL AND REPRODUCTIVE HEALTH
- unwanted pregnancy
- abortion
- HIV
- other STIs
- gynaecological problems

▶ NONCOMMUNICABLE DISEASES
- cardiovascular disease
- hypertension

▶ SOMATOFORM
- irritable bowel
- chronic pain
- chronic pelvic pain

DISABILITY

DEATH
· homicide · suicide · others

Note: STI – sexually transmitted infections; PTSD – post-traumatic stress disorder.
Source: WHO, 2013.

The millions of African women and girls suffering daily from violence are barely discernible. The individuals involved, both men and women, remain mostly silent. Institutions also remain silent, in part because of the widespread belief in many countries that domestic violence is a purely private concern. This makes it difficult for victims to seek help outside of the family from officials such as the police, lawyers and social workers. Only 6 per cent of African women report being victims of intimate partner violence, while it is estimated to affect an average of 37 per cent of women in sub-Saharan Africa (AfDB, 2015). Other barriers to reporting that are tied to social norms include under-standing the problem as "part of life", or trying to avoid the social shame and stigma of violence survivors (World Bank, 2014a). This social and institutional silence combines to exacerbate gender violence in Africa.

Women's acceptance of violence is decreasing but still prominent. In Guinea and Mali, more than 75 per cent of women report acceptance of wife beating as a normal practice. Here, physical violence against wives is justified for reasons such as burning food, refusing sex, neglecting children, arguing with the husband or leaving the house without informing him (ibid.). Awareness must be increased so that sexual violence and other forms of violence within the household are no longer accepted as normal. Gender-based violence has multiple negative impacts on women's health, but also on other less obvious spheres, such as the economic sphere. A study recently undertaken in the United Republic of Tanzania found that women experiencing intimate partner violence (IPV) and those experiencing severe IPV earned 29 per cent less income and 43 per cent less income, respectively, than women who had never been abused by a partner,

Social norms related to sexuality are strongly connected to domestic violence. For young men in Africa, just as for many young men worldwide, sexual experience is frequently associated with initiation into socially recognized manhood. This fosters a perception of sex as performance, specifically a means by which to demonstrate masculine prowess. Young men in many cultures, Africa included, experience pressure from peers to be sexually active and have multiple partners in order to be perceived as men. This pattern of sexual bravado as a means to peer acceptance often continues into manhood. Patriarchy grants men privilege over women regarding sexuality. Socially accepted thinking about sexuality includes the belief that women exist to satisfy men's desire on demand. Within marriages, this notion can fuel undesired and non-consensual sexual relationships.

Gender-based violence poses specific dangers to men and boys as well as women. In many instances, males engage in risky behaviours that are damaging to themselves and their communities. In Lesotho and Seychelles, for example, girls are overtaking boys in enrolment and performance in secondary and tertiary education because social norms and expectations discriminate against boys' educational attainment. In other parts of Africa, such as the Democratic Republic of the Congo, cultural norms of masculinity place young men at risk of being either victims or perpetrators of gender-based violence, as well as at risk of being violated by other men (AfDB, 2014b:11).

BOX 6.3

The Berhane Hewan Programme for decreasing early marriage in Ethiopia

The Berhane Hewan Programme in Ethiopia (2004-2008) sought to delay marriage among unmarried girls at risk and to support child wives. A wide coalition of actors cooperated to make it possible, including the Ethiopian Ministry of Youth and Sport (that became Ministry of Women, Children and Youth Affairs), the Amhara Regional Bureau of Youth and Sport, the United Nations Population Fund (UNFPA), the United Nations Foundation, the Nike Foundation, local authorities and the Population Council.

The programme engaged elders in dialogue, provided adult female mentors for young girls, as well as financial incentives in the form of cash transfer conditional on girls being kept in school and school supplies. Close collaboration and implementation with the government contributed to its success.

An evaluation of the 2004-2006 period showed that school attendance of girls aged 10-14 improved from 72 to 96 per cent. Young adolescents aged 14 or less were three times more likely to be in school and 90 per cent less likely to be married. Girls participating in the programme also improved their knowledge of HIV transmission and family planning. Based on the success of the programme, a second-generation project was initiated to identify the most cost-efficient approach to prevent child marriage in Africa. Burkina Faso and the United Republic of Tanzania joined this initiative.

Source: Erulkar, 2015.

The problem of early marriage is closely related to gender-based violence. Although it violates several international and African declarations, it is persistent in Africa and is nourished by traditional norms and social behaviours. In sub-Saharan Africa, early marriage is a socially accepted practice based on traditional and religious beliefs. According to local customary beliefs, early marriage protects daughters against dangerous events such as rape that would compromise their purity and reduce the probability of future marriage. Economic factors also amplify early marriage practice. Girls of poor households are almost twice as exposed to early marriage as girls in wealthier households (World Bank, 2014a). One of the reasons is that women are sometimes viewed as an economic burden in some African cultures where daughters are considered additional mouths to feed. The marrying off a daughter, reduces the economic burden on the family and is a source of economic benefits, such as a dowry, and even psychological benefits. At the same time, age differences between married men and women lead to power imbalances between husbands and wives, as well as less communication. Thus, if strategies to reduce early marriage are to deconstruct age-old beliefs rooted deeply in social norms, communities must be engaged in dialogue (box 6.3).

Social stigmatization, female genital mutilation and HIV/AIDS

Sexuality-related social beliefs are also at the base of one of the most disturbing forms of violence and human rights violation faced by millions of African women: FGM. Parents, mothers included, feel strong pressure to perform FGM on their daughters and to hold beliefs concerning its positive effects. These beliefs are based on tradition and include mutilation as a way of preventing sexual promiscuity, as a rite of passage for girls into womanhood, and also as a condition for marriage. In some communities, girls are considered unworthy to marry if not previously mutilated. FGM is also wrongly understood as a technique to increase fertility and better performance of women in their role as mothers. It is also believed that the female genitals in their natural form are unhealthy and unclean. The problem does not affect the entire continent, but FGM is the standard in certain areas and communities. Challenging this tradition is a very difficult task. Addressing this calls for a communal approach involving community, religious and traditional leaders. The example from Burkina Faso (box 6.1) is one very good practice.

In the context of HIV/AIDS, the social roles and norms governing masculinity may predispose men towards risky behaviours. Acting responsibly and practising safe sex or no sex may be considered in some societies as unmanly, thus leading men to practise unsafe sex with multiple partners. This association between sexual activity, manhood and identity has numerous direct implications for HIV/AIDS prevention. Uganda is a model in its HIV/AIDS prevention programmes with a gender perspective. The approach seeks in particular to reduce male vulnerability. Uganda has had astonishing success rates, given that behavioural programmes have had a very mixed success elsewhere on the Continent. The reason may be that these programmes have made excellent use of alternative male role models.

The most salient factor in changing the behaviour of younger men has been older men willing to assume a more responsible model of masculinity. The most effective approach has been that of person-to-person communication. "Our findings indicate that substantial HIV reductions in Uganda resulted from public-health interventions that triggered a social process of risk avoidance manifested by radical changes in sexual behaviours. The outcome was equivalent to a highly effective vaccine" (Stoneburner and Low-Beer, 2004: 717). This approach also seems to have yielded sustained, long-term results, and reinforced the belief that successful transformation of behavioural patterns requires participatory exercises of dialogue and consensus.

Research conducted in different countries has documented associations between HIV/AIDS and physical and/or sexual violence, both seen as risk factors for HIV infection. A decade of cross-cutting research from African

In patriarchal societies that countenance violence, conflict resolution is sometimes based on violence. In many African countries, war, civil conflict and local atrocities have become prevalent.

BOX 6.4

The cultural factors at play in Africa's HIV crisis: Lessons from Zambia

Lusaka, Zambia – Mary, who is 24 but barely looks 18, has already experienced more than enough betrayal for any lifetime. Shyly but deliberately, she told of feeling sick at 16 and being diagnosed with HIV. After her mother – her only provider – was sent to prison, an aunt took Mary in, but forced her to sleep in an open-walled shed behind the house. Then she was raped by a boyfriend. "I went home crying and bleeding," she recalled. Mary told no one, fearing she would be turned out on the street. "I kept quiet, by myself." Four months later, she learned that she was pregnant [and HIV positive].

For the sake of the child, a girl who was born HIV-free, she took antiretroviral drugs. But then a friend introduced her to a Christian pastor. "He lays his hands on you and says the sickness will go [away]," Mary remembered. "I believed him." She put her medicines down the toilet and stopped treatment for two years.

Last year, Mary got married and initially did not reveal her medical history to her spouse, fearing another rejection. "It is difficult to stand up and say you are HIV-positive," Mary explained. "It was my secret." But a counsellor persuaded her to be tested again along with her husband. When her test came back positive and his negative, she ran crying from the clinic, convinced she would be abandoned. But her husband followed after her. "He said to me, 'This is not the end of the world.'"

True enough. Yet it is hard to imagine why the world – family, pastor, rapist – should be so relentlessly cruel to such a sweet and gentle young woman. Gentle, but not fragile. Just revealing her status and story to strangers, in a place where stigma is strong, took some of the greatest personal courage I've witnessed.

Stories like Mary's – in the millions – add up to one of the most urgent health crises of our time. While vast progress has been made in AIDS treatment in sub-Saharan Africa, barely a dent has been made in HIV infection rates among young women (which are significantly higher than among young men). With the youth population of Africa booming (40 per cent of Zambians are under 16), a realization is dawning: the AIDS epidemic will be uncontrollable unless the number of infections among young women is rapidly and dramatically reduced.

In Zambia, about 11 per cent of women become HIV-positive by the age of 24. A sad variety of cultural factors are implicated. These include gender-based violence, child marriage (in spite of national laws against it) and a male-dominated society means that young women often lack the power to negotiate safer sex or to access health services without the permission of male partners. Extreme poverty can also lead young women to engage in transactional sex, but so can the desire for consumer goods that demonstrate status among girls from wealthier backgrounds.

High rates of HIV-infection among young women are a medical crisis for which there is no purely medical answer. Norms need to be changed. The empowerment of young women has become an essential health priority.

Source: The Washington Post, The cultural factors at play in Africa's HIV crisis, 22 April 2016.

countries, including Rwanda, United Republic of Tanzania and South Africa, and more recently outside the region, in India, has consistently found women who have experienced partner violence to more likely be infected with HIV.

This particular interlinkage between violence and HIV/AIDS infection is complemented by widespread stigma and persecution of people who are open about their status (box 6.4). Women and men with certain stigmatized conditions, such as HIV/AIDS infection, are subject to persecution when openly claiming their status. Infected people may decide to remain silent to avoid social violence at the cost of life-threatening consequences. In addition to the psycholo-gical and physical trauma, victims of rape also face stigmatization and have no legal resources to hold perpetrators accountable.

Political violence against women

Electoral-related violence in Africa has also been a growing concern in the past few years. This has been the case in countries such as Côte d'Ivoire, Kenya, Nigeria and Zimbabwe. Electoral violence is a barrier to political participation in a context where democratic elections are increasing in Africa, and a record number of women have successfully run for political office. A 2009 report from an Electoral Institute for Sustainable Democracy (EISA) symposium explained that conflict can exacerbate patterns of discrimination and violence against women, and that, in situations of conflict, habitual abuses take on new dimensions and distinctive patterns, since all forms of violence increase for people in vulnerable situations (EISA, 2009).

Nonetheless, the region has registered several successful strategies in strengthening the electoral and democratic processes. In the 2010 presidential elections in Guinea, for example, civil society and women's groups in particular multiplied efforts to educate the electorate about the democratic process and to facilitate women's participation in the elections after decades of authoritarian rule. Also,

BOX 6.5

Women in the Ugandan conflict

The return of ex-combatants in post-conflict settings has had an impact on the female population. In the context of the northern Uganda conflict, it was found that 72 per cent of girls in the Lord's Resistance Army (LRA) received weapons and military training but were often the last to be released due to their critical role. However, little is known about how the LRA war has impacted the female population, particularly women who were abducted. It seems clear that the female experiences of abduction, violence and even return have been fundamentally different from those of their male counterparts (Annan et al., 2008).

While the conflict in Uganda has brought suffering to the whole population, women and children were the ones who suffered the most. Women were sexually assaulted, maimed, abducted and forcefully recruited into the armed forces. The exploitation and victimization of women has led to prolonged emotional trauma, unwanted pregnancies and sexual diseases including HIV/AIDS. As culturally designated caregivers, women struggle to support their families and keep their households together while their husbands, sons and daughters are caught up in the fighting and are unable to provide for the remaining family members. Moreover, they have had limited access to benefits in their recipient communities (De Watteville, 2002). Also, the reinsertion packages are the same for men and women, failing to take into account the particular dynamics of returning females.

The fact that many of these girls have children is ignored, and the failure to address the real needs of the female returnees renders the process of reintegration weak. This has also been true for those females who were not abducted by the LRA. Many of the girls admitted that they had been subjected to social exclusion and abuse. Hence, without a greater understanding of who is at risk of violence (and from whom), what factors affect violence and acceptance, and a sense of the long-term impacts of war violence, it will be impossible to design effective and relevant reintegration programmes (Annan et al., 2008). In short, women and girls have specific needs that should be taken into consideration in the course of reintegration if the process is to be considered effective.

Source: Carrasco, 2015.

in Kenya, post-election violence prompted activists to propose several initiatives that would ensure a peaceful electoral process during the run-up to the March 2013 elections.

Because of its track record in other African countries as an effective tool in preventing and minimizing electoral violence, the Women's Situation Room (WSR) was among the selected initiatives. The WSR is an innovative real-time intervention that works with communities in advocating, mediating and intervening to protect voters and help keep the peace before and after an election. Daisy Amdany, the co-convener of the National Women Steering Committee, a consortium of women's advocacy groups, said that she felt that the establishment of the WSR in Kenya was good for women, but that it should have been brought in earlier than a month before the elections. According to Amdany, "[I]t was a good platform to enforce women's rights and give women a voice because it was able to get the attention of the police and the elections body. ...It can be useful if put in place once again for the 2017 general election."

Sexual violence has been all too common in the context of war, civil conflict and local atrocities. During conflict situations, additional social norms related to gender arise. In the Rwanda civil war and genocide, women were targeted not only on the basis of their ethnicity, but also their sex: they were subjected to sexual assault, torture, rape, forced incest and breast oblation [sic]. Various estimates suggest that up to 2,500,000 women and children were raped during the 1994 Rwanda genocide (United Nations, 2014). The use of Rwandan women and girls as weapons of war was not an isolated case; it is not uncommon that they became frequent casualties of sexual violence for reasons that involve humiliating and punishing the enemy. During war, rape and sexual violence are seen as minor crimes. Sexual and gender-based violence is particularly challenging and heartrending, with non-state actors, government forces and even peacekeepers and humanitarian workers being among the perpetrators, as in the case of the Democratic Republic of the Congo. As box 6.6 recounts, the array of perverse consequences of conflict on women and girls persists long beyond the end of conflict.

A study of child soldiers in four African countries noted, "With low levels of material and human capital, children are typically unable to provide food and shelter for themselves. Former child soldiers often end up on the street, in gangs, or are drawn back into conflicts" (Young, 2007:20). Child soldiers will then not find themselves only subject to post-traumatic stress disorders, but will also face the day-to-day immediate practical problems of all adult veterans: finding work and a place to live. Yet, these children face them without having the resources an adult has.

Overall Policy and Implementation Issues:
Implications of Legal and Social Norms for Promoting Gender Equality

The Africa region has made significant strides in contextualizing international legal norms for promoting gender equality and women's empowerment, but detrimental social norms continue to limit the full benefits of women's legal and human rights.

- The African legal framework for gender equality is still only theoretical for too many African countries. The challenge for the AU, African governments and African citizens is not to fine-tune existing legal standards, but rather, to ensure that regional standards are accepted and assimilated into national laws and regulations, and then fully implemented and enforced.

- A wide range of social norms continue to have a negative impact on the attainment of gender equality in Africa. Despite a number of international and regional laws and declarations concerning human rights and gender equality, these standards are often negated or diminished at the national and community level because of pervasive social norms.

- Social norms that are detrimental to gender equality are manifest across the Africa region in the form of job and education discrimination, sexual violence, early marriage, social stigma, harmful traditional procedures such as female genital mutilation, and other gender-based practices that limit women's opportunities.

- The impact of social norms that limit women has also shown to have deleterious effects on men and boys, and communities as a whole, essentially holding everyone back from achieving higher human development.

- Experience suggests that ignoring or minimizing the role of social norms in actions aimed at improving gender equality will likely limit the potential for success.

Forging alliances and institutional collaboration
for gender equality

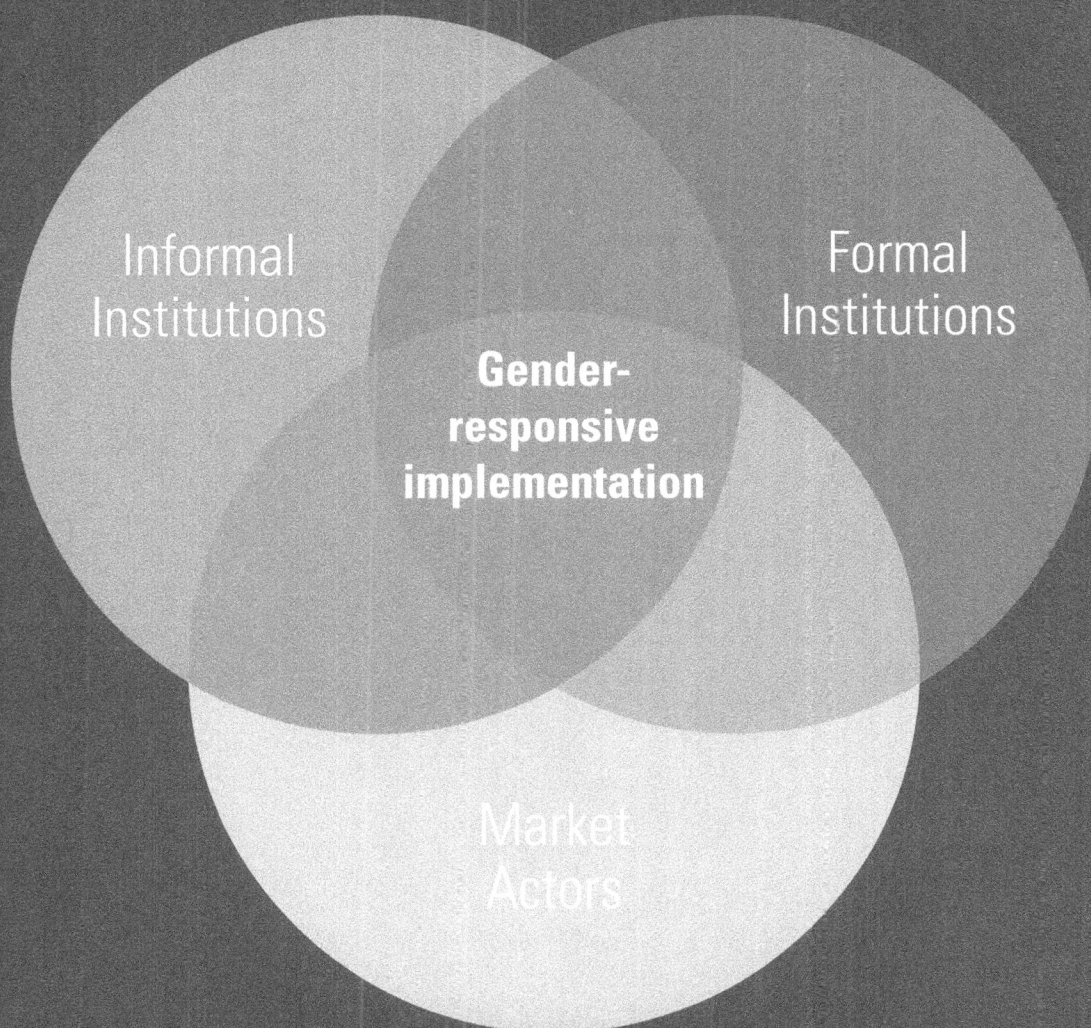

Informal
Institutions

Formal
Institutions

**Gender-
responsive
implementation**

Market
Actors

Chapter 7

Policy and Institutional Responses to Address Gender Inequality

Chapter 7
Policy and Institutional Responses to Address Gender Inequality

This chapter explores the ways in which governments have sought to respond to gender inequality through a range of policy and institutional approaches. It also documents key lessons and good practices that could help accelerate gender equality and women's empowerment in Africa.

Assuming that the political commitment exists, governments have a range of options in promoting gender equality. These include, but are not limited to, five overlapping and mutually reinforcing options:

- **macro policy and public expenditures;**

- **gender-focused institutions;**

- **integrated programmes, targeted interventions and social transfers;**

- **legal and regulatory policies; and**

- **social norms.**

Before looking at these policy and institutional tools, it may be useful to first lay the groundwork by briefly highlighting the channels by which policies and institutions can impact issues affecting gender equality

and women's empowerment. As figure 7.1 implies, there are basically three avenues through which policies and institutions can focus on working within the household, with the economy and markets, and within society at large. In effect, these contexts reflect achieving gender equality in terms of rights, resources and voice.

From this perspective, a government's policy and institutional response directed at the household, market and societal contexts is a process requiring constant refinements and adjustments over time to reflect changing economic and social dynamics for both women and men. With this in mind, the chapter will now focus on the different policy and institutional responses used by African governments, as well as examples from LAC and Asia that are relevant to the African experience.

FIGURE 7.1

Policy and institutional conduits for gender equality

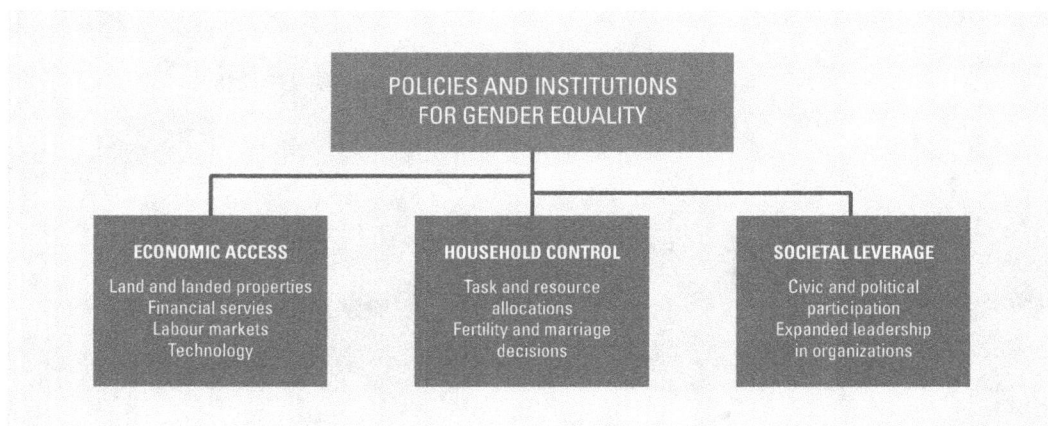

POLICIES AND INSTITUTIONS
FOR GENDER EQUALITY

ECONOMIC ACCESS
Land and landed properties
Financial servies
Labour markets
Technology

HOUSEHOLD CONTROL
Task and resource
allocations
Fertility and marriage
decisions

SOCIETAL LEVERAGE
Civic and political
participation
Expanded leadership
in organizations

Source: Adapted from WHO, 2015.

Macro policy and public expenditures

From a macroeconomic perspective, all governments seek to articulate economic policies that are internally driven and sustainable over time. The ensuing policy debates must consider such questions as the role of the state in economy, monetary and fiscal policies including taxation, industrial and trade policies, as well as social and equity issues. While policies are generally assumed to be gender-neutral, such debates have often failed to adequately consider the unintended or unexpected differential impacts on women. Given the expanding body of research demonstrating that gender (in)equality is a macroeconomic variable with significant effects on development and on rates of economic growth, this represents a major gap in the way macroeconomic policy is formulated in many African countries. The size and direction of these effects have been found to vary with the structure of the economy, the degree and type of job segregation, and the macro-level policies in force.

As part of macro policy, fiscal policy and public expenditures may be the first and most important litmus test of a government's commitment to gender equality. Gender equality may in theory be mainstreamed in laws, policies, programmes and institutions, but the test of commitment is ultimately a function of resources made available and the efficacy in their use. While financial and human resources allocated to gender equality have increased since 1995, that amount remains very small.

Table 7.1 suggests the nature of the problem in understanding the impacts of macro and fiscal policy on gender. The calculations infer that what is being measured at the country level are programmes and expenditures that are classified as gender-specific. The calculations do not capture the way that general public expenditures are differentially benefitting or limiting women's empowerment. The table also raises questions about how African governments are classifying budget allocations for gender as a percentage of total budget expenditures,

TABLE 7.1

Expenditure allocation for gender equality in selected African countries

Country	National budget allocated for promotion of gender equality (%)
Chad	20
Cameroon	10
Guinea	10
Lesotho	5.9
Botswana	5
Namibia	2.9
Burkina Faso	>2
Sao Tome and Principe	0.5
Mali	0.30-0.40
Rwanda	0.24
Liberia	0.23
Republic of the Congo	0.20
Togo	0.12

Source: UNECA, 2014.

ranging from 20 per cent in Chad to 0.12 per cent in Togo. However, not all governments explicitly mentioned allocation to gender issues in their budgets, even when such resources are dedicated to such expenses.

The gaps in the information from table 7.1 thus demonstrate the importance of analysing the impact of overall national budgets on gender outcomes. Government commitments to gender - across all expenditure categories - must be monitored both to establish the proportion of expenditures and identify desired outcomes. In 2009, gender budgeting was being used in just over 20 per cent of African countries, either at the initiative of civil society or of govern-ment. In 2014, gender budgeting was a key recommendation of the 9th African Regional Conference on Women, showing that there is significant room for improvement on this front. In addition to gender analysis by budget categories, greater attention is needed to understand the role of other economic policy choices, such as the impact of tax policies on women, the positive as well as potentially negative impacts of decentralized revenue generation, and the ability of budget planning and modelling to be gender-sensitive.

Gender equality may in theory be mainstreamed in laws, policies, programmes and institutions, but the test of commitment is ultimately a function of resources made available and how effectively they are used.

The LAC region offers a useful lesson on budget commitment for Africa. For the past 15 years, the region has been allocating approximately 0.4 per cent of its GDP to fund various kinds of conditional cash transfer CCT programmes (ECLAC, 2013: 50). To contextualize this investment effort, CCT fund allocations were about 10 per cent of all public educational expenditures, which have fluctuated between 3.9 and 4.5 per cent of GDP since 2000. CCT programmes in LAC have been financed both through regular national budgets and through World Bank or Inter-American Development Bank (IDB) loans.

CCTs have become the prime policy instrument to combat poverty and extreme poverty and inequality; however, they are not necessarily aimed at reducing gender inequalities per se, but poverty more broadly defined. In LAC, these fund allocations reflect a renewed political will to operationalize human development and poverty reduction. Only with such levels of financial commitment has it been possible for CCT programmes to cover over 25 million households and over 100 million people. This represents almost 20 per cent of the LAC region's total population, a rate that implies true national development efforts beyond the more common small-scale and pilot dimension of many interventions (ECLAC, 2013:50).

African governments and development agencies need to tap further into the potential of public investments for promoting additional inclusive growth for women at the local level. Mozambique provides a useful example for other African states. There, the power of women was leveraged to participate in urban development projects during the post-war reconstruction era in the 1990s (box 7.1). By partnering with local communities, governments can provide them with a voice to define and defend their interests and needs. Designed in partnership, public work projects can provide new jobs and also demand local inputs that may be provided by the local population, especially women, with significant economic and social benefits for the communities. Housing and community

BOX 7.1

Peri-urban development programme in Mozambique

In 1991, *Associação Moçambicana para o Desenvolvimento Urbano* (AMDU, Mozambican Association for Urban Development), as part of its urban programme, a study was conducted in peri-urban areas of Maputo to determine the priorities of communities and to gather socio-economic data.

A key finding of the study was that pre-schools were considered by all members of the community to be a priority. This partly reflected the conditions of urban overcrowding and the prevalent poverty towards the end of the war in 1992, with children often left unsupervised while parents went to farm or work outside the home. AMDU took pre-schools as a focal point for mobilizing communities in urban neighbourhoods and involved many members of the community, outside experts and local administrations in building and organizing pre-schools.

In Maputo, women were in the majority of those involved in the construction of AMDU projects. In 1996, 300 women and 78 men were employed in labour-intensive construction work of various kinds. In total, around 4,100 people had temporary employment in the urban programme during the 1993-1996 period. A training centre as well as six training schools in six neighbourhoods were built. In addition, one cultural centre, two schools and a health centre were rehabilitated. Also, 15 pit latrines, three community bread ovens and roads were constructed.

Income-generating activities for women were linked to some of the pre-schools. Other urban activities promoted by AMDU included new systems of garbage collection, latrine construction and urban road maintenance. As a result of AMDU activities, the municipal government took interest in peri-urban development.

Source: Carrasco, 2015.

building projects offer additional sorts of investments that can also be leveraged in support of national efforts to correct social inequalities.

Engaging resources from private firms and international organizations in support of gender equality is an ongoing requirement. The African Development Bank's (AfDB) involvement in initiatives such as the African Women in Business Initiative and ILO's Growth-Oriented Women Entrepreneurs are positive examples that must continue to expand in the continent. The financial requirements to advance gender equality and human development in Africa are considerable, and therefore private resources are also important to supplement public expenditures.

Gender-focused institutions

Most African countries have followed international practice by setting up institutions for the advancement of women. These new organizational mechanisms for gender issues have taken many forms, including thematic ministries or ministerial departments for women, designated in some countries as lead institutional mechanisms. The record of such gender-focused institutions is mixed. In some cases, there is concern that these institutions have not received full backing of the government, resulting in the marginalization of the institution by delegating gender issues to a single ministry or agency outside of mainstream government.

The other institutional model is to employ a framework in which multiple institutions are responsible for women's rights. This approach has also met with varying degrees of success. In South Africa, multiple mechanisms have been cited as a positive example, but in other places, such as Benin, confusion around the duplication of mandates between institutions has reportedly hampered the effectiveness of programmes. Different state institutions have different levels of political commitment as well as varying degrees of collaboration with other stakeholders, including civil society, international donors, and regional and international bodies.

FIGURE 7.2

Institutional collaboration for gender equality

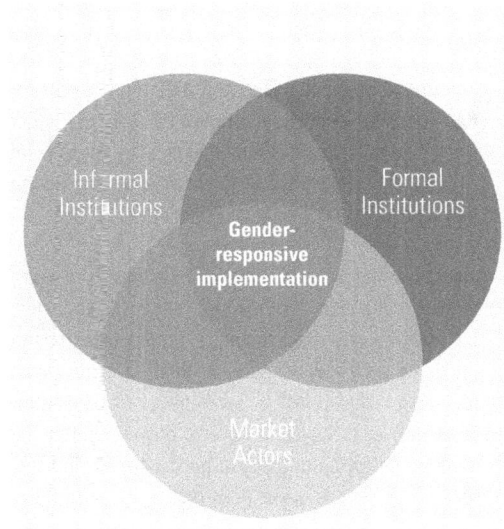

Note: The interaction of these three elements comes together to yield gender-responsive implementations.

Source: Prepared by the AfHDR Team.

Developing effective institutional models to achieve greater social equality must also be understood as a shared responsibility involving the private sector and civil society, which consists of many informal and formal institutions (figure 7.2). In the LAC region, the IDB's Women Entrepreneurship Banking (weB) has been providing incentives for financial institutions in Latin America to stimulate their lending to women-owned SMEs.

Other significant interventions along this line involve organizations such as the ILO or private companies such as Coca-Cola and Goldman Sachs. In 2002, ILO launched the Women's Entrepreneurship Development initiative to support women entrepreneurs in starting, strengthening and expanding their enterprises in developing countries; to date, over 60,000 women have benefitted from this initiative. By the end of 2012, about 300,000 women had been assisted by Coca-Cola with business training, financial services, mentoring and networking opportunities to start and expand small businesses, and join the company's supply chains. The number of women supported is expected to rise to

Most African countries have followed international practice by setting up institutions for the advancement of women, including specialized ministries, departments and agencies. However, the record of such gender-focused institutions is mixed.

Stronger voices for reproductive health in the United Republic of Tanzania

The United Republic of Tanzania's Stronger Voices for Reproductive Health project, which ran in Geita District from 2001 to 2006, empowered women by giving them a stronger voice in securing information and health services.

The project began with meetings to establish, in a participatory manner, a consensus among stakeholders on identifying the community's reproductive health problems and how to address them. The problems identified included lack of awareness of the need for condom use, of women's right to privacy, and of the need for follow-up to cases of gender-based violence. Village workshops were then organized and efforts made to achieve gender balance and include particularly vulnerable people among the participants.

Training modules were developed that covered a range of health topics: the male and female anatomy as it relates to sexual and reproductive health, pregnancy, family planning, sexually transmitted diseases and HIV/AIDS prevention. The modules also covered the gender dimensions of the epidemic, human rights related to sexual and reproductive health, and gender-based violence. The project also provided training to public officials and health service providers and institutional support to help them better meet women's needs and demands at the community level.

Source: UNFPA and Harvard School of Public Health, 2008: 19-25.

5 million women by 2020. In the case of Goldman Sachs, in 2008, the firm launched a five year, $100 million initiative to provide business education, networking and mentoring opportunities to 10,000 female entrepreneurs in developing regions (Goldman Sachs, n.d.).

International agencies, private corporations and civil society have prominent roles to play in committing resources to foster new opportunities for women and balance the playing field. Their scale of action may never reach the universal coverage of public services, but their leverage capacity can yet make a difference. For this reason, it is necessary to engage their purchasing and investment power in the fight against gender inequality. Although the coverage of these programmes seems of minor relevance when compared with Africa's equality challenge, they do realize vital contributions. Commitment of private investment to foster women's opportunities has proven to empower participating women's groups, creating new opportunities for them, their families and communities while facilitating new institutional models to replicate.

Integrated programmes, targeted interventions and social transfers

Clearly, larger expenditure allocations are a much needed element of any sustainable national commitment toward gender equality. Yet, equally important to the availability of funds is the quality and effectiveness of new or existing programmes and initiatives targeting gender equality. This section reviews some of the programmes that have been implemented in Africa in an effort to improve women's economic benefits and that also result in important social co-benefits. The kinds of programmes and projects highlighted below may be directly or indirectly targeted at women, with an overall goal of creating community benefits using women as the change agent.

Participatory programme design, implementation and monitoring

In Africa, as in Asia and Latin America, the concept of women's participation in project and programme decision-making is not novel. Regardless of the kind of project or programme, women as well as men should be involved in the decision-making that impacts their well-being.

Effective beneficiary participation improves the likelihood of project success. Box 7. 2 provides an example of the role of expanding women's partici-patory space in a community reproductive health project in the United Republic of Tanzania. The project included women in the identification of problems and needs as well as the interventions to address them.

The participatory process described in the United Republic of Tanzania's community health project is not limited to small-scale projects. The potential for large-scale projects is demonstrated by a World Bank project in Viet Nam, for the equivalent of $250 million. There was an opportunity in this project for poor, local indigenous communities - mainly women - to participate in the self-assessment and design stages. With an adequate division of labour and access to appropriate technology, women as well as men participated in the implementation. This approach triggered notable development outcomes such as increased awareness, higher household incomes and uptake of useful technical skills, all of which were based on women's participation.

Monitoring and evaluation (M&E) represents another key component of project and programme design and execution. It not only increases transparency and accountability, and generally empowers women as subjects of development, but it also continuously informs gender analysis on the effects of implementation based on empirically driven data.

Gender-disaggregated data have been key in LAC at the base of their progress in gender equality. Many Latin American countries have established observatories, research centres and think tanks exclusively dedicated to the collection, analysis and publication of gender-disaggregated data and indicators related to women's empowerment and gender equality. Gender-disaggregated data are crucial to accurately understand women's issues and design effective measures to address them. Public and private entities generating gender-disaggregated data can be found in Bolivia, Argentina, Colombia, Mexico, Bolivarian Republic of Venezuela, Chile and many other countries in the region. These monitoring entities regularly produce evidence-based public policy recommendations that provide a very solid support to women's voice and opinions.

In Africa, an increasing number of countries are using gender-disaggregated data to help inform policy. Some countries have partnered with national universities or international organizations to improve the gender content of their statistical data. In 2014, UNECA worked with Cameroon, Cabo Verde, Ethiopia, Tunisia and Zambia to review their capacity to collect, analyse and report on gender statistics and gender-disaggregated data at the country level. These are positive first steps. To enable effective interventions, however, efforts to extend gender-disaggregated data need to continue. Moreover, data should be disaggregated not just by sex, but also by factors such as location or ethnicity in order to differentiate between the situations of rural and urban women.

Technology has proved to be a crucial ally in LAC to increase efficiency and effectiveness in monitoring gender equality achievements. The CCT programmes described above have been at the forefront of the technological modernization of social assistance. Technology has been successfully applied to geographic and household targeting methods and to payments to women, which today are reliable, in the right amounts at the right times and at very low transaction costs. Technology also monitors compliance with payments' conditionality. This has required the development of extensive and fast information flows among numerous actors with appropriate management information systems and M&E systems. Since cash transfer programmes need to coordinate actions of many parties – the programme itself, the providers of health and education services, the payment agency, and often sub-national governments at one or more levels – the need for information sharing has been paramount. CCT programmes in LAC have been able to foster citizen participation and social auditing systems through their monitoring mechanisms. Important lessons can be drawn from the LAC experience to be replicated in Africa in order to improve gender-focused investments in their respective economies.

Finally, monitoring progress in gender equality needs to involve the private sector. It is necessary to track advancement in the ability of private firms to provide discrimination-free working environments. Leveraging private firms' resources to fund the monitoring of their own progress is another LAC experience worth replicating. During the last decade, the region has successfully tested a certification model tracking and promoting gender equality for workers in firms and institutions. The model produces outcomes and impacts that are reported, communicated and presented at national and sub-national levels, showcasing good practices for gender equality while keeping track of the achievements being made. Box 7.3 highlights some details of the model. African countries

could adopt similar certification schemes that promote greater gender equality at the workplace while leveraging private resources to monitor achievements. Efforts could start at the country level, engaging international corporations in certifying themselves with a gender equality seal in order to ignite a cascade effect with large- and medium-size firms first, and with others in the formal sector following later.

Gender-responsive social transfers

Social security programmes are a means to reimburse women, who bear most of the responsibilities for unpaid care work and who are disadvantaged economically. Cash transfer programmes are thus emerging in Africa in response to poverty and vulnera-bilities. As articulated in the Progress of the 2015 World Women's Report, unpaid care work constitutes a 'subsidy' to governments. While it is difficult to estimate the size of these subsidies across countries, they are significant. As the need for care has increased with HIV/AIDS,

---

BOX 7.3

UNDP's gender equality seal in Latin America: lessons learned

The Gender Equality Seal for Public and Private Enterprises (GES) is a collective effort involving national governments, private sector companies and civil society to establish and achieve standards that empower women. Participating companies that successfully complete the certification requirements are awarded the Seal – a recognized symbol of gender equality in the workplace that certifies that a company actively promotes equality among its employees.

The Gender Equality Seal presents opportunities for both implementing governments and the companies with which they partner. For governments, the seal represents a concrete means of mainstreaming gender equality to achieve progress in reducing gender gaps. And private companies that have participated in the initiative report numerous advantages, including greater staff performance and commitment, and a positive public image as a leader in corporate responsibility. UNDP lends support to both governments and companies throughout the process.

Since 2007, UNDP has supported governments and companies in Latin America participating in the Gender Equality Seal programme. Beginning with Costa Rica, Uruguay, Brazil and Chile, the GES programme is now active in 12 countries in the region, involving over 400 companies. Designed as a means for the private sector to embrace gender equality and enhance women's economic and social empowerment, the seal offers support to a growing number of corporations to make their human resources management systems more equitable and gender sensitive.

Furthermore, companies report that adopting measures related to the certification requirements has resulted in an increase in employee commitment and a reduction in absenteeism, and attracts a greater diversity of talent. By levelling the playing field for women, economies also prosper, driving national GDP growth.

Source: UNDP, 2016.

the Ebola epidemic and ageing populations, women face an overwhelming responsibility to provide unpaid care.

The programmes are diverse, including emergency one-time transfers, unconditional non-contributory social pensions, and CCT programmes. For example, Ethiopia's Productive Safety Net Programme's Direct Support component and Kenya's Hunger Safety Net Programme were both developed in response to food insecurity situations in the countries. Ghana's Livelihood Empowerment against Poverty (LEAP) Programme is another social cash transfer scheme, providing cash and health insurance to extremely poor households across Ghana as a short-term poverty reduction strategy with a view to encouraging long-term human development. As of July 2013, the programme had reached over 70,000 households across the country with an annual expenditure of approximately US$20 million, 50 per cent of which is funded from the Government's general revenues.

The 2011 African MDG Report discussed the evolution of social protection programmes in the African context and highlighted some key areas that require attention. The AU's Social Policy Framework for Africa (2008) proposed a minimum package of essential social protection, targeting healthcare, and benefits for children, informal workers, the unemployed, the elderly, and persons with disabilities. The launch of the African Civil Society Platform for Social Protection contributed to the growing impetus towards establishing pan-African social protection. In 2010, the Khartoum Declaration on Social Policy Action towards Social Inclusion was launched, which sets out a comprehensive approach to social protection in Africa (AfDB et al., 2011).

A desk review of 123 social protection programmes in sub-Saharan Africa shows positive impacts on reducing poverty and social exclusion. Some of the programmes' impacts include: increased school enrolment for children; reduced grade repetition and reduced absenteeism; reduced teenage pregnancies; increased household food security; and female employment, among others. In Mozambique, for instance, the probability of women's employment increased by 24 per cent with the programme (Soares and Teixeira, 2010). Basic social protection floors are inexpensive ways to reduce vulnerability and destitution, often with multiplier effects on economic growth.

Modelling results for Senegal and the United Republic of Tanzania show that basic social protection benefits can indeed play an important role in poverty reduction strategies in low-income countries. Introducing basic old-age and disability pensions in Senegal and the United Republic of Tanzania would not only improve the living standards of the beneficiaries, but also of the other members living in the same household, especially children, since transfers are typically shared within the household. In Senegal, a combination of a basic old-age and disability pension, and a child benefit for school-age children would reduce food poverty rates by 40 per cent and reduce the poverty gap by more than half. While child benefits affect all groups of individuals to a similar extent, old-age and disability pensions have a more pronounced effect on older persons, especially women, and their family members.

A study in the United Republic of Tanzania estimated that a universal old-age pension would cut poverty rates by 9 per cent, with considerably stronger effects on older women (36 per cent) and men (24 per cent) living in multi-generational households. A more balanced effect would be achieved by a child benefit for school-age children, which would decrease poverty rates by about 30 per cent. The combination of these two benefits would reduce poverty rates by 35 per cent, with even more substantial effects for individuals living in households with children and elderly persons (a drop of 46 per cent). Targeted cash transfers achieve an overall reduction of poverty of 7 per cent. For older men and women, the reduction is more significant, at 12 per cent and 18 per cent, respectively, and for individuals living in households without working members, 46 per cent (Gassmann and Behrendt, 2006).

TABLE 7.2

Early childhood development indicators by family wealth quintile, 2005-2013

Country	% of families with at least three children's books			% of families with at least two toys at home			% of children left in inadequate care		
	Total	Poorest wealth quintile	Richest wealth quintile	Total	Poorest wealth quintile	Richest wealth quintile	Total	Poorest wealth quintile	Richest wealth quintile
Cameroon	3.6	0.4	12.9	41	30	57			
Central African Republic	0.7	0	3	49	41	51	61	58	60
Chad	0.5	0	2.2	43	38	50	56	58	56
Rep. of the Congo	1.2	0.3	4.9	39	24	51	37	38	38
Côte d'Ivoire	4.8	3	12.7	39	44	35	59	62	51
Democratic Rep. of the Congo	0.6	0.4	1.8	29	21	40	60	69	39
Djibouti	14.7	–	–	24	–	–	8	–	–
Gambia	1.2	0.1	4.3	42	28	50	21	25	18
Ghana	6.2	0.6	22.7	41	31	51	21	27	15
Mali	0.4	0	2	40	33	49	33	33	36
Mauritania	–	–	–	40	42	39	26	24	25
Morocco	21.1	8.5	52.3	14	19	7	11	–	–
Mozambique	2.8	1.5	9.6	–	–	–	33	–	–
Nigeria	6	0.3	18.7	38	29	48	40	40	34
Sierra Leone	2.1	0.4	10	35	24	50	32	29	28
Swaziland	3.8	1.1	12.2	69	64	74	15	20	9
Togo	1.5	0	7	31	26	41	41	45	35
Tunisia	17.8	2.6	39.7	53	46	56	13	18	9

Source: Compiled by the AfHDR Team based on the UNICEF 2015 database.

The ILO estimated that the initial gross annual cost of the overall basic social transfer package (excluding access to basic health care) was 2.3 to 5.5 per cent of GDP in 2010. The cost of targeted cash transfers was 3.3 per cent of Senegal's GDP and 3.2 per cent of that of the United Republic of Tanzania.

Paid maternity leave and provision of childcare

As noted in chapter 3, the ILO Maternity Protection Convention (No. 183) provides for mothers, including those in the informal sector, to be entitled to maternity leave of not less than 14 weeks, which should be paid for collectively, by employers and social insurance, at a rate of at least two-thirds the normal wage of the employee.

Paid maternity leave not only serves to preserve the health of a mother and her newborn, but it also provides a measure of job security guaranteeing that women of childbearing age have access to jobs and maintain their wages and benefits during maternity. Using 2010 data on female labour force participation and the 2012 Social Institutions Gender Index (SIGI), Cerise et al. (2013) estimate a linear regression model for understanding how women's employment is related to maternity leave and discriminatory social practices. They found that government-funded paid maternity leave has a greater positive effect on female employment in countries with higher levels of discriminatory social practices such as in Africa and South Asia. The predicted values of female labour force participation

FIGURE 7.3

Early childhood education: net pre-primary enrolment for children below primary school age, by sex, 2005-2014

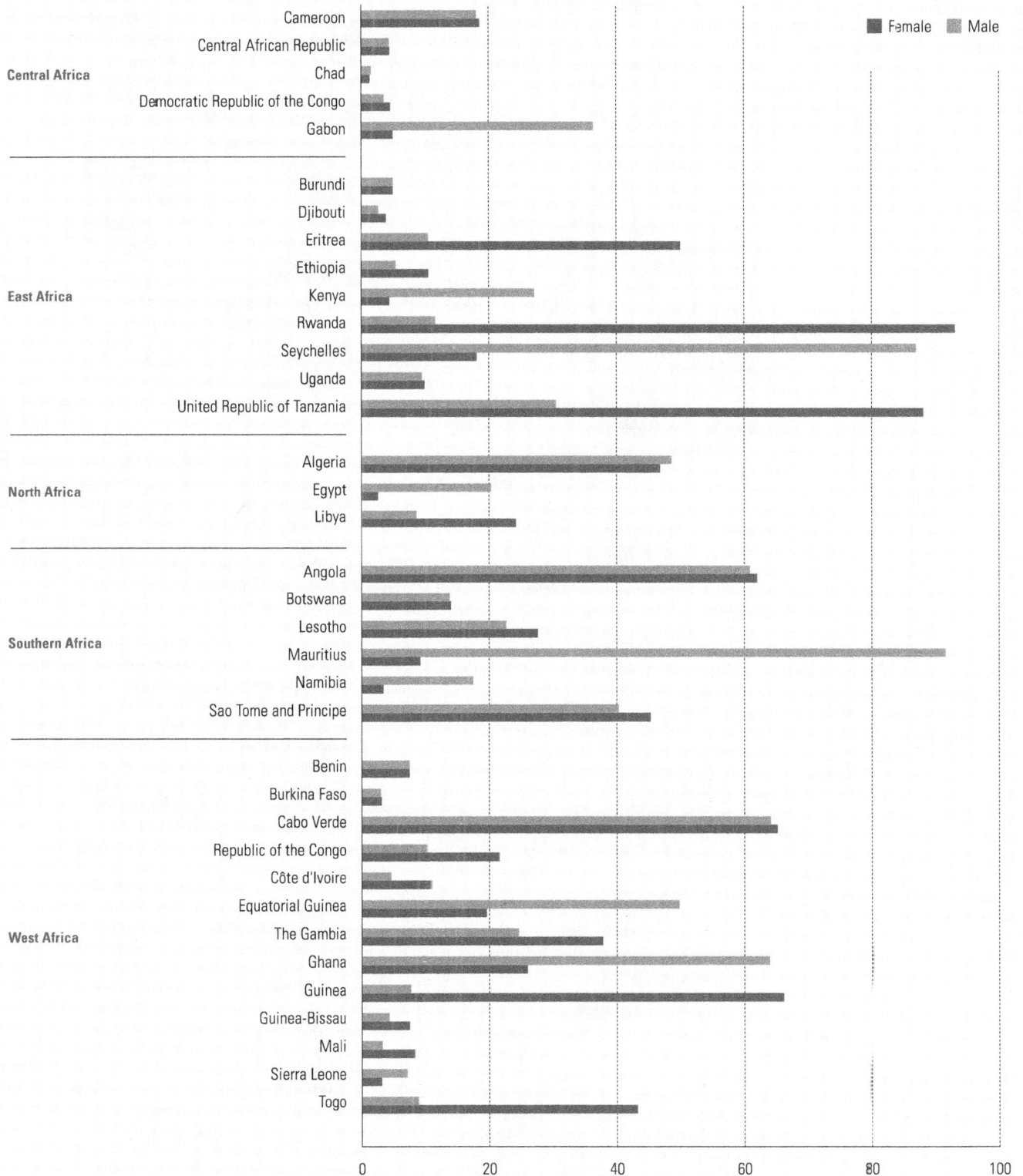

Source: Compiled by the AfHDR Team based on data from the UNESCO Institute for Statistics. 2015.

increase by 20 per cent in such countries if governments provide paid maternity leave.

In the public provision of childcare, the government funds childcare facilities and services, or subsidizes the use of private childcare facilities and services as well as the hiring of child-minders. Data on public provision of childcare for children below primary school age are available for only 35 countries; in just over half (18 countries), the families enjoy government-provided child services (World Bank Group, 2015).

In the absence of public facilities and workplace childcare programmes, women from poor households commonly opt out of the labour market, engage in the informal sector where they can combine work and childcare, or rely on informal networks for support. For example, when asked, "Who takes care of your child while you are working?", 51 per cent of women from the poorest wealth quintile households in sub-Saharan Africa (with DHS data) responded that they relied on their partners, other relatives, older children and neighbours, while 43 per cent combined working with childcare (ICF International, 2015). Women are also more likely than men to cite childcare responsibilities as the reason for not being in the labour force.

There is increasing recognition that the first few years of a child's life are a particularly sensitive period in the development process, laying a foundation in childhood and beyond for cognitive functioning; behavioural, social and self-regulatory capacities, and physical health. Gaps in skills between rich and poor children begin early in life, yet many children from poor families have little or no access to early childhood services. Where user fees are attached to early childhood development services and there are no child support credits for mothers with young children, poor women and their children are at risk of overlapping deprivations when they are unable to access critical early childhood development tools at home. For example, children from poor households are less likely to have children's books or toys at home (table 7.2). State provision of early childhood education programmes may be an equalizer between rich and poor children in cognitive functioning, allowing children from poor households to begin primary education on a more equal footing with those from rich homes. The right public investments at the right time could reduce disadvantages and vulnerabilities in adulthood, and break the vicious cycle of inter-generational poverty.

On average, only 16 per cent of girls and 15 per cent of boys below primary school age are enrolled in pre-primary education services, with a wide variation across countries. This situation must change if inequality in labour market outcomes between the rich and the poor, and women and men in future generations is to be reduced.

Regarding the costs of childcare services, experience from Kenya and South Africa shows that workplace provision of childcare services provides a triple win – for employers, employees and communities. To cite three examples, the BMW Automobile Company, First National Bank, Johannesburg, and Old Mutual, Cape Town are among the large companies in South Africa providing workplace childcare services for employees. The programmes have reduced family-related absenteeism and increased productivity, worker welfare and the ability to attract and retain workers. At the same time, workplace initiatives are most beneficial to children when they provide services beyond child minding. Such services need to fit within a broader public strategy for the provision of childcare and follow national standards related to the qualifications of the staff and the content of the programmes. (See box 4.3 for a Kenyan example of workplace childcare services.)

Legal and regulatory policy

Virtually all of the policies and programmes described in the previous section are based on some set of legal or regulatory norms, which form the legal foundation for their enactment.

The legal environment within which women and men engage in society underscores the fact that more effective non-discriminatory labour institutions, family-friendly policies and work environment standards could contribute greatly towards reducing women's economic and social disadvantages. As of 2014, for example, a significant number of African countries had passed laws prohibiting discrimination based on gender. Thirty-nine countries had laws providing for maternity leave, and 15 had legislation on equal remuneration for work of equal value. There was also legislation requiring equal inheritance between sons and daughters in 26 countries. While eight countries have specific tax credit deductions applicable to male employees, no such laws exist for women employees. Only two countries – Angola and Côte d'Ivoire – have passed laws allowing employees with young children to have flexible or part-time work hours (figure 7.3). With respect to the gender wage gaps, minimum wage legislation is another important avenue to bridge gender gaps in earnings. Minimum wages can play an important role in reducing inequality in wages and in supporting the wages of low-paid women and men. In a number of countries, minimum wage coverage has been extended to workers in both the formal and the informal sector.

Legal provision for gender equality, both in the social and economic arenas, is an important basis for demanding and achieving gender equality in labour market outcomes. In practice, however, women are still held back by societal perceptions of their roles, limiting them to low-paid jobs in the informal sector as well as informal work in the formal sector. In essence, there is an unwritten code among men regarding barriers to women's career advancement, which is

FIGURE 7.4

No. of African countries with non-discriminatory gender laws, 2014

a.   Laws mandating paid or unpaid maternity leave

b.   Laws penalizing or preventing the dismissal of pregnant women

c.   Married men and women have equal ownership rights to property

d.   Laws requiring employers to provide break time for nursing mothers

e.   Laws allowing married women to choose where to live in the same way as a man

f.   Sons and daughters have equal inheritance rights to property

g.   Legislation that specifically addresses sexual harassment

h.   Laws mandating equal remuneration for men and women for work of equal value

i.   Laws mandating paid or unpaid paternity leave

j.   Public provision of childcare for children under primary school age

k.   Laws requiring employers to give employees an equivalent position when they return from maternity leave

l.   Laws providing for valuation of non-monetary contributions during marriage

m.   Laws mandating non-discrimination based on gender in hiring

n.   Specific tax deductions or credits that are applicable only to men

o.   Laws allowing employees with minor children to have rights to a flexible/part-time schedule

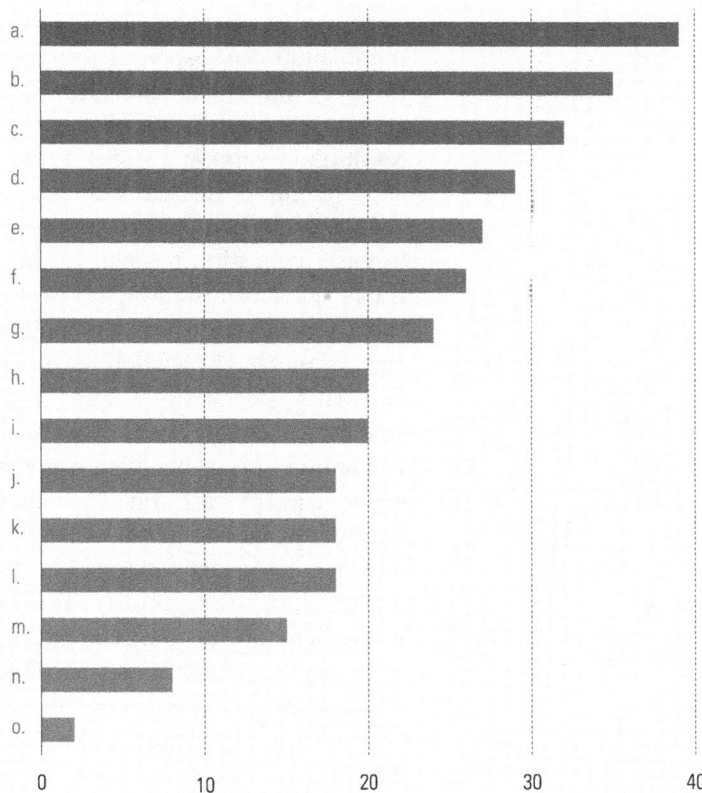

Source: Compiled by the AfHDR Team based on World Bank, 2015a.

also referred to as 'male-occupational reserve' a 'glass ceiling' and 'feminized jobs' or 'sticky floors'. Women's disproportionate responsibility for unpaid care and domestic work, discriminatory practices such as unequal access to education and training, productive resource constraints and lack of voice limit their options in the economic and social arenas. Just as quota systems have been a useful tool for improving gender gaps in parliamentary representation, it would take affirmative action including mentorship programmes and on-the-job training to bridge the gender gap in the upper echelons of the employment ladder.

The efficacy and reach of laws are closely related to the institutions that are expected to implement and enforce them. The previous chapter refers to the Maputo Protocol, which requires signatory states to draft a range of legislative measures aimed at supporting gender equality and women's empowerment. The Protocol constitutes a useful blueprint whose implementation success is still contingent on the enforcement of its standards. There are, however, no guidelines on developing institutional responses to implement the Protocol. Individual states have been left to choose the mechanisms that best suit them, resulting in varying degrees of effectiveness and strengths of institutional responses.

As a result, gaps still exist in states' efforts to pass legislation to achieve the women's rights set out in the Maputo Protocol. This should include not just new legislation, but also a thorough gender-sensitive review of existing legislations. For many African countries, there are four key areas of the law that require special attention when promoting gender equality and women's empowerment: family law, land tenure law, labour and employment laws, and customary laws.

The first area, **family law**, requires strengthening the legal recognition of non-monetary contributions to marriage and removing, in family codes and other statutes, head-of-household and related provisions that diminish women's legal capacity and economic autonomy. The second area is **land tenure law**, which has the potential to facilitate and encourage mandatory joint land titling and other means to allow women greater access to land. **Labour and employment laws** are key to addressing existing restrictions on women, including married or pregnant women, that limit the type of work that women may engage in or the hours they may work.

Finally, **customary law** deserves special attention at the national level in terms of enforcement. A recent survey conducted by the World Bank in 2014 indicates that, in more than a quarter of African countries surveyed, customary law is considered a valid source of law – even if it violates constitutional provisions on non-discrimination or equality (World Bank, 2015).

In general, it is necessary to strengthen the effective application of the non-discrimination principle, especially for marital property and land, while offsetting areas of gender bias in the application of customary law. Mechanisms are needed to reconcile any gaps between statutory, customary and religious law in the protection and realization of the rights of women and girls. Deconstruction of harmful social norms that sanction discrimination in customary law is critical in order to hasten gender equality.

In short, legal frameworks at the continental level are generally robust, but national laws generally need more specificity and better adaptation to local conditions and circumstances, as well as a stronger commitment to implementation and enforcement.

Policy and programme responses to harmful social norms

Clearly related to customary law is the issue of harmful social norms. As suggested in Chapter 6, African governments face policy and programme dilemmas in seeking to overcome harmful social norms. The power of social norms cannot be overestimated; they represent ethical and moral basis of a society. Social norms are reflected in African laws, institutions and policies. At the same time, they are the root of some of Africa's biggest achievements and greatest challenges.

In more than a quarter of African countries, customary law is considered a valid source of law – even if it violates constitutional provisions on non-discrimination or equality.

BOX 7.4

Reconciling customary and statutory law in Zambia

Like most African countries, the Government of Zambia has committed itself to the goal of gender equality and women's empowerment. Yet, reconciling existing national policies, strategies and institutional frameworks with customary laws and traditions represents an ongoing problem. Low women's participation in decision-making positions and the political arena (only 13 per cent of parliament are women), lack of affirmative action frameworks, and inherent contradictions between customary and statutory laws work to the disadvantage of women and girls. While the Constitution of Zambia forbids discrimination on the basis of sex, it has allowed for the application of customary law in matters of marriage, divorce and disposal of property. It permits discrimination in customary laws related to early marriage, dowry payment and inheritance, resulting in high levels of violence against women and the unacceptably high incidence of early marriage, at a national average of 45 per cent.

Efforts to support the realization of the Government's commitment towards gender equality and women's empowerment have prioritized legal and policy frameworks, the improvement of institutions and the engagement of communities and local leaders to counter negative social and cultural norms that inhibit women's rights. Early results from UNDP-supported interventions for resolving conflicts between statutory and customary laws include a strengthened legal and policy environment for gender equality and women's empowerment.

In addition, the initiative has tackled customary laws and negative cultural practices related to gender-based violence and child brides in partnership with chiefs, religious and traditional leaders, and has included the establishment of one-stop shops on gender-based violence in seven villages in Eastern, Western and Central Provinces. Community forums to end violence against women engage both women and men in discussing issues that contribute to violence against women, such as alcoholism, gambling, domestic violence and polygamy, and help men in the community work towards non-violent and more equal relationships with women and girls. These men act as 'community police' by engaging, in collaboration with the local authorities, in discussions with known perpetrators on the negative effects of gender-based violence. As a result, local leaders are paying more attention to ending child marriage, and there is a gradual change of men's behaviour toward their wives. Men who have participated in these discussions are demonstrating a better understanding of the costs of violence against women and are making positive changes.

Source: Case study prepared by UNDP Zambia Country Office, 2015.

As a starting point, universally agreed human rights represent a useful framework for deconstructing harmful social norms. Universal human rights symbolize the first-ever global consensus on what is right and wrong for humankind. Such rights have become a solid benchmark against which to compare and judge particular social norms of given communities. The moral authority of universal human rights comes from the unanimity of acceptance by almost all nations around the globe, who have legally ratified them. The ratifying nations represent all of the world's major religions and traditions in the North and Global South.

The exercise of deconstructing beliefs needs to be paired with the simultaneous construction of new (i.e. replacement) social norms able to mitigate potential tension. These reconstructed social norms that can mitigate the national legal framework, gender-sensitive policies and institutions, and the demands of society – as is the case in Zambia (box 7.4).

Another basic departure point is the realization that societal resistance to gender equality impedes progress. This resistance not only negatively affects women, but also men as they adapt to the new norms and the new institutions that were created to pursue gender equality. In countries with entrenched views about women's roles, institutions for gender equality and women's empowerment can be confronted with unsupportive public attitudes. To avoid conflict they may tend towards less controversial needs-focused work rather than tackle power inequalities between genders. Societal resistance to institutions extends as far as deliberate attempts to establish laws, policies and programmes that directly counter gender equality and women's empowerment.

The last 70 years, nonetheless, show a positive track record in the creation of positive social norms that replace older social norms that were once unthinkable for women. Voting, holding high political office and having separate financial dealings are all commonly accepted realities for women in most African countries. In Africa, opposition to the concept of gender equality that today is felt by a quarter of Africans already represents an improvement from 2002, when over a third of the population opposed gender equality.

As suggested by previous chapters, policies and programmes that increase assets and improve women's capabilities are necessary but not sufficient. On their own, they may fall short in advancing gender equality unless ways are found to deconstruct harmful social norms in the debate and action plans aimed at increasing equality. Unless and until harmful social norms are changed, they will continue to drive inequality in areas as fundamental as labour markets, political participation and leadership. They will continue to fuel gender-based violence in all its forms. Although Africans have changed their beliefs regarding the inferiority of women, a serious challenge remains. It is therefore important to deconstruct social norms, pointing out which ones are discriminatory, and discuss how to make conditions better for women. Recent evidence brings to light promising directions for reshaping social norms that undermine gender equality and inhibit human development.

Overall Policy and Implementation Issues:
Implications of Policy and Institutional Responses in Promoting Gender Equality

African countries have used a range of policy and institutional means to promote gender equality and women's empowerment. But the record of success is mixed, and there is ample room to expand such efforts both in scale and intensity.

- Fiscal policy and public expenditures are possibly the first and most important litmus test of a government's commitment to gender equality. Gender equality may be mainstreamed in laws, policies, programmes and institutions, but the test of commitment is ultimately a function of resources made available.

- African governments have begun using various kinds of cash transfer programmes and subsidies to promote gender equality and poverty reduction. Still, there is considerable room for expanding a number of cash transfer and social service programmes that would have a direct impact on improving women's economic and social well-being. These include paid maternal leave, provision of childcare services, and some form of income support or cash transfers for women's unpaid work, which is usually carried out in the home or in the family field.

- In order to better apply international and regional legal norms for gender equality, many African countries may be at a crossroads in fully articulating, implementing and enforcing their laws, statutes and regulations that could have a profound impact on improving women's access to equal rights and entitlements.

- Gender-sensitive reviews of existing legislation in the areas of family law, land law, labour and employment law, and customary law are necessary to identify and remove ongoing gender discrimination.

- Reconciling national laws and regulation with customary laws and traditions remains a monumental challenge.

Agenda for **action**

Use gender equality as the organizing policy lens for all development planning and implementation.

Deploy strong leadership and accountability to directly tackle destructive norms.

Make critical choices and investments to give priority to gender equality.

Create adaptive national institutional capacities and representative institutions.

Use gender disaggregated data and gender responsive analysis for improved decision-making.

Promote alliances including regional and South-South cooperation in designing and implementing gender-focused policies and initiatives.

Chapter 8

An Agenda for Action to Accelerate Gender Equality

Chapter 8
An Agenda for Action to Accelerate Gender Equality

This chapter suggests four pathways and six accelerators that could speed up gender equality and women's empowerment in Africa. It also proposes some concrete actions such as the establishment of an African Women Investment Bank and the implementation of Gender Equality Seal certification standards in Africa.

Achieving gender equality and empowering women are still very much an unfinished agenda.

This report has sought to explore the challenges and options facing Africa in forcefully addressing the need for greater gender equality across the continent. The previous chapters examined the kinds of social and economic advances and disadvantages that women face, their political voice and role in decision-making, as well as the interaction of legal and social norms in both expanding and impeding women's rights and opportunities. Chapter 7 reviewed some of the policy and institutional responses that governments have used to address gender inequality. The basic conclusion from this review is that progress has been made in all African countries, but more concerted efforts are needed, both across the African region and within countries. Achieving gender equality and empowering women are still very much an unfinished agenda.

This chapter proposes some elements for developing an agenda for action to accelerate gender equality and women's empowerment. The first section below outlines four broad pathways that offer a policy and programme construct to accelerate gender equality and fully integrate gender into the broader development agenda. The second section then offers six operating guidelines or benchmarks for developing an agenda for action at the individual country level and for measuring the pace of change and eventual success.

Policy and strategic pathways

In the previous chapters, several policy and programme areas were discussed including examples for other regions such as LAC and Asia. Four broad strategic pathways are highlighted in figure 8.1 and briefly summarized below.

Pathway 1: Supporting the adoption of legal reforms, policies and regulations to advance women's empowerment. Women's and girls' lives are improved when countries formulate and then fully implement a combination of laws and regulations, policies and programmes that provide equal opportunities for all, regardless of sex, and promote gender – going beyond legal equality to substantive gender equality. There is a clear need for African governments to move beyond small-scale initiatives and silo approaches to gender equality, and invest considerably in building national and local capacities to ensure that women's empowerment is addressed in a much more systematic manner.

Pathway 2: Supporting national institutions to promote and increase women's voice, participation and leadership in decision-making in the home, the economy and in society. Evidence demonstrates that when a critical mass of women participates in decision-making, their contributions and needs are more likely to be recognized and addressed. Even though attention has largely focused on women's leadership and participation in national parliaments, there is a pressing need to realize women's leadership throughout the daily lives of all Africans – in the home, in the economy and markets, and in society as broadly defined. To this end, this report calls on both public and private institutions, and CSOs to commit to implementing UNDP's Gender Equality Seal (GES) in Africa. GES helps to promote standards that foster equality among employees and empower women.

Pathway 3: Supporting capacity to implement multi-sectoral approaches to mitigate the impacts of discriminatory health and education practice. Reducing inequalities in access to health and education, in addition to giving women greater choice in family decision-making, can have significant benefits for women and important inter-generational benefits. In this regard, eliminating sexual and gender-based violence is a critical component to enable women to live healthy and more productive lives. Undertaking health and education improvements is not limited to merely re-designing services available through the health and education ministries, but also involves collaboration across ministries and with the private sector and civil society, based on their comparative advantages.

Pathway 4: Supporting women to gain ownership and management of economic and environmental assets. The combination of the socio-cultural barriers faced by women, their lack of access to resources and decision-making power, and their heavy reliance on natural resources puts women on the front line of social-economic, environmental and climate risks. However, women are also on the front line to defend against the effects of climate change. Consequently, African governments need to ensure that women have access to and ownership of the economic and environmental assets upon which their lives depend. To this end, governments will need to work in close collaboration with NGOs, the private sector and their international development partners in order to ensure the kind of collaboration and consistency of purpose that will allow women to gain control over economic and environmental assets that can profoundly improve their lives. This report calls for an urgent need to make critical choices and investments that give priority to gender equality including the establishment of an African Women Investment Bank and opening women's investment windows in development banks.

FIGURE 8.1

Strategic pathways for addressing gender inequality

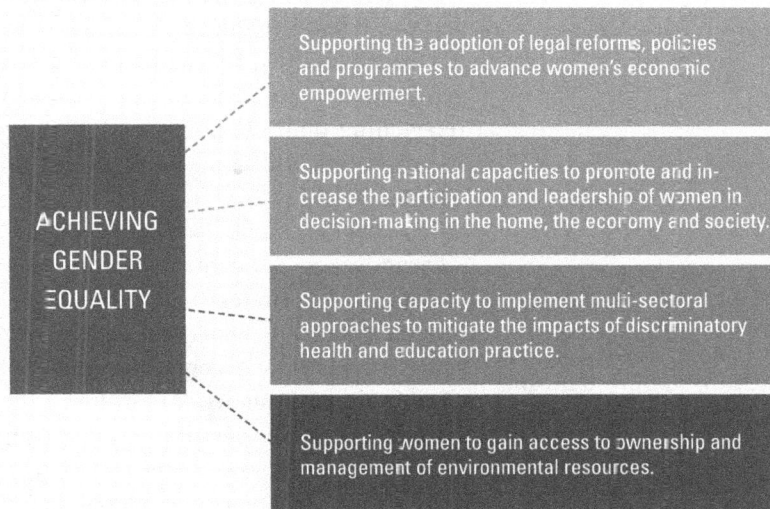

Source: Adapted from UNDP, 2013b.

A gender-focused agenda for action

With these four pathways in mind, an overriding strategic question faces African governments wishing to accelerate women's rights and entitlements.

Assuming political commitment exists, how can African leaders and policymakers more forcefully address gender inequalities in the face of competing national priorities?

Given the pressures on leaders and policymakers to maintain the pace of economic growth, diversify the economy for integration into global markets, meet the rising demands of a growing middle class and address national security concerns, tough decisions must often be made in competing for the use of scarce resources. At the same time, African governments need to consider and weigh a wide range of policy recommendations and priorities that come from multiple sources – the governments themselves, the international community and African regional organizations. Similarly, African governments are also

This report calls for the establishment of an African Women Investment Bank and opening of women's investment windows in national and regional development banks.

party to global commitments, such as those most recently articulated in the Sendai Framework for Disaster Risk Reduction (March 2015), the Addis Ababa Action Agenda (July 2015), the SDGs agreed to in September 2015 and the Paris Agreement on climate change in December 2015. Taken as a whole, African governments must address the challenge of reconciling multiple policy and programme prescriptions and courses of action at the national level.

To provide some policy guidance for African leaders concerned with this ongoing dilemma, six strategic considerations are offered as an organizational framework for action in addressing gender inequality. This organizational framework is in line with the argument that accelerating gender equality and women's empowerment simultaneously represents a practical operational approach for African governments to tackle the challenge of achieving the SDGs as well as move forward on the AU's Agenda 2063. To the extent that gender inequalities are being addressed, then, in effect, progress is being made across the wide spectrum of development goals found in the SDGs. Addressing gender equality is not separate from addressing the SDGs.

From this perspective, the six strategic considerations are outlined below.

Gender equality as an organizing policy lens for the formulation, planning and implementation of development agenda.

It is a false assumption to assume that giving higher priority to gender equality means giving lower priority to other development priorities. Focusing on gender issues is not a zero-sum choice where choosing one priority comes at the expense of another. Irrespective of the policy objective (e.g. inclusive growth and economic diversification, eradicating extreme poverty, revitalizing the agricultural sector, improving national health services, tackling climate change), if half the population (i.e. women and girls) is not benefitting equally from the policies and initiatives, then they cannot be considered a success, regardless of the aggregated data that mask different gender outcomes. Development, if not engendered, is endangered.

The previous chapters highlighted a number of examples where programmes and policies that benefitted women and girls had the result of benefitting all of society, not simply females. The reverse is not necessarily true: programmes that do not account for existing gender discrimination will continue to perpetuate it.

Discarding this false assumption and using gender equality as the policy lens for planning and implementation changes the debate on national priorities. The debate is no longer about adding in special policies and programmes for women or having separate women's ministries or agencies, but rather, ensuring that all policies and programmes are aimed at achieving equal outcomes for men and women. Realizing gender equality and women's empowerment is not an inadvertent outcome, but a key design feature. African governments must still make difficult choices in agreeing on national spending priorities, but gender equality is not a separate category or sector to choose from; rather, it is an integral component of any agreed priority, whether related to the economy, the provision of social services, environment and natural resource management, or legal safeguards and protections.

In this regard, a gender lens also represents an organizing approach for addressing many, if not all, of the Sustainable Development Goals (SDGs) that transcend the one Goal that specifically mentions gender equality (SDG 5). This report proposes that gender equality should be the lens for operationalizing a "leave no one behind" agenda. Addressing poverty and inequality by 2030 without engendering development plans, strategies, policies, programmes and budgets remains a grossly inadequate approach.

All government policies, programmes and expenditures are ultimately aimed at increasing human capacity and promoting inclusive human development. From a purely cost-benefit perspective, government initiatives should be measured in terms of cost-effectiveness in reaching the highest number of people as possible, or targeting

All policies and programmes must aim at achieving equal outcomes for men and women.

those segments of the population who are left behind – the poor, the marginalized, and above all, women who can leverage any received benefits to other family members and across generations. While the economic costs of any particular policy or programme are important, they are not the only consideration. Addressing women's equality is first and foremost a human rights issue that is not bounded by a price tag, but rather, driven by gender equity concerns.

Tackling harmful social norms directly

Reversing the social norms that impede women's and girls' equal opportunities will be a long-term and difficult process. As noted in Chapter 6, social norms are the cornerstone of a person's and a society's identity. They define what is normal and what is not, what is right and wrong, and what is appropriate or unacceptable in most aspects of life. Consciously or unconsciously, social norms are the under- lying factor affecting how individuals process information, make decisions and take actions. Therefore, pushing to deconstruct harmful social norms and cultural barriers is no doubt a morally demanding, socially difficult and politically risky course of action, or more precisely, multiple and overlapping courses of actions.

Chapter 6 further noted that the existence of social norms does not make them fair or non-discriminatory. Over the last 70 years, a whole body of human rights and entitlements, which have been defined and accepted by the international community and the African region, transcend political, economic, social and cultural differences among countries. These international and regional legal standards set the bar for gender equality and women's empowerment.

Many African governments have made progress in codifying these standards at the national level, but implementation and enforcement are often lacking. Leaders and policymakers therefore need to understand the long-term nature of deconstructing harmful social norms and replacing them with positive social norms. In many instances, the approach will entail reconciling legal and social norms. And it will most likely entail a series of deliberate and explicit steps incrementally induced over time. Diluting harmful social norms may require – to borrow from an old Persian saying – 'death by a thousand cuts'; i.e. small or incremental changes being made across multiple fronts, none of which is seen as socially damaging by itself, but which over time leads to the demise of the harmful social norm and its replacement with social norms that enhance women's and girls' opportunities, not distract from them.

From a practical standpoint, African governments must seek the best combination of laws and regulations, policies and programmes that create both incentives and disincentives to accelerate the reduction of harmful norms that limit women's economic and social potential. These actions, illustrated in Chapter 6, will need to be carried out across a broad range of social, economic and political arenas where women's rights are being limited. African governments can no longer abdicate their responsibilities to address harmful social norms in a straightforward and unambiguous manner.

Prioritization of plans and budgets for gender equality

There is no shortage of policy advice and reports written by governments, donor agencies, NGOs, think tanks, and advocacy groups that lay out a whole range of options for encouraging and promoting gender equality. These different policy and programme prescriptions certainly warrant careful consideration; yet, ultimately, African governments will invariably need to identify and then implement a strategic set of policy and programme choices that are deemed priorities in the national context, that have the highest likelihood of making important changes, that can work synergistically, and that have the best chance of being successfully implemented. It is not the objective of this report to state that the policy and programme priorities in the previous chapters are the only ones that should be considered; different governments can arrive at a different set of priorities. The objective, then, is

Addressing women's equality is first and foremost a human rights issue

African governments must seek the best combination of laws and regulations, policies and programmes that create both incentives and disincentives to accelerate the reduction of harmful norms that limit women's economic and social potential.

> A robust data collection and analysis is needed to monitor implementation and assess gender-related outcomes effectively.

> Accelerating gender equality and women's empowerment simultaneously represents a practical operational approach for African governments to tackle the challenge of achieving the SDGs.

to suggest that African governments must develop a process that gives priority to achieving gender equality, given the tremendous needs and resource constraints facing each country. To be successful, the prioritization process must have the full backing of society, based on consultation and consensus. Whatever the policies chosen, there will be a need for more robust data collection and analysis in order to monitor implementation and assess gender-related outcomes, as discussed below.

In short, the task does not necessarily entail selecting and implementing a wide range of policy options, but rather, following an orderly and transparent process of prioritizing among multiple (and often contending) policy options – all of which place competing demands on scarce public resources.

To achieve the kind of transformation needed to address gender inequalities, African governments will need to practise the discipline of linking short-term priorities to the long-term view of their respective countries. This translates into the ability to visualize different kinds of futures than the current trajectories that continue to impede women's progress, while still addressing challenges and issues in the medium term. Linking the short to the long term consists of engaging in the tough political economy choices on an almost daily basis that are involved in seeking long-term benefits by foregoing short-term politically and economically expedient decision-making. Closely related to the notion of linking the short- to the long-term view is the understanding that 'business as usual' cannot be sustained as an implicit governing construct. If this construct is maintained, then all social and economic classes would continue to be negatively affected, not just the poor in general and poor women in particular.

The importance of linking short- and long-term prioritization cannot be overstated. Yet how is the process of prioritization among multiple demands manifested in government decision-making? While the priorities selected are ultimately decisions taken by individual governments, some analytical guidelines are offered to inform the policy and

implementation debate that is required. Three guidelines are suggested, as follows:

- Which policies and programmes are most likely to improve the lives of women and bring them into the economic mainstream through productive employment opportunities and improved social welfare? Are there opportunities to exploit multiplier effects where one intervention can lead to multiple objectives for gender equality?

- In what ways are the views and concerns of stakeholders, particularly women and other beneficiaries, being factored into the decision-making process?

- In situations where resources are shifted from one programme or initiative to another, can the shift be justified in terms of improved economic and social outcomes for women?

Strengthening adaptive policies and institutional capacities

Achieving gender equality and accelerating the pace of human development will require African governments to incorporate a commitment to strong, proactive and responsible governance frameworks that develop policies for both the public and private sectors — based on a long-term vision and leadership, shared norms and values, and rules and institutions that build trust and cohesion. At the same time, governments will need to have the capacity for flexibility and adaptation. In complex societies such as those in Africa, the outcome of any particular policy is inevitably uncertain. African governments will need to follow a governance framework that is pragmatic and able to problem-solve and adapt collectively and rapidly.

Examples abound in Africa, Asia and LAC, and throughout the Global South of countries that have begun to transform the way their governments identify challenges, develop appropriate policy responses, and follow through with focused implementation strategies and articulated fiscal commitments. Similarly, it is a characteristic of these countries that they are adept at modifying and shifting their policies and budget priorities as circumstances change. In most instances, such modifications are undertaken with full support of the country's development partners.

What are some of the characteristics of highly flexible and adaptive governments that are relevant to making a systemic push for gender equality and other human development goals? A few suggestions based on international experience are as follows:

- An adaptive government is consistent in its pursuit of developmental objectives, including gender equality, and is committed to them. Failing to achieve certain developmental objectives may be an opportunity to learn, adapt and re-engage.

- An adaptive government is proactive. The state is not relegated to the role of overseer, but rather, it actively participates in the development process, often serving as an entrepreneur of last resort.

- The adaptive state evolves as the needs of the society in which it is embedded change. Change is welcomed provided that it does not detract from the overall development objectives that the nation as a whole has set for itself.

- An adaptive government is well-staffed, risk-taking and socially legitimate. It includes a competent and neutral bureaucracy that is performance- and outcome-oriented to ensure implementation and that actively engages with other stakeholders.

- An adaptive government values the presence and contribution of viable and vocal stakeholders including the private sector, NGOs, civil society organizations and communities.

- An adaptive government is committed to reducing corruption and rent-seeking because of their detrimental effects on inclusive growth and human development.

Adding value to data for improved decision-making

In order for African governments to fully address gender inequalities and understand the outcomes of chosen policies and programmes, more robust data collection, monitoring, analysis and dissemination systems will be required. Having effective capacity in statistics and monitoring and evaluation is the 'lubricant' by which governments are able to perform as an adaptive state and undertake necessary policy changes and make mid-course corrections. Data collection and analysis should not be considered an after-thought, but rather, a core function of governmental services.

In several of the previous chapters, examples were cited where insufficient data collection, analysis and dissemination limited governments and their partners from knowing precisely how women and girls were being affected by current realities and why existing services were not being used effectively. The data gaps were found in both the formal and informal sectors. Problems of limited data are not unique to gender issues, but represent a pervasive problem affecting all kinds of economic and social statistics. Many governments are now assessing their capabilities for monitoring the new Sustainable Development Goals, together with traditional economic and social statistics.

This assessment and stock-taking exercise represents a window of opportunity for African governments to evaluate how their statistical agencies and line ministries (including finance ministries) can improve their data gathering and analysis functions to fully capture the gender implications of current policies and initiatives, and how, over time, they can be modified and enhanced. The assessment process can reveal whether or not current data gathering processes are sufficient, and if so, whether the data need to be analysed differently. It can also reveal if entirely new survey and monitoring tools are required to capture underlying trends and outcomes that were previously missed or under-reported. Similarly, more attention will be needed for data disaggregation in order to delineate

African governments should be adept at modifying and shifting their policy and budget priorities as circumstances change.

Data collection and analysis should not be considered an after-thought, but rather, a core function of governmental services.

the district and local impacts of policies and programmes within countries, not just national-level analysis.

In any case, an examination is required of the kinds of 'common data platforms' on which robust statistical systems can be built. Understandably, resource constraints and lack of institutional capacity have been, and potentially will remain, a major challenge for the statistical services of African governments. However, the process of assessing the overall data requirements presents an opportunity to dovetail data requirements with available resources and plan accordingly. Here, too, the donor community will need to ensure that the statistical support it requires as part of their assistance programmes is congruent with the national statistical system.

Prioritizing regional and South-South cooperation

It is important to underline the importance of regional and South-South cooperation in designing and implementing gender-focused policies and initiatives. African countries have much to learn from each other – about both what has worked and what has not. The previous chapters offered many successful and innovative examples of initiatives from other regions and from across the African continent. The focus of such cooperation should be on sharing tools, strategies and experiences across sectors – from large infrastructure projects to community-based interventions – all of which need to drive innovation, learning and upscaling.

It is also important to understand that African governments and the donor community have undertaken countless conferences and workshops aimed at sharing experience and lessons learned. The task ahead does not entail holding more conferences and workshops, but rather expanding the audience and participation of these kinds of meetings in addition to the kinds of South-South and regional exchanges. The audience needs to include not just gender specialists and managers in dialogue (often women dialoguing with women), but also senior managers and policymakers (usually men) from key ministries

including finance and planning, as well as the president or prime minister's office and parliamentary leaders who together, have the means for shifting the policy debate. These senior officials have historically been outside discussions or only occasionally involved, or have not thought the discussion important enough to attend. An example of this need to broaden discussion was noted in a speech, entitled 'Why Should Finance Ministers Care about Gender Equality?', given to an international meeting of finance ministers by Ms. Ngozi Okonjo-Iweala, a former Managing Director of the World Bank, who served twice as Nigeria's Finance Minister (World Bank, 2016). If gender issues are to become the policy lens by which development plans are designed and implemented, as proposed above, then having a larger audience for sharing experience is crucial.

With regard to the kinds of South-South and regional exchanges, there is considerable scope for expanding intra-African and inter-regional training and study tours, secondment of staff and other types of experiential learning opportunities that place managers and policymakers more directly in the fulcrum of on-the-ground change.

Some concluding observations

This report has focused on the continuing problem of gender equality facing the women and girls of Africa. Despite the growing recognition that improvements in women's and girls' education, health and workplace opportunities result in economic and social progress for an entire country and for the African region as a whole, removing inequalities for women has not kept pace. Significant gaps between men's and women's opportunities remain a major challenge and a severe impediment to the kinds of structural economic and social transformation that is still the goal of all African countries.

The report noted that there is widespread recognition of the importance of gender equality in promoting African human development, which dates back many decades. Yet, international and regional statements of solidarity for women's empowerment have

African countries have much to learn from each other – about both what has worked and what has not.

not been translated into concrete actions on the ground on a broad scale. While progress has been made in certain areas and within many countries, change has not kept pace with regional and national requirements or expectations.

A key conclusion of this report is that gender equality is not achieved by having gender-specific ministries or women-only projects and programmes (although they can be important), but rather, by tackling gender equality as a wide-ranging effort across multiple sectors that engages all segments of society. The report has further emphasized the inter-linkages between the social well-being of women and their economic opportunities for more productive lives. Underpinning all these efforts will be the necessary but understandably difficult task of breaking down harmful social norms and cultural barriers that have a particularly serious impact on poor women and their families.

Another conclusion is that accelerating gender equality will entail highly collaborative efforts involving not only national and local governments, but also NGOs, the private sector, advocacy groups, and effective community-based organizations. The obstacles to achieving gender equality are too immense to be tackled unless the entire range of national and local stakeholders is fully committed during all phases – from design and formulation of action to be taken to how implementation and follow-through are assured.

Finally, it will be important for African governments to articulate time-bound benchmarks to measure progress, make adjustments as needed, and maintain a common vision of why achieving gender equality has such important ramifications for all of society. In this regard, the implementation of Gender Equality Seal standards in public and private organizations that promotes equality among employees and empower women is vital.

The peoples of Africa must hold themselves and their governments accountable for making progress on improvements within a sufficient timeframe in order not to dilute the urgency for action. The 15-year timeframe of the Sustainable Development Goals and the ten-year plan of Agenda 2063 represent two viable targets to which African governments have already committed themselves.

The implementation of Gender Equality Seal certification standards in public and private organizations is vital to accelerating gender equality.

Annexes

BACKGROUND PAPERS	AUTHOR(S)	TITLE
	Yvette Abrahams	Socio-cultural gaps: mapping gaps and country benchmarking
	Sajjad Akhtar	Analyzing the multiplier effect of gender equality on the achievement of MDGs and the post-2015 Development Agenda in Africa
	Gisela Carrasco	Political gaps: mapping gaps and country benchmarking, including women's empowerment for building peace, security and resilience
	Amie Gaye	Economic gender gaps: mapping gaps and country benchmarking
	Paige Jennings	A rights-based approach to gender equality and women empowerment in the African context
	Angela Lusigi Ahmadou Mboup Yumna Omar	The political economy of gender equality in labour force participation and leadership in public and private institutions
	Arsene Nkama	Estimating the cost of gender gaps in sustainable growth and structural transformation in Africa
	Alejandro Rausch	The role of politics, partnerships, resources, technology and innovation in women's empowerment: lessons from Asia and Latin America
	Eleni Yitbarek Theophile Azoumahou	Advancing women's empowerment, gender equality and sustainable human development: linkages between empowerment, gender equality and sustainable development

ADVISORY GROUP	NAME	TITLE, INSTITUTION
High Level Advisory Group	Abdoulaye Mar Dieye	Co-Chair, Regional Director, UNDP Africa
	H. E. Fatima H. Acyl	Co-Chair, Commissioner, Trade and Industry, African Union Commission
	Ayo Ajayi	Director, Africa Programme, Bill & Melinda Gates Foundation
	Aminata Dibba	Economic Community of West African States (ECOWAS) Gender Development Centre, Dakar, Senegal
	Leymah Gbowee	Nobel Peace Prize Winner, Gbowee Peace Foundation USA
	Geraldine Fraser-Moleketi	African Development Bank (AfDB) Special Envoy on Gender
	Beatrice Hamusonde	Gender and Social Affairs Division, Common Market for East and Southern Africa (COMESA)
	Amy Jadesimi	Managing Director, Lagos Deep Offshore Logistics Base (LADOL)
	Jeni Klugman	Lecturer, Harvard Kennedy School of Government
	Ndioro Ndiaye	Coordinator, Réseau Femmes Africaines Leaders pour la Paix et le Développement (RFALPD)
	Justine Diffo Tchunkam	Coordinator, Network for More Women in Politics (Cameroon)
UNDP Internal Oversight Group	Selim Jahan	Co-Chair, Human Development Report Office
	Ayodele Odusola	Regional Bureau for Africa
	Pedro Conceição	Bureau for Policy and Programme Support
	Randi Davies	Bureau for Policy and Programme Support
	Odette Kabaya	Regional Service Centre Africa
	Thangavel Palanivel	Regional Bureau for Asia and Pacific

Continued

ADVISORY GROUP	NAME	TITLE, INSTITUTION
UN Readers' Group	Anthony Ngororano	UN Women
	Thokozile Ruzvidzo	United Nations Economic Commission for Africa (UNECA)
	Moa Westman	United Nations Environment Programme (UNEP)
	Simonetta Zarrilli	United Nations Conference on Trade and Development (UNCTAD)
UNDP Field Sounding Board	Lamin Maneh	UNDP Rwanda
	Eugene Owusu	UNDP South Sudan
	Amarakoon Bandara	UNDP Zimbabwe
	Ginette Camara	UNDP Republic of Congo / Brazzaville
	Amata Diabate	UNDP Burcna Faso

REGIONAL CONSULTATIONS	
Addis Ababa Regional Consultation	
NAME	**TITLE, INSTITUTION**
Mahawa Wheeler	Co-Chair, Director, Women, Gender and Development, African Union Commission
Lebogang Motlana	Co-Chair, Director, UNDP Regional Service Centre Africa
Noubatour Adoumtar	African Union Commission
Floride Ahitungye	Search for Common Ground (Burundi)
Helen M. Apila	Africa Women's Development and Communication Network (FEMNET) (Regional)
Regina Bafaki	Action for Development (ACFODE) (Regional)
Pauline Bullen	Women's University (South Africa)
Samuel Bwalya	UNDP Ethiopia
Beatrice Hamusonde	Common Market for Eastern and Southern Africa
Botswelelo John	Young Women's Christian Association (YWCA) (Botswana)
Gamer Khalifa Habbani	Sudanese Women's General Union (SWGU) (Sudan)
Mzati Kidney-Mbeko	Women & Law in Southern Africa (Malawi)
Rafava Machava	Women, Law and Development Association (Mozambique)
Patricia McFadden	Southern Africa Political and Economic Series (SAPES) TRUST (Regional)

REGIONAL CONSULTATIONS	
Dakar Regional Consultation	
NAME	**TITLE, INSTITUTION**
Bintou Djibo	Co-Chair, UN Resident Coordinator and UNDP Resident Representative Senegal
Ibrahima Aidara	Co-Chair, Head Economic Governance, Open Society Initiative in West Africa
Jacqueline Bisimwa Murangaza	Association des Femmes Entrepreneurs Chefs d'Entreprises (ASSOFE) (Democratic Republic of the Congo)
Souleman Boukar	UNDP Senegal
Amadou Diallo	New Partnership for Africa's Development (NEPAD) Agency, West Africa
Yacine Diagne	Enda Tiers Monde
Anne Marie Engouma	ONG Malachie (Gabon)
Sesneica Fernandes	Associação Sao-tomeses das Mulheres Juristas (Cabo Verde)
Rebecca Nodjiti Ganbe	Union des Femmes pour la Paix (UFEP, Women's Union for Peace) (Chad)
Rebecca Wright Gaye	African Women's Entrepreneurship Program (AWEP) (Liberia)
Rachel Gogoua	Chair, Groupement des Organisations Féminines pour l'Egalité Homme-Femme (GOFEHF) (Côte d'Ivoire)
Djehounke Hermann	Chair, Association de jeunes pour le développement des initiatives de base (AJDIB) (Benin)

Continued

REGIONAL CONSULTATIONS

Addis Ababa Regional Consultation

NAME	TITLE, INSTITUTION
Clotilde Noa	Women, Law and Development (MULEIDE) (Mozambique)
Fikile Nkosi	Federation of Swaziland Employers and Chamber of Commerce (FSE&CC) (Swaziland)
Mamakhete Phomane	She-Hive (Lesotho)
Thokozile Ruzvidzo	United Nations Economic Commission for Africa (UNECA)
Naemy Sillayo	Legal and Human Rights Centre (LHRC) (United Republic of Tanzania)
James Wakiaga	UNDP Ethiopia
Ambassa Yodi	Rwanda Women Network (Rwanda)

Continued

REGIONAL CONSULTATIONS

Dakar Regional Consultation

NAME	TITLE, INSTITUTION
Meteteiton Houmey	Groupe de réflexion et d'action, Femme, Démocratie et Développement (GF2D, Action and Reflection Group for Women, Democracy and Development)
Oumoulkhairy Kane	Chair, Association for Women's Rights Defense in Mauritania (ADDFM)
Nantènin Koné	Réseau des Femmes du Fleuve Mano pour la Paix (REFMAP, Mano River Women's Peace Network) (Guinea)
Euphrasie Kouame	United Nations Capital Development Fund (UNCDF)
Aisha Fofana Ibrahim	President, The 50/50 Group of Sierra Leone
Odette Kabaya	UNDP Regional Service Centre Africa
Monica Maduekwe	Economic Community of West African States (ECOWAS) Regional Centre for Renewable Energy and Energy Efficiency
Fatime Christiane N'Diaye	International Labour Organization (ILO)
Safiatou Alzouma Nouhou	International Renewable Energy Agency (IRENA)
Ndioro Ndiaye	Réseau Femmes Africaines Leaders pour la Paix et le Développement (RFALPD)
Fatou Sow Sarr	University of Cheikh Anta Diop de Dakar (UCAD)
Rufina Dabo Sarr	Réseau International des Femmes Scientifiques et Ingénieures (INWES) – Direction Afrique Francophone
Louis Seck	Global Village Energy Partnership (GVEP) International
Mary Small	The Gambia Committee on Traditional Practices Affecting the Health of Women & Children (GAMCOTRAP) (The Islamic Republic of The Gambia)
Khady Fall Tall	Chair, Bureau Régional de l'Association des Femmes de l'Afrique de l'Ouest (AFAO-WAWA)
Valérie-Blandine Tanga	Head of Programme, Réseau des Femmes Croyantes Médiatrices de la Paix (RFCMP) (Central African Republic)
Olaifa Abimbola Temitope	Stephanie Peace-building and Development Foundation (Nigeria)
Bouba Oualy	UNDP Regional Service Centre – Dakar (Senegal)

The UNDP team responsible for the preparation of this report has given considerable attention to using a range of data sources and kinds of analysis in order to fully cover a topic as broad as gender equality in Africa. As explained in chapter 1, the underlying approach was to take a 'political economy' perspective in analysing gender issues and women's empowerment. The goal has been to understand the way that ideas, resources and power are conceptualized, negotiated and implemented by different social groups in relation to gender inequality – whether in the workplace, the marketplace, or at home. 'Political economy analysis' is thus concerned with the interaction of political, social (including norms and institutions) and economic processes in a society, including the distribution of power and wealth between groups and individuals, and the processes that create, sustain and transform these relationships over time. This definition recognizes that power is essentially about relationships – between the state, social groups and individuals, or between the state, market forces and civil society.

Toward this end, the report has sought to balance quantitative and qualitative analysis of gender equality as evidenced by the background papers listed in Annex A. The nine background papers prepared for the report deepened the evidence on the human development costs of gender disparities in work, markets, politics, leadership and social outcomes. These studies used country benchmarking and regional analysis to identify development areas, examples of successful reforms and proposed institutional responses.

This analysis was complemented by qualitative analysis of the role of social norms and institutions in perpetuating the cycle of gender inequality using in-country investigative interviews, focus group discussions and country case studies, including Cabo Verde, Guinea Bissau, Kenya, Rwanda, Mali, Morocco, Mozambique, Togo and Tunisia, among others. Similarly, an Africa-wide online survey was used to collect further insights.

In addition, considerable attention has been given to the data collected by UNDP for different human development indicators and efforts to disaggregate these data looking specifically at Africa and in making cross-regional comparisons. This effort includes the report's further disaggregation of the human development data to the African sub-regional level.

A key methodological objective in the report's preparation was to ensure a very high level of collaboration and consultation with multiple organizations, policy-makers, practitioners and researchers. At various stages during the preparation, regional consultations were held in Addis Ababa, Ethiopia and Dakar, Senegal, as well as two policy dialogues in Lusaka, Zambia and Johannesburg, South Africa. The meetings were held in close collaboration with the African Union and United Nations organizations, as well as civil society organizations, regional economic institutions, and representatives from women and youth organizations across Africa.

In addition, the report preparation process benefitted from further reviews and recommendations by a High Level Advisory Group, a UNDP Internal Oversight Group, a UN Readers' Group, and a UNDP Field Sounding Board.

It is hoped that the collaborative approach used in the preparation of this report will lay the groundwork for a network of change agents who will contribute to supporting and advocating for the implementation of the policy agenda and recommendations put forward in the final chapter of this report.

Central Africa
Africa
World

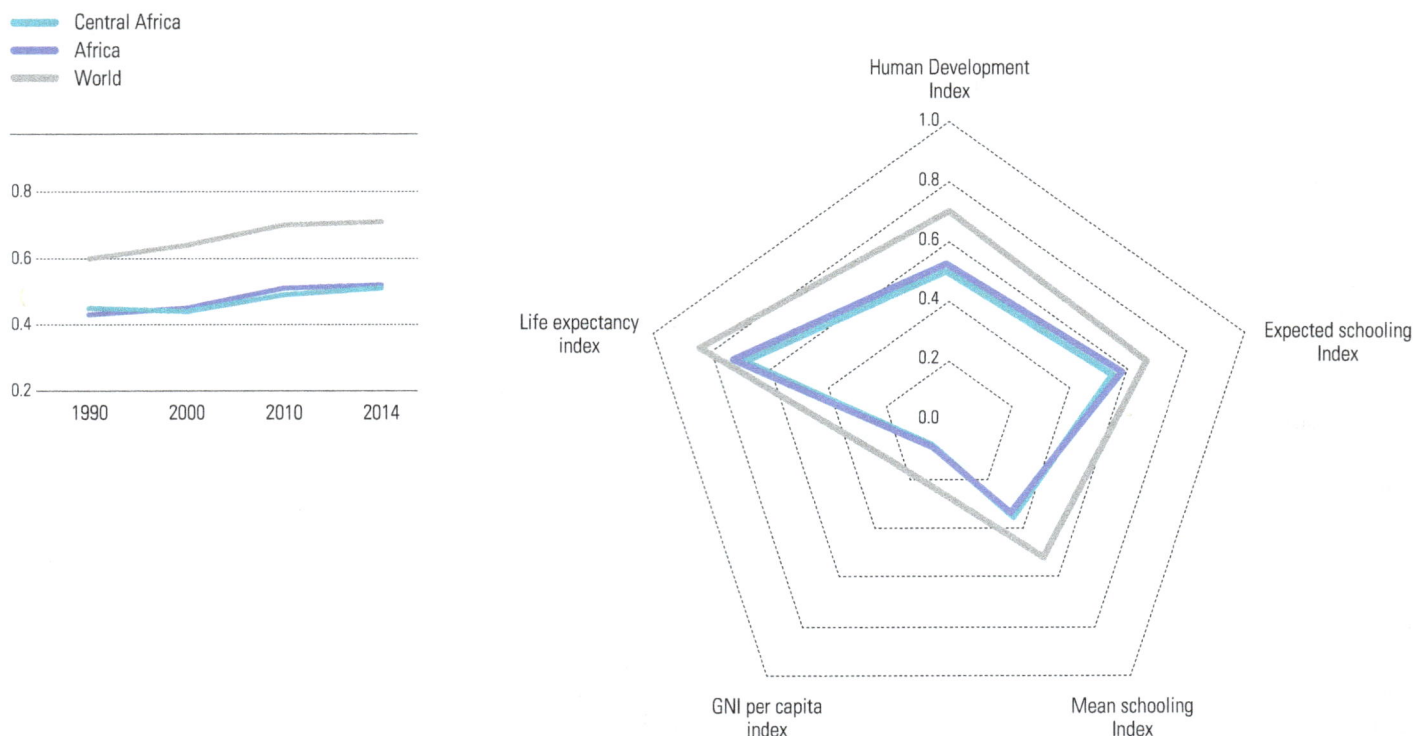

0.8

0.6

0.4

0.2

1990   2000   2010   2014

Human Development
Index
1.0
0.8
0.6
0.4
0.2
0.0

Life expectancy
index

Expected schooling
Index

GNI per capita
index

Mean schooling
Index

Source: Computed by the AfHDR Team based on data from UNDP, 2015.

Human Development Index and Trends

The **Human Development Index** (HDI) is a summary measure for assessing long-term progress in three basic dimensions of human development: a long and healthy life, access to knowledge and a decent standard of living. Knowledge is measured by mean years of education among the adult population, and access to learning and knowledge by expected years of schooling for children of school-entry age. Standard of living is measured by gross national income (GNI) per capita expressed in constant 2011 international dollars converted using purchasing power parity (PPP) rates.

The Central Africa sub-region has an average Human Development Index (HDI) value of 0.507, which is below the African average value of 0.524. However, there is a wide variation between the highest value of 0.585 for Republic of the Congo and the lowest value of 0.348 in Central African Republic. Equatorial Guinea, Gabon and the Republic of the Congo have achieved medium

human development with living standards indicated by GNI per capita that are above the African average. Nevertheless, even with lower standards of living, Madagascar, a low human development country, has achieved the highest life expectancy in the sub-region, while the Democratic Republic of the Congo and Cameroon, also low human development countries, have achieved higher than average education outcomes for this sub-region. Since 2010, Republic of the Congo, the Democratic Republic of the Congo, Chad and Cameroon have made the biggest strides in improving their level of human development.

The **Inequality-adjusted Human Development Index** (IHDI) takes into account inequality in all three dimensions of the HDI by 'discounting' each dimension's average value according to the level of inequality across the population. The 'loss' in human development due to inequality is given as the difference between HDI and IHDI expressed

Human development index, inequality and change

Country	Human Development Index (HDI)	Inequality-adjusted HDI (IHDI)	Overall loss in HDI from Inequality	Life expectancy at birth	Expected years of schooling	Mean years of schooling	GNI per capita	Average annual HDI growth (%)	
	Value	Value	(%)	(Years)	(Years)	(Years)	(2011 PPP $)	2000-2010	2010-2014
Gabon	0.684	0.519	24.0	64.4	12.5	7.8	16.367	0.48	0.76
Republic of the Congo	0.591	0.434	26.6	62.3	11.1	6.1	6.012	1.25	1.61
Equatorial Guinea	0.587	–	–	57.6	9.0	5.5	21.056	1.18	-0.18
Cameroon	0.512	0.344	32.8	55.5	10.4	6.0	2.803	1.07	1.32
Democratic Rep. of the Congo	0.433	0.276	36.2	58.7	9.8	6.0	680	2.18	1.52
Chad	0.392	0.236	39.9	51.6	7.4	1.9	2.085	1.12	1.37
Central African Republic	0.350	0.198	43.5	50.7	7.2	4.2	581	1.58	-0.84
Central Africa	0.507	0.340	32.8	58.2	9.7	5.4	6.364	1.23	0.73
Africa	0.524	0.349	32.89	61.2	10.3	5.0	5.126	1.55	0.86

Source: Compiled by the AfHDR Team based on data from UNDP, 2015.

as a percentage. On average, there is a 33 per cent loss in human development due to inequality in the Central Africa sub-region, which is similar to the African average. The Central African Republic, Chad and the Democratic Republic of Congo have the highest loss in human development from inequality in the sub-region, whereas Gabon, Republic of the Congo and Madagascar have the lowest.

A review of inequality in each sub-index of the HDI shows that in most countries in this sub-region, the inequality in life expectancy within countries is higher than inequality in income and education. The exceptions are Madagascar and Central African Republic, with higher inequality in the income distribution of income per capita across the population.

Gender Inequality and Women's Empowerment

The Gender Development Index (GDI) is based on the sex-disaggregated HDI and defined as a ratio of the female to the male HDI. The GDI measures gender inequalities in achievement in terms of health (measured by female and male life expectancy at birth), education (measured by female and male expected years of schooling for children and mean years for adults aged 25 years and older) and command over economic resources (measured by female and male estimated GNI per capita). The GDI of the Central Africa sub-region (0.85) is slightly below the African average (0.87), with a wide variation. The GDI indicates that women in Madagascar achieve up to 95 per cent of the human development outcomes of men, while in Chad and Central African Republic, women attain only 77 per cent of male achievements in education, health and command over resources.

The **Gender Inequality Index** (GII) reflects gender-based inequalities in three dimensions – reproductive health, measured by maternal mortality and adolescent birth rates; empowerment, measured by the share of parliamentary seats held by women, and attainment in secondary and higher education by each gender; and economic activity, measured by the labour market participation rate for women and men. The GII can be

Cameroon
Central African Republic
Chad
Rep. of the Congo
Democratic Rep. of the Congo

Trends in gender inequality

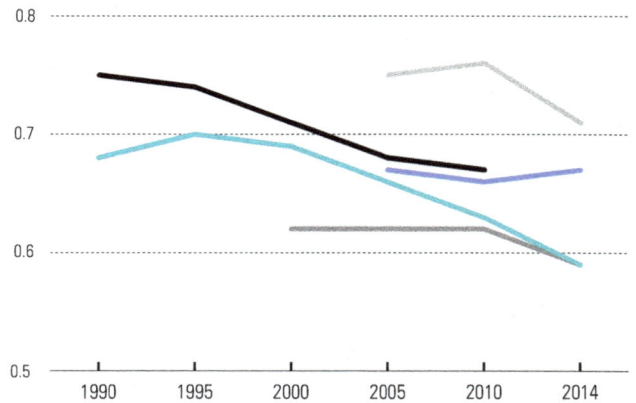

GENDER DEVELOPMENT INDEX

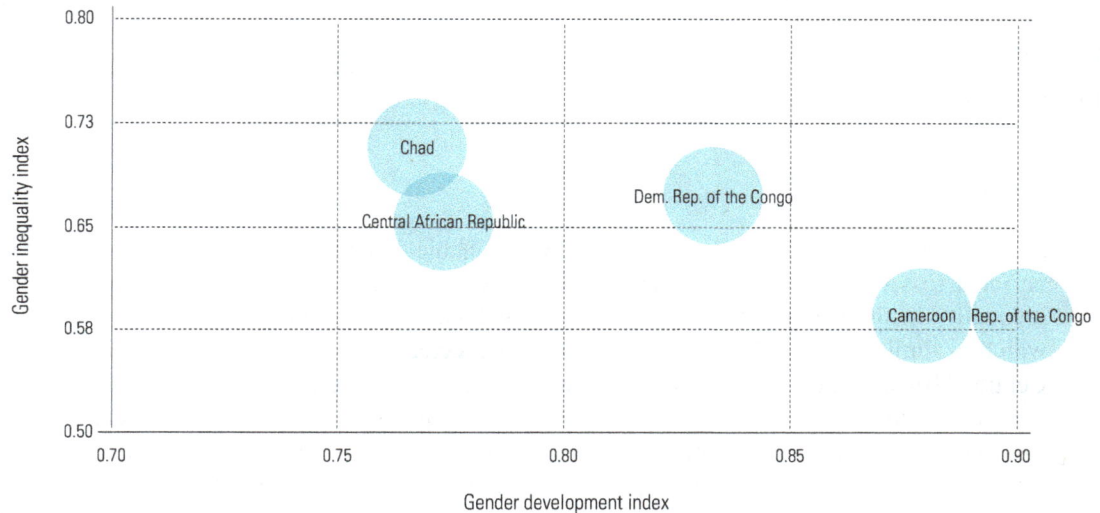

Gender inequality index

Gender development index

Source: Computed by the AfHDR Team based on data from UNDP, 2015.

interpreted as the loss in human development due to inequality between female and male achievements in the three GII dimensions. Countries with higher gender inequality, such as the Democratic Republic of Congo, Central African Republic and Chad, tend to have a larger gap between female and male HDI outcomes. In these countries, the maternal mortality rates are over three times the average of developing countries. In addition, the gender gap in secondary education attainment is high; less than 4 women for every 10 men over 25 years of age have obtained at least some secondary education.

Countries with high gender inequality and the presence of discriminatory social institutions, as illustrated in the **Social Institutions and Gender Index** (SIGI), tend to have poorer human development outcomes for women than for men. These social institutions limit women's decision-making power and status in the home, increase their vulnerability to violence, lead to unequal care for children (favouring sons) and reduce women's access to resources and participation in politics and public life. Chad and the Democratic Republic of the Congo are considered to have highly discriminatory social institutions. In these

Gender equality, social institutions and women's empowerment

Country	Gender Development Index	Gender Inequality Index	Social Institutions and Gender Index	Female/ male GNI per capita	Maternal mortality gap	Adolescent birth rate gap	Gender gap in secondary education attainment (25+)	Labour force participation gap (15+)	Female share of seats in parliament
	Value	Value	Value	Ratio	Ratio	Ratio	Ratio	Ratio	(%)
	2014	2014	2014	2014	2015	2010-2015	2005-2014	2015	2016
Republic of the Congo	0.922	0.593	0.20	0.8	1.8	2.5	0.8	0.9	13.4
Cameroon	0.879	0.587	0.28	0.7	2.5	2.2	0.6	0.9	25.6
Democratic Republic of the Congo	0.833	0.673	0.43	0.8	2.9	2.6	0.4	1.0	6.8
Central African Republic	0.773	0.655	0.33	0.7	3.7	1.9	0.4	0.9	8.6
Chad	0.768	0.706	0.47	0.7	3.6	3.0	0.2	0.8	14.9
Gabon	–	0.514	0.40	0.7	1.2	2.0	1.5	0.7	16.2
Equatorial Guinea	–	–	–	0.7	1.4	2.2	–	0.8	18.9
Central Africa	0.853	0.621	0.32	0.7	2.3	2.3	0.6	0.9	15.5
Africa	0.871	0.548	0.28	0.6	2.1	1.7	0.7	0.8	20.8

Source: Compiled by the AfHDR Team based on data from GDI and GII, UNDP (2015), Women in Parliament, IPU (2016), Labour force, ILO (2016), Maternal Mortality, WHO, (2016), SIGI, OECD (2015)

Notes:

a. Female and male GNI per capita, UNDP (2015).

b. Maternal mortality gap is actual deaths per 100,000 live births in each country benchmarked against developing country average of 239, WHO (2015).

c. Adolescent birth rate gap is the number of actual births per 1,000 women aged 15-19 in each country benchmarked against developing country average (2010/2015), UNDP (2015).

d. Population with at least some secondary education gap is the female to male ratio of secondary education attainment for the population aged 25 and older, UNDP (2015).

e. Female share in parliament is the average percentage of women parliamentarians in each country, across all chambers (single, lower and upper houses) at May 2016. The average for sub-Saharan Africa (SSA) is 23.1 per cent and 20.8 per cent including North Africa, IPU (2016).

f. Labour force participation gap is the female-male ratio (Ratio of female to male shares) for the female and male population aged 15 and above, ILO (2016).

References:

UNDP. 2015. Human Development Report 2015: Work for Human Development. New York.

IPU (International Parliamentary Union). 2016. International Parliamentary Union: Women in National Parliaments Database. Accessed 16 June 2016. www.ipu.org/wmn-e/world.htm

ILO (International Labour Organization). 2015. Key Indicators of the Labour Market (KILM) Database, 9th edition. Accessed 16 June 2016. www.ilo.org/global/statistics-and-databases/research-and-databases/kilm/WCMS_422090/lang--en/index.htm

WHO (World Health Organization). 2015. Trends in Maternal Mortality 1990-2015, Estimates by WHO, UNICEF, UNFPA, World Bank Group and the United Nations Population Division. www.who.int/reproductivehealth/publications/monitoring/maternal-mortality-2015/en

OECD (Organisation for Economic Co-operation and Development). 2015. Social Institutions and Gender Index 2014. OECD Development Centre. www.genderindex.org

countries, there are low levels of female representation in parliament and higher levels of adolescent births. By contrast, countries such as Madagascar and Cameroon, with lower levels of social discriminatory institutions, have a higher share of women in parliament.

East Africa
Africa
World

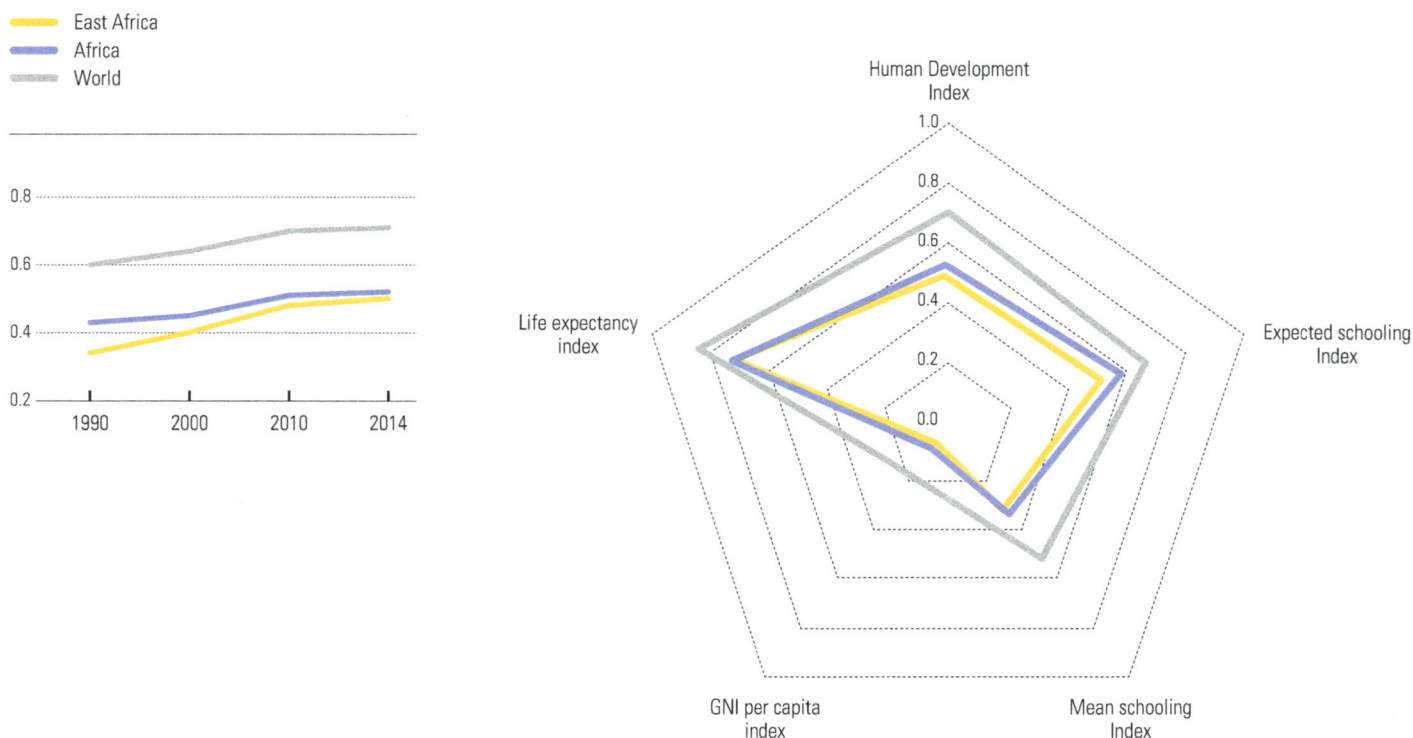

Source: Computed by the AfHDR Team based on data from UNDP, 2015.

Human Development Index and Trends

The **Human Development Index** (HDI) is a summary measure for assessing long-term progress in three basic dimensions of human development: a long and healthy life, access to knowledge and a decent standard of living. Knowledge is measured by mean years of education among the adult population, and access to learning and knowledge by expected years of schooling for children of school-entry age. Standard of living is measured by gross national income (GNI) per capita expressed in constant 2011 international dollars converted using purchasing power parity (PPP) rates.

East Africa sub-region has an average human development value of 0.497, which is below the African average value of 0.524. There is a wide variation between the highest value of 0.770 for Seychelles and the lowest value of 0.391 in Eritrea. Although Comoros, Rwanda and Ethiopia have broadly similar levels of income per capita, both Comoros and Rwanda have better health and education

outcomes, which increase their level of human development relative to Ethiopia. Countries with relatively lower income per capita such as Kenya and United Republic of Tanzania fare better than Sudan and Djibouti, mainly due to better education outcomes implying better efficiency in the utilization of resources. Since 2010, Ethiopia, Rwanda, Burundi and United Republic of Tanzania have made the biggest strides in improving their level of human development.

The **Inequality-adjusted Human Development Index** (IHDI) takes into account inequality in all three dimensions of the HDI by 'discounting' each dimension's average value according to the level of inequality across the population. The 'loss' in human development due to inequality is given as the difference between HDI and IHDI expressed as a percentage. On average, due to inequality, the sub-region has a similar level of loss to the African region average. Comoros has

Human development, inequality and change

Country	Human Development Index (HDI)	Inequality-adjusted HDI (IHDI)	Overall loss in HDI from Inequality	Life expectancy at birth	Expected years of schooling	Mean years of schooling	GNI per capita	Average annual HDI growth (%)	
	Value	Value	(%)	(Years)	(Years)	(Years)	(2011 PPP $)	2000-2010	2010-2014
Seychelles	0.772	–	–	73.1	13.4	9.4	23.300	0.39	0.97
Kenya	0.548	0.377	31.30	61.6	11.0	6.3	2.762	1.70	0.92
Tanzania (United Republic of)	0.521	0.379	27.30	65.0	9.2	5.1	2.411	2.46	1.05
Comoros	0.503	0.268	46.70	63.3	11.5	4.6	1.456	–	0.75
Rwanda	0.483	0.330	31.60	64.2	10.3	3.7	1.458	3.13	1.61
Uganda	0.483	0.337	30.20	58.5	9.8	5.4	1.613	1.86	0.51
Sudan	0.479	–	–	63.5	7.0	3.1	3.809	1.52	0.74
Djibouti	0.470	0.308	34.30	62.0	6.4	3.8	3.276	2.17	0.97
South Sudan	0.467	–	–	55.7	7.6	5.4	2.332	–	-0.15
Ethiopia	0.442	0.312	29.40	64.1	8.5	2.4	1.428	3.78	1.78
Burundi	0.400	0.269	32.60	56.7	10.1	2.7	758	2.62	0.66
Eritrea	0.391	–	–	63.7	4.1	3.9	1.130	–	0.62
East Africa	0.497	0.323	32.96	62.1	9.1	4.7	3.811	2.18	0.87
Africa	0.524	0.349	32.89	61.2	10.3	5.0	5.126	1.55	0.86

Source: Compiled by the AfHDR Team based on data from UNDP, 2015.

the highest loss in human development from inequality in the sub-region, whereas the United Republic of Tanzania has the lowest. A review of inequality in each sub-index of the HDI shows that in Kenya, Comoros and Rwanda, the inequality in income per capita contributes most to human development inequality. By contrast, in United Republic of Tanzania and South Sudan, higher inequality in both education and health outcomes contributes more than inequality in income per capita. In Ethiopia and Djibouti, the main driver of inequality is unequal distribution in education outcomes.

Gender Inequality and Women's Empowerment

The **Gender Development Index** (GDI) is based on the sex-disaggregated HDI and defined as a ratio of the female to the male HDI. The GDI measures gender inequalities in achievement in terms of health (measured by female and male life expectancy at birth), education (measured by female and male expected years of schooling for children and mean years for adults aged 25 years and older) and command over economic resources (measured by female and male estimated GNI per capita). The East Africa sub-region has a higher GDI than the African average, which indicates that in East Africa, there is a higher ratio of female to male HDI values. The GDI reveals that women in Rwanda attain up to 96 per cent of the human development outcomes of men, while in Comoros and Sudan, women attain only 81 per cent of male achievements in education, health and command over resources.

The **Gender Inequality Index** (GII) reflects gender-based inequalities in three dimensions – reproductive health, measured by maternal mortality and adolescent birth rates; empowerment, measured by the share

Uganda
Tanzania
Sudan
Rwanda
Kenya
Burundi

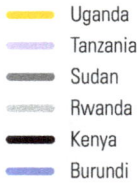

Trends in gender inequality

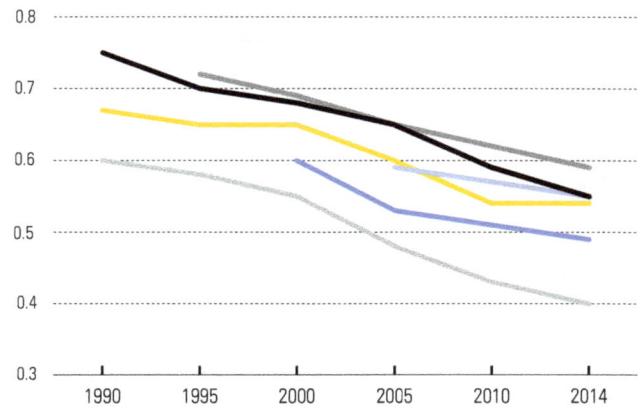

GENDER DEVELOPMENT INDEX

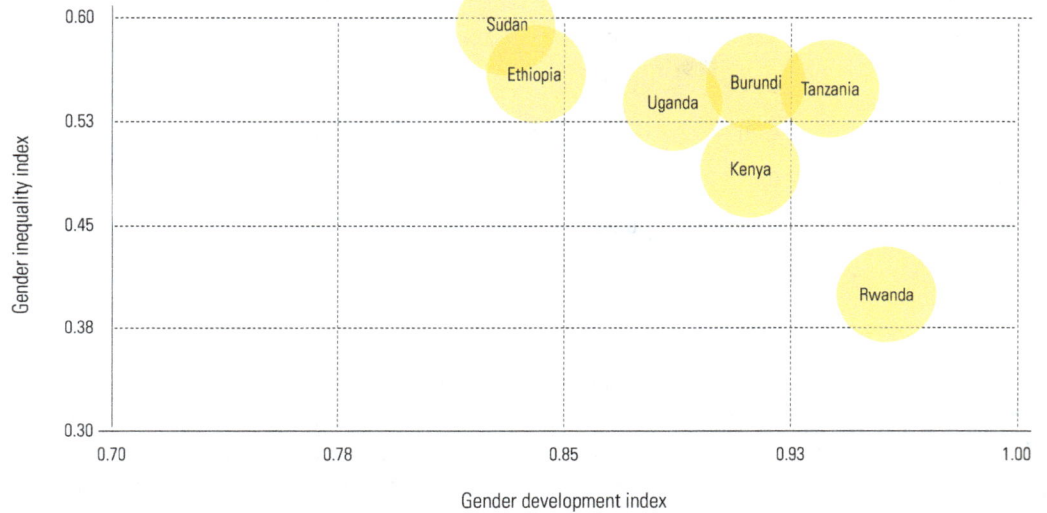

Gender inequality index

Sudan

Ethiopia

Uganda

Burundi

Tanzania

Kenya

Rwanda

Gender development index

Source: Computed by the AfHDR Team based on data from UNDP, 2015.

of parliamentary seats held by women and attainment in secondary and higher education by each gender; and economic activity, measured by the labour market participation rate for women and men. The GII can be interpreted as the loss in human development due to inequality between female and male achievements in the three GII dimensions. Rwanda and Burundi have the lowest levels of gender inequality in the sub-region, whereas Sudan has the highest.

Countries with high gender inequality and the presence of discriminatory social institutions, as illustrated in the **Social Institutions and Gender Index** (SIGI), tend to have poorer human development outcomes for women than for men. Rwanda, with the lowest level of gender inequality and low levels of discriminatory social institutions, also has the lowest gap in human development between women and men, as demonstrated by the highest GDI. In Rwanda, women's economic empowerment is high, with a low gap in terms of GNI per capita for women compared to men, a lower maternal mortality rate than the sub-regional average, lower adolescent births, and an almost equal share of women with secondary education and participating in the labour force as men. The opposite is true for Comoros and Sudan,

Gender equality, social institutions and women's empowerment

	Gender Development Index	Gender Inequality Index	Social Institutions and Gender Index	Female/ male GNI per capita	Maternal mortality gap	Adolescent birth rate gap	Female share of seats in parliament	Gender gap in secondary school attainment (25+)	Labour force participation gap (15+)
	Value	Value	Value	Ratio	Ratio	Ratio	%	Ratio	Ratio
	2014	2014	2014	2014	2015	2010/2015	2016	2005–2014	2015
Rwanda	0.957	0.40	0.13	0.8	1.2	0.7	51.2	0.9	1.0
Tanzania	0.938	0.55	0.25	0.9	1.7	2.4	36.6	0.6	0.9
Kenya	0.913	0.55	0.22	0.7	2.1	1.8	23.1	0.8	0.9
Burundi	0.911	0.49	0.17	0.8	3.0	0.6	39.2	0.6	1.0
Uganda	0.886	0.54	0.22	0.6	1.4	2.5	33.5	0.7	0.9
Ethiopia	0.840	0.56	0.25	0.6	1.5	1.5	35.4	0.4	0.9
Sudan	0.830	0.59	0.56	0.3	1.3	1.6	32.9	0.7	0.3
Comoros	0.813	–	–	0.4	1.4	1.0	3.0	–	0.4
Somalia	–	–	0.46	–	3.1	2.1	13.8	–	0.4
Seychelles	–	–	–	–	–	1.1	43.8	1.0	–
Djibouti	–	–	–	0.4	1.0	0.4	12.7	–	0.5
South Sudan	–	–	–	–	3.3	1.5	18.3	–	0.9
Eritrea	–	–	–	0.8	2.1	1.3	22.0	–	0.9
East Africa	0.886	0.53	0.28	0.6	1.9	1.4	28.1	0.7	0.8
Africa	0.871	0.55	0.28	0.6	2.1	1.7	20.8	0.7	0.8

Source: Compiled by the AfHDR Team based on data from GDI and GII, UNDP (2015), Women in Parliament, IPU (2016), Labour force, ILO (2016), Maternal Mortality, WHO, (2016), SIGI, OECD (2015).

Notes:

a. Female and male GNI per capita, UNDP (2015).

b. Maternal mortality gap is actual deaths per 100,000 live births in each country benchmarked against developing country average of 239, WHO (2015).

c. Adolescent birth rate gap is the number of actual births per 1,000 women ages 15-19 in each country benchmarked against developing country average (2010/2015), UNDP (2015).

d   Population with at least some secondary education gap is the female to male ratio of secondary education attainment for the population aged 25 and older, UNDP (2015).

e   Female share in parliament is the average percentage of women parliamentarians in each country, across all chambers (single, lower and upper houses) at May 2016. The average for sub-Saharan Africa (SSA) is 23.1 per cent and 20.8 per cent including North Africa, IPU (2016).

f. Labour force participation gap is the female-male ratio (Ratio of female to male shares) for the female and male population aged 15 and above, ILO (2016).

References:

UNDP. 2015. Human Development Report 2015: Work for Human Development. New York.

IPU (International Parliamentary Union). 2016. International Parliamentary Union: Women in National Parliaments Database. Accessed 16 June 2016. www.ipu.org/wmn-e/world.htm

ILO (International Labour Organization). 2015. Key Indicators of the Labour Market (KILM) Database, 9th edition. Accessed 16 June 2016. www.ilo.org/global/statistics-and-databases/research-and-databases/kilm/WCMS_422090/lang--en/index.htm

WHO (World Health Organization). 2015. Trends in Maternal Mortality 1990-2015, Estimates by WHO, UNICEF, UNFPA, World Bank Group and the United Nations Population Division. www.who.int/reproductivehealth/publications/monitoring/maternal-mortality-2015/en

OECD (Organisation for Economic Co-operation and Development). 2015. Social Institutions and Gender Index 2014. OECD Development Centre. www.genderindex.org

where indicators of women's political, social and economic empowerment are low. These countries with lower human development outcomes for women face high gender inequality and highly discriminatory social institutions. These social institutions limit women's decision-making power and status in the home, increase their vulnerability to violence, lead to unequal care for children (favouring sons) and reduce women's access to resources and participation in politics and public life.

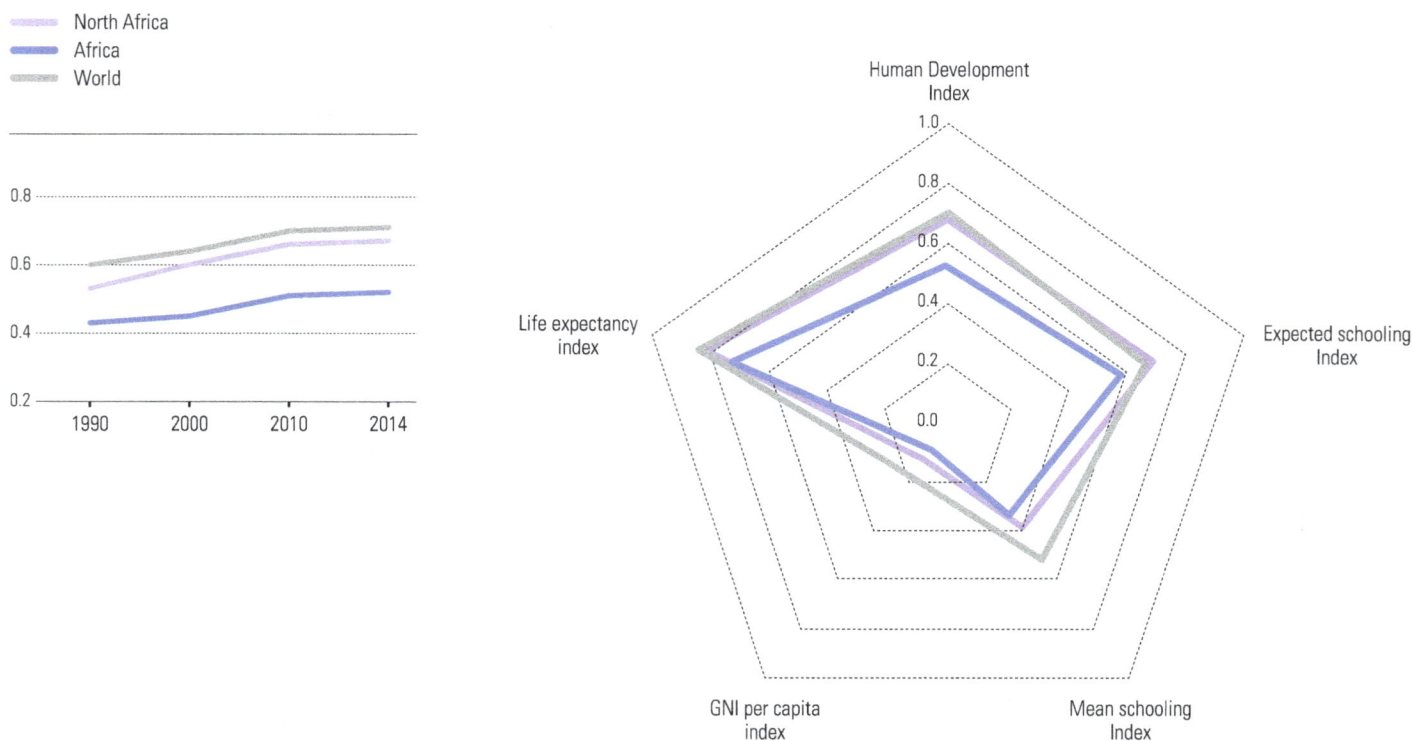

North Africa
Africa
World

Human Development
Index

Life expectancy
index

Expected schooling
Index

GNI per capita
index

Mean schooling
Index

Source: Computed by the AfHDR Team based on data from UNDP, 2015.

Human Development Index and Trends

The **Human Development Index** (HDI) is a summary measure for assessing long-term progress in three basic dimensions of human development: a long and healthy life, access to knowledge and a decent standard of living. Knowledge is measured by mean years of education among the adult population, and access to learning and knowledge by expected years of schooling for children of school-entry age. Standard of living is measured by gross national income (GNI) per capita expressed in constant 2011 international dollars converted using purchasing power parity (PPP) rates. North Africa has an average HDI value of 0.668, which is well above the African average of 0.524. There is a wide variation between the highest value of 0.736 for Algeria and the lowest value of 0.506 for Mauritania. Three countries – Algeria, Libya and Tunisia – have achieved high human development status. Egypt and Morocco are medium human development countries, and only Mauritania

is a low human development country. In this sub-region, the average life expectancy and income per capita are higher than the African average. However, the years of schooling in Morocco and Mauritania are lower than the African average. Since 2010, improvement in human development values has been modest except in Mauritania, which achieved the African average rate of annual HDI growth.

The **Inequality-adjusted Human Development Index** (IHDI) takes into account inequality in all three dimensions of the HDI by 'discounting' each dimension's average value according to the level of inequality across the population. The 'loss' in human development due to inequality is defined as the difference between HDI and IHDI expressed as a percentage. On average, North Africa has a much lower level of loss due to inequality than the African average, although there are missing values for Algeria and Libya. Tunisia and Egypt have the lowest losses in

Human development, inequality and change

Country	Human Development Index (HDI)	Inequality-adjusted HDI (IHDI)	Overall loss in HDI from Inequality	Life expectancy at birth	Expected years of schooling	Mean years of schooling	GNI per capita	Average annual HDI growth (%)	
	Value	Value	(%)	(Years)	(Years)	(Years)	(2011 PPP $)	2000-2010	2010-2014
Algeria	0.736	–	–	74.8	14.0	7.6	13.054	1.26	0.35
Libya	0.724	–	–	71.6	14.0	7.3	14.911	0.34	-1.07
Tunisia	0.721	0.562	22.0	74.8	14.6	6.8	10.404	0.88	0.26
Egypt	0.690	0.524	24.0	71.1	13.5	6.6	10.512	0.90	0.33
Morocco	0.628	0.441	29.7	74.0	11.6	4.4	6.850	1.48	0.69
Mauritania	0.506	0.337	33.4	63.1	8.5	3.8	3.560	0.98	0.92
North Africa	0.668	0.466	27.3	71.6	12.7	6.1	9.882	0.97	0.25
Africa	0.524	0.349	32.9	61.2	10.5	5.0	4.827	1.55	0.86

Source: Compiled by the AfHDR Team based on data from UNDP, 2015.

human development from inequality, whereas Mauritania has the highest.

A review of inequality in each sub-index of the HDI shows that in all countries for this sub-region, inequality in education outcomes across the population contributes more to inequality in human development outcomes than inequality in income per capita and health.

Gender Inequality and Women's Empowerment

The **Gender Development Index** (GDI) is based on the sex-disaggregated HDI and defined as a ratio of the female to the male HDI. The GDI measures gender inequalities in achievement in terms of health (measured by female and male life expectancy at birth), education (measured by female and male expected years of schooling for children and mean years for adults aged 25 years and older) and command over economic resources (measured by female and male estimated GNI per capita). North Africa has a similar GDI value to the African average, with some variation across countries. For instance, women in Libya attain up to 95 per cent of the human development outcomes of men, compared to women in Mauritania, at 82 per cent.

The **Gender Inequality Index** (GII) reflects gender-based inequalities in three dimensions – reproductive health, measured by maternal mortality and adolescent birth rates; empowerment, measured by the share of parliamentary seats held by women and attainment in secondary and higher education by each gender; and economic activity, measured by the labour market participation rate for women and men. The GII can be interpreted as the loss in human development due to inequality between female and male achievements in the three GII dimensions.

Tunisia
Morocco
Mauritania
Egypt
Algeria

Trends in gender inequality

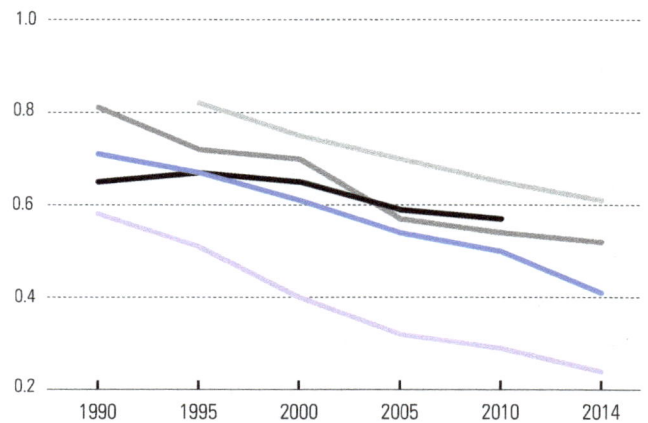

GENDER DEVELOPMENT INDEX

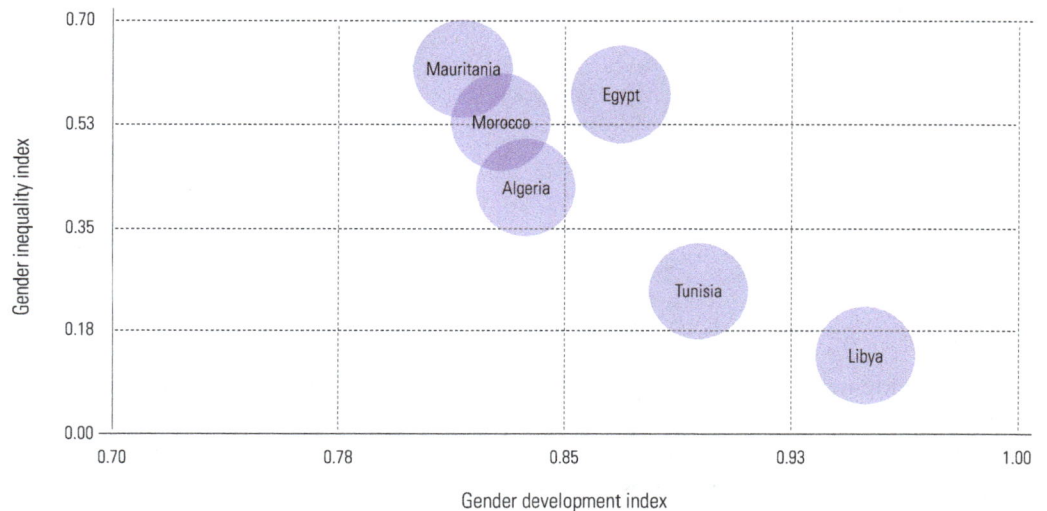

Source: Computed by the AfHDR Team based on data from UNDP, 2015.

Although the sub-region has lower levels of gender inequality compared to the African average, gender inequality in Mauritania, Egypt and Morocco is particularly high. For instance, the gap between female and males aged 25 and older who have achieved at least a secondary education is highest in Mauritania, where there are 4 women for every 10 men with secondary education. The adolescent birth rates in Algeria, Egypt and Mauritania are also higher than the sub-regional average, which may indicate a higher rate of early marriage. In Algeria, there is near parity in secondary education attainment, whereas in Libya, the share of women in secondary education is higher than for men. Maternal mortality in this sub-region is 50 per cent lower than the average for all developing countries except in Mauritania, where it is 1.4 times higher. A key driver of gender inequality in this sub-region is that women earn only 30 per cent of men's income per capita, which is related to the low levels of labour force participation.

Countries with high gender inequality and the presence of discriminatory social institutions, as illustrated in the **Social Institutions and Gender Index** (SIGI),

Gender equality, social institutions and women's empowerment

	Gender Development Index	Gender Inequality Index	Social Institutions and Gender Index	Female/ male GNI per capita	Maternal mortality gap	Adolescent birth rate gap	Female share of seats in parliament	Gender gap in secondary school attainment (25+)	Labour force participation gap (15+)
	Value	Value	Value	Ratio	Ratio	Ratio	%	Ratio	Ratio
	2014	2014	2014	2014	2015	2010-2015	2016	2005–2014	2015
Libya	0.950	0.134	–	0.3	0	0	16.0	1.3	0.4
Tunisia	0.894	0.240	0.20	0.3	0.3	0.1	31.3	0.7	0.4
Egypt	0.868	0.573	0.43	0.3	0.1	0.8	14.9	0.7	0.3
Algeria	0.837	0.413	–	0.2	0.6	0.2	19.3	0.9	0.2
Morocco	0.828	0.525	0.11	0.3	0.5	0.7	11.7	0.7	0.3
Mauritania	0.816	0.610	0.40	0.3	2.7	1.4	14.3	0.4	0.5
North Africa	0.865	0.416	0.28	0.3	0.7	0.5	19.3	0.8	0.3
Africa	0.871	0.548	0.28	0.6	1.9	1.7	20.8	0.7	0.8

Source: Compiled by the AfHDR Team based on data from GDI and GII, UNDP (2015), Women in Parliament, IPU (2016), Labour force, ILO (2016), Maternal Mortality, WHO, (2016), SIGI, OECD (2015).

Notes:

a. Female and male GNI per capita, UNDP (2015).

b. Maternal mortality gap is actual deaths per 100,000 live births in each country benchmarked against developing country average of 239, WHO (2015).

c. Adolescent birth rate gap is the number of actual births per 1,000 women ages 15–19 in each country benchmarked against developing country average (2010/2015), UNDP (2015).

d. Population with at least some secondary education gap is the female to male ratio of secondary education attainment for the population aged 25 and older, UNDP (2015).

e. Female share in parliament is the average percentage of women parliamentarians in each country, across all chambers (single, lower and upper houses) at May 2016. The average for sub-Saharan Africa (SSA) is 23.1 per cent and 20.8 per cent including North Africa, IPU (2016).

f. Labour force participation gap is the female-male ratio (Ratio of female to male shares) for the female and male population aged 15 and above, ILO (2016).

References:

UNDP. 2015. Human Development Report 2015: Work for Human Development. New York.

IPU (International Parliamentary Union). 2016. International Parliamentary Union: Women in National Parliaments Database. Accessed 16 June 2016. www.ipu.org/wmn-e/world.htm

ILO (International Labour Organization). 2015. Key Indicators of the Labour Market (KILM) Database, 9th edition. Accessed 16 June 2016. www.ilo.org/global/statistics-and-databases/research-and-databases/kilm/WCMS_422090/lang--en/index.htm

WHO (World Health Organization). 2015. Trends in Maternal Mortality 1990-2015 Estimates by WHO, UNICEF, UNFPA, World Bank Group and the United Nations Population Division. www.who.int/reproductivehealth/publications/monitoring/maternal-mortality-2015/en

OECD (Organisation for Economic Co-operation and Development). 2015. Social Institutions and Gender Index 2014. OECD Development Centre. www.genderindex.org

tend to have poorer human development outcomes for women than for men. The level of discriminatory social institution is highest in Egypt and Mauritania with lower levels in Tunisia and Morocco. These discriminatory social institutions may contribute to lower levels of parliamentary representation for females in parliament in Egypt and Mauritania. However, Libya and Morocco with relatively less discriminatory social institutions also have low levels of female representation in parliament and in the labour force, which may indicate more structural barriers to women's participation in political and public life. Discriminatory social institutions and practices limit women's decision-making power and status in the home, increase their vulnerability to violence, and in many cases, reduce their access to resources and decision-making platforms in public and private life.

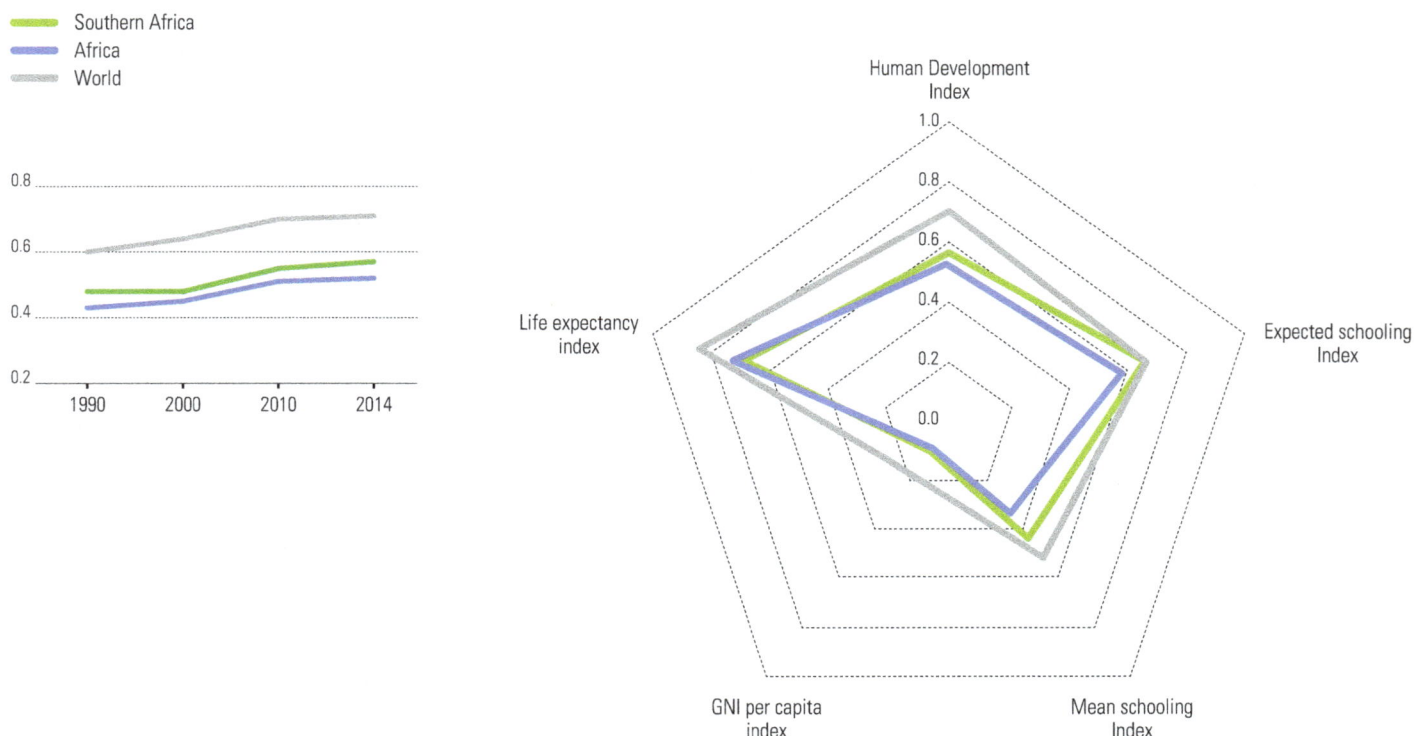

Legend:
- Southern Africa
- Africa
- World

Source: Computed by the AfHDR Team based on data from UNDP, 2015.

Human Development Index and Trends

The **Human Development Index** (HDI) is a summary measure for assessing long-term progress in three basic dimensions of human development: a long and healthy life, access to knowledge and a decent standard of living. Knowledge is measured by mean years of education among the adult population and access to learning and knowledge by expected years of schooling for children of school-entry age. Standard of living is measured by gross national income (GNI) per capita expressed in constant 2011 international dollars converted using purchasing power parity (PPP) rates.

The Southern Africa sub-region has an average HDI value of 0.57, which is above the African average value of 0.52. This is driven by higher than average income per capita and education, although average life expectancy is lower than the African average for many countries. There is also a wide variation in HDI values between countries. Mauritius has already achieved high medium

development status, while Botswana, South Africa, Zambia, and Sao Tome and Principe are medium human development countries. However, although Mauritius, Botswana, South Africa and Namibia have higher income per capita, the life expectancy in low-income per capita countries such as Sao Tome and Principe and Malawi are higher. Education outcomes in Southern Africa surpass the average for Africa in all countries except Angola, Sao Tome and Principe, Malawi and Mozambique. Zimbabwe, despite having a relatively low income per capita, has relatively high education outcomes but poor health. Since 2010, Angola, Lesotho, Malawi, Zambia and Zimbabwe have improved their levels of human development faster than the sub-regional average.

The **Inequality-adjusted Human Development Index** (IHDI) takes into account inequality in all three dimensions of the HDI by 'discounting' each dimension's average

Human development, inequality and change

Country	Human Development Index (HDI)	Inequality-adjusted HDI (IHDI)	Overall loss in HDI from Inequality	Life expectancy at birth	Expected years of schooling	Mean years of schooling	GNI per capita	Average annual HDI growth (%)	
	Value	Value	(%	(Years)	(Years)	(Years)	(2011 PPP $)	2000-2010	2010-2014
Mauritius	0.777	0.666	14.2	74.4	15.6	8.5	17.470	1.15	0.68
Botswana	0.698	0.431	38.2	64.5	12.5	8.9	16.646	1.96	0.61
South Africa	0.666	0.428	35.7	57.4	13.6	9.9	12.122	0.18	0.87
Namibia	0.628	0.354	43.6	64.8	11.3	6.2	9.418	0.94	0.70
Zambia	0.586	0.384	34.4	60.1	13.5	6.6	3.734	2.52	1.36
Sao Tome and Principe	0.555	0.418	24.7	66.5	11.3	4.7	2.918	1.02	0.52
Angola	0.532	0.335	37.0	52.3	11.4	4.7	6.822	2.70	1.11
Swaziland	0.531	0.354	33.3	49.0	11.3	7.1	5.542	0.57	0.28
Zimbabwe	0.509	0.371	27.0	57.5	10.9	7.3	1.615	0.75	2.50
Lesotho	0.497	0.32	35.6	49.8	11.1	5.9	3.306	0.62	1.30
Malawi	0.445	0.299	32.9	62.8	10.8	4.3	747	2.14	1.49
Mozambique	0.416	0.273	34.3	55.1	9.3	3.2	1.123	2.96	0.94
Southern Africa	0.570	0.386	32.6	59.5	11.9	6.5	6.789	1.46	1.03
Africa	0.524	0.349	32.9	61.2	10.5	5.0	4.827	1.55	0.86

Source: Compiled by the AfHDR Team based on data from UNDP, 2015.

value according to the level of inequality across the population. The 'loss' in human development due to inequality is defined as the difference between HDI and IHDI expressed as a percentage. The Southern Africa sub-region has similar human development losses due to greatest losses as the African average. The highest losses in human development due to inequality are in Namibia, Botswana and Angola, whereas Mauritius, Sao Tome and Principe, and Zimbabwe have the smallest. A review of inequality in each sub-index of the HDI reveals that the unequal distribution of income per capita across the population is the main driver of inequalities in human development in this sub-region except in Angola, Malawi and Mozambique. In these countries, inequality in the distribution of education and health outcomes is higher than the unequal distribution of income.

Gender Inequality and Women's Empowerment

The **Gender Development Index** (GDI) is based on the sex-disaggregated HDI and defined as a ratio of the female to the male HDI. The GDI measures gender inequalities in achievement in terms of health (measured by female and male life expectancy at birth), education (measured by female and male expected years of schooling for children and mean years for adults aged 25 years and older) and command over economic resources (measured by female and male estimated GNI per capita). The Southern Africa sub-region has a higher GDI value than the rest of Africa, which indicates that human development outcomes for women and men are more equal. For instance, women in Botswana and Namibia achieve up to 98 per cent of the

Botswana
Lesotho
Malawi
Mauritius
Mozambique
South Africa
Swaziland
Zambia
Zimbabwe

Trends in gender inequality

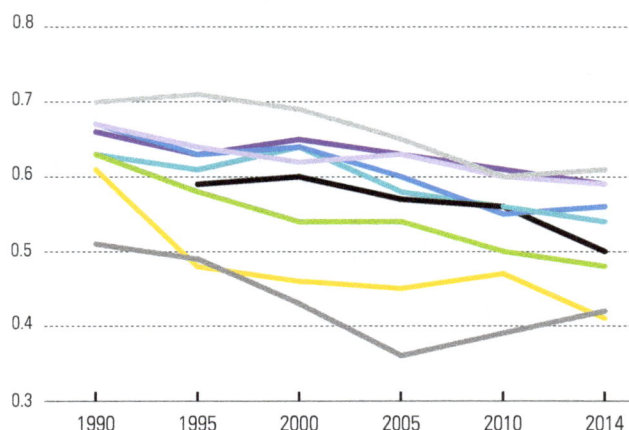

GENDER DEVELOPMENT INDEX

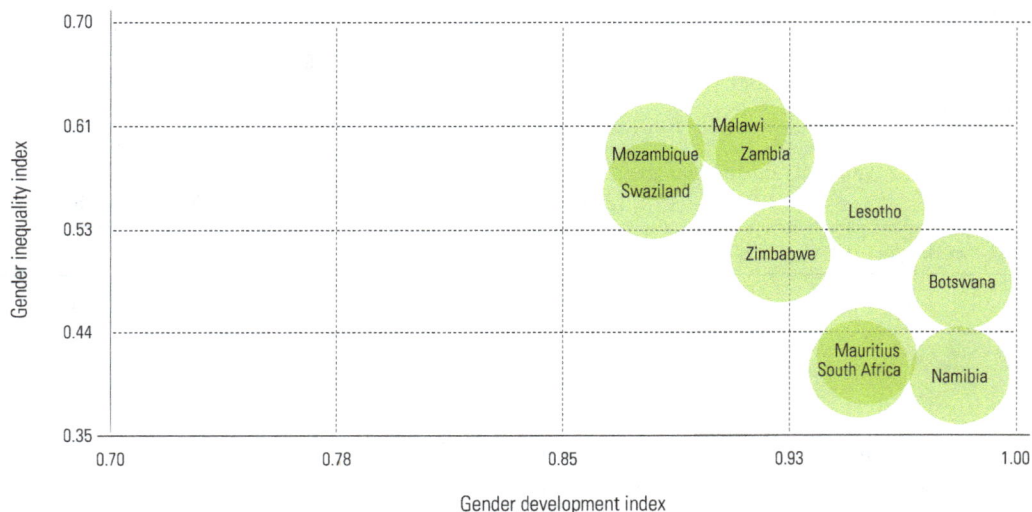

Source: Computed by the AfHDR Team based on data from UNDP, 2015.

human development outcomes of men, while in Swaziland and Mozambique, women attain close to 88 per cent of male achievements in education, health and income per capita.

The **Gender Inequality Index** (GII) reflects gender-based inequalities in three dimensions – reproductive health, measured by maternal mortality and adolescent birth rates; empowerment, measured by the share of parliamentary seats held by women and attainment in secondary and higher education by each gender; and economic activity, measured by the labour market participation rate for women and men. The GII can be interpreted as the loss in human development

due to inequality between female and male achievements in the three GII dimensions. For instance, the ratio of women to men aged 25 and older in the category 'population with at least a secondary education' indicates that Mozambique and Malawi have the highest levels of gender inequality in the sub-region, with 2 and 4 women, respectively, to every 10 men with secondary school education. In contrast, in Namibia and South Africa, the proportion of women with secondary education is the same as for men, whereas in Lesotho, there are more women than men with secondary education.

Gender equality, social institutions and women's empowerment

	Gender Development Index	Gender Inequality Index	Social Institutions and Gender Index	Female/ male GNI per capita	Maternal mortality gap	Adolescent birth rate gap	Female share of seats in parliament	Gender gap in secondary school attainment (25+)	Labour force participation gap (15+)
	Value	Value	Value	Ratio	Ratio	Ratio	%	Ratio	Ratio
	2014	2014	2014	2014	2015	2010-2015	2016	2005–2014	2015
Botswana	0.982	0.480	–	0.8	0.5	0.9	9.5	0.9	0.9
Namibia	0.981	0.401	0.12	0.7	1.1	1.1	32.6	1.0	0.9
Lesotho	0.953	0.541	0.09	0.7	2.0	1.7	24.6	1.2	0.8
Mauritius	0.950	0.419		0.4	0.2	0.6	11.6	0.9	0.6
South Africa	0.948	0.407	0.06	0.6	0.6	1.0	38.8	1.0	0.8
Zimbabwe	0.922	0.504	0.14	0.7	1.9	1.2	39.5	0.8	0.9
Zambia	0.917	0.587	0.45	0.7	0.9	2.4	12.7	0.6	0.9
Malawi	0.907	0.611	0.21	0.8	2.7	2.8	16.7	0.5	1.0
Sao Tome and Principe	0.891	–	–	0.5	0.7	1.3	18.2	–	0.6
Mozambique	0.881	0.591	0.14	0.9	2.0	2.7	39.6	0.2	1.1
Swaziland	0.879	0.557	0.21	0.5	1.6	1.4	19.8	0.8	0.6
Angola	–	–	0.17	0.7	2.0	3.3	36.8		0.8
Southern Africa	0.928	0.510	0.18	0.7	1.4	1.7	25.0	0.8	0.8
Africa	0.871	0.550	0.28	0.6	2.1	1.7	20.8	0.7	0.8

Source: Compiled by the AfHDR Team based on data from GDI and GII, UNDP (2015), Women in Parliament, IPU (2016), Labour force, ILO (2016), Maternal Mortality, WHO, (2016), SIG , OECD 2015).

Notes:

a. Female and male GNI per capita, UNDP (2015).

b. Maternal mortality gap is actual deaths per 100,000 live births in each country benchmarked against developing country average of 239, WHO (2015).

c. Adolescent birth rate gap is the number of actual births per 1,000 women ages 15–19 in each country benchmarked against developing country average (2010/2015), UNDP (2015).

d. Population with at least some secondary education gap is the female to male ratio of secondary education attainment for the population aged 25 and older, UNDP (2015).

e. Female share in parliament is the average percentage of women parliamentarians in each country, across all chambers (single, lower and upper houses) at May 2016. The average for sub-Saharan Africa (SSA) is 23.1 per cent and 20.8 per cent including North Africa, IPU (2016).

f. Labour force participation gap is the female-male ratio (Ratio of female to male shares) for the female and male population aged 15 and above, ILO (2015).

References:

UNDP. 2015. Human Development Report 2015: Work for Human Development. New York.

IPU (International Parliamentary Union). 2016. International Parliamentary Union: Women in National Parliaments Database. Accessed 16 June 2016. www.ipu.org/wmn-e/world.htm

ILO (International Labour Organization). 2015. Key Indicators of the Labour Market (KILM) Database, 9th edition. Accessed 16 June 2016. www.ilo.org/global/statistics-and-databases/research-and-databases/kilm/WCMS_422090/lang--en/index.htm

WHO (World Health Organization). 2015. Trends in Maternal Mortality 1990-2015, Est mates by WHO, UNICEF, UNFPA, World Bank Group and the United Nations Population Division. www.who.int.reproductivehealth/publications/monitoring/maternal-mortality-2015/en

OECD (Organisation for Economic Co-operation and Development). 2015. Social Institutions and Gender Index 2014. OECD Development Centre. www.genderindex.org

Countries with high gender inequality and the presence of discriminatory social institutions, as illustrated in the **Social Institutions and Gender Index** (SIGI), tend to have poorer human development outcomes for women than for men. Although the average level of gender discrimination in social institutions is lower than the African average, Zambia, Swaziland and Malawi have particularly high levels of discrimination. These countries with discriminatory institutions have twice the maternal mortality and over twice the rate of average adolescent births for developing countries. In addition, women's representation is much lower than in Namibia, Mozambique, South Africa and Zimbabwe, which have lower levels of discriminatory social institutions. Discriminatory social institutions and practices limit women's decision-making power and status in the home, increase vulnerability to violence, and in many cases, reduce women's access to resources and decision-making platforms in public and private life.

West Africa
Africa
World

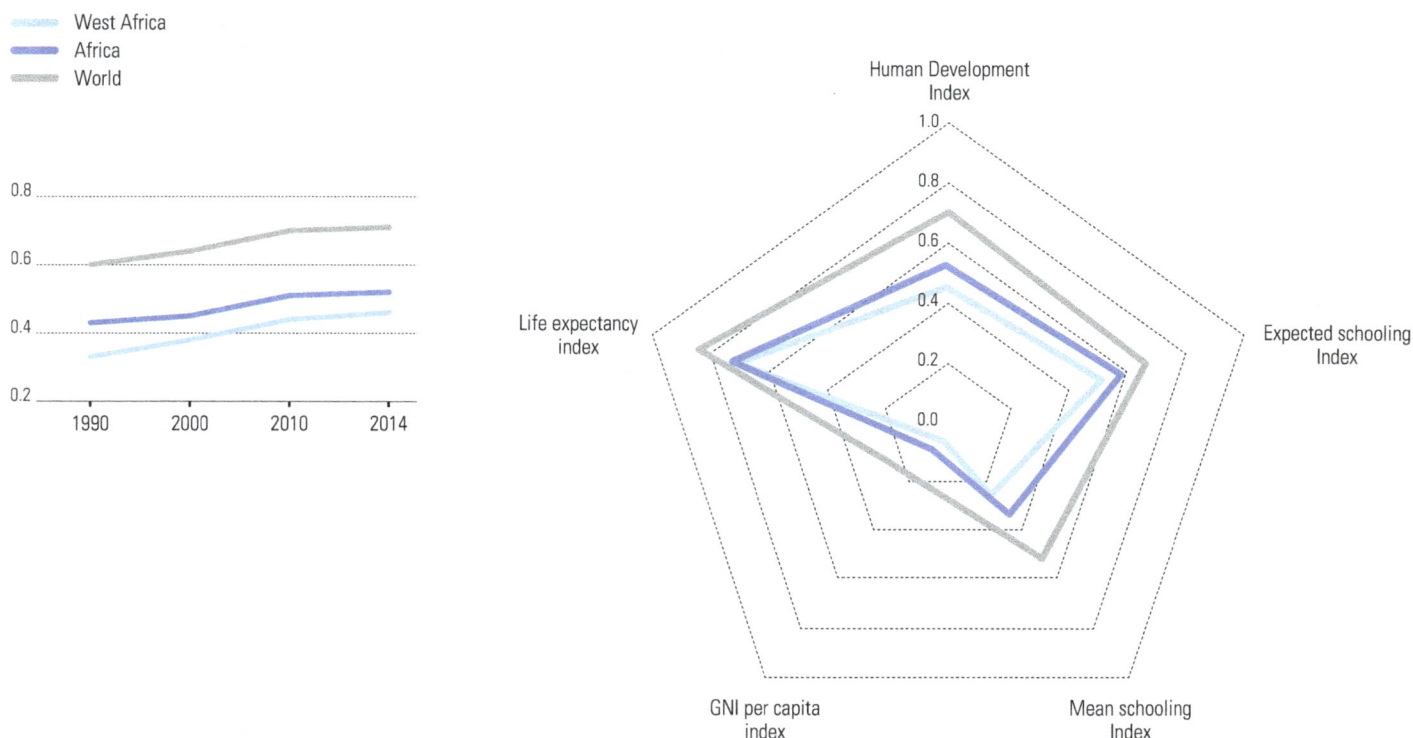

Human Development
Index

Life expectancy
index

Expected schooling
Index

GNI per capita
index

Mean schooling
Index

Source: Computed by the AfHDR Team based on data from UNDP, 2015.

Human Development Index and Trends

The **Human Development Index** (HDI) is a summary measure for assessing long-term progress in three basic dimensions of human development: a long and healthy life, access to knowledge, and a decent standard of living. Knowledge is measured by mean years of education among the adult population and access to learning and knowledge, by expected years of schooling for children of school-entry age. Standard of living is measured by gross national income (GNI) per capita expressed in constant 2011 international dollars converted using purchasing power parity (PPP) rates.

The West Africa sub-region has an average human development value of 0.461, which is below the African average value of 0.524, with a wide variation across countries. Cabo Verde has the highest HDI value, at 0.646, whereas Niger has the lowest value, at 0.348. Ghana and Cabo Verde are the only countries in the sub-region to have achieved medium

human development status. In some countries, poorer education and health outcomes outweigh the benefits of income per capita. Although the Islamic Republic of The Gambia, Mali, Burkina Faso, Benin and Sierra Leone have broadly similar levels of income per capita, the Islamic Republic of The Gambia and Benin have much better health and education outcomes, which increases their level of human development relative to Mali and Burkina Faso, for instance. Countries with relatively lower income per capita, such as Liberia and Guinea, fare better than Burkina Faso and Mali due to better education outcomes, among other factors, implying better efficiency in the utilization of resources. Since 2010, Niger, Sierra Leone, Burkina Faso and Guinea have made the biggest strides in improving their level of human development.

The **Inequality-adjusted Human Development Index** (IHDI) takes into account inequality in all three dimensions of the HDI

Human development, inequality and change

Country	Human Development Index (HDI)	Inequality-adjusted HDI (IHDI)	Overall loss in HDI from Inequality	Life expectancy at birth	Expected years of schooling	Mean years of schooling	GNI per capita	Average annual HDI growth (%)	
	Value	Value	(%)	(Years)	(Years)	(Years)	(2011 PPP $)	2000-2010	2010-2014
Cabo Verde	0.646	0.519	19.7	73.3	13.5	4.7	6,094	0.96	0.66
Ghana	0.579	0.387	33.1	61.4	11.5	7.0	3,852	1.33	1.13
Nigeria	0.514	0.320	37.8	52.8	9.0	5.9	5,341	–	1.06
Togo	0.484	0.322	33.4	59.7	12.2	4.5	1,228	0.76	1.29
Benin	0.480	0.300	37.4	59.6	11.1	3.3	1,767	1.78	0.64
Senegal	0.466	0.305	34.5	66.5	7.9	2.5	2,188	1.83	0.55
Côte d'Ivoire	0.462	0.287	38.0	51.5	8.9	4.3	3,171	1.12	0.98
The Gambia	0.441	–	–	60.2	8.8	2.8	1,507	1.38	-0.02
Liberia	0.430	0.280	34.8	60.9	9.5	4.1	805	1.20	1.50
Guinea-Bissau	0.420	0.254	39.6	55.2	9.0	2.8	1,362	–	0.42
Mali	0.419	0.270	35.7	58.0	8.4	2.0	1,583	2.73	0.61
Sierra Leone	0.413	0.241	41.7	50.9	8.6	3.1	1,780	2.63	1.59
Guinea	0.411	0.261	36.5	58.8	8.7	2.4	1,096	1.83	1.50
Burkina Faso	0.402	0.261	35.0	58.7	7.8	1.4	1,591	–	1.58
Niger	0.348	0.246	29.2	61.4	5.4	1.5	908	2.40	1.69
West Africa	0.461	0.304	34.7	59.3	9.4	3.5	2 285	1.66	1.01
Africa	0.524	0.349	32.9	61.2	10.3	5.0	5 126	1.55	0.86

Source: Compiled by the AfHDR Team based on data from UNDP, 2015.

by 'discounting' each dimension's average value according to the level of inequality across the population. The 'loss' in human development due to inequality is defined as the difference between HDI and IHDI expressed as a percentage. The sub-region has a higher level of loss in human development due to inequality compared to the African average. Sierra Leone, Guinea Bissau and Côte d'Ivoire have the highest loss in human development from inequality in the sub-region, whereas Cabo Verde has the lowest. A review of inequality in each sub-index of the HDI reveals that inequality in this sub-region is driven by inequality in the distribution of education and health outcomes relative to income inequality in all countries except Cabo Verde. In Cabo Verde, inequality in income per capita is the main driver of inequality in human development.

Gender Inequality and Women's Empowerment

The **Gender Development Index** (GDI) is based on the sex-disaggregated HDI and defined as a ratio of the female to the male HDI. The GDI measures gender inequalities in achievement in terms of health (measured by female and male life expectancy at birth), education (measured by female and male expected years of schooling for children and mean years for adults aged 25 years and older) and command over economic resources (measured by female and male estimated GNI per capita). The West Africa sub-region has a slightly lower GDI than the African average. The GDI further indicates that women in the Islamic Republic of The Gambia and Ghana attain up to 89 per cent of the human development outcomes of men, while in Guinea, Mali

Benin
Côte d'Ivoire
Gabon
The Gambia
Ghana
Liberia
Mali
Niger
Senegal
Sierra Leone
Togo

Trends in gender inequality

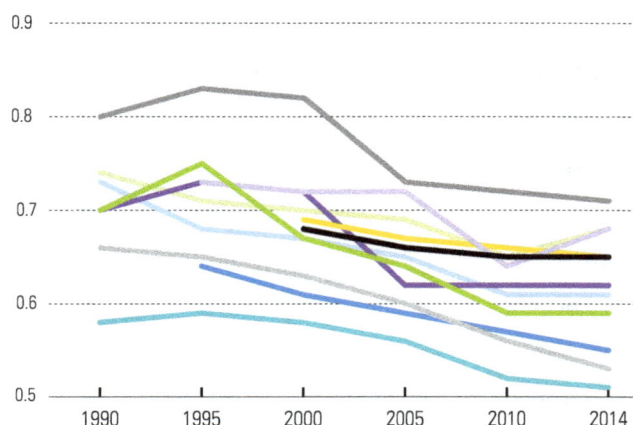

GENDER DEVELOPMENT INDEX

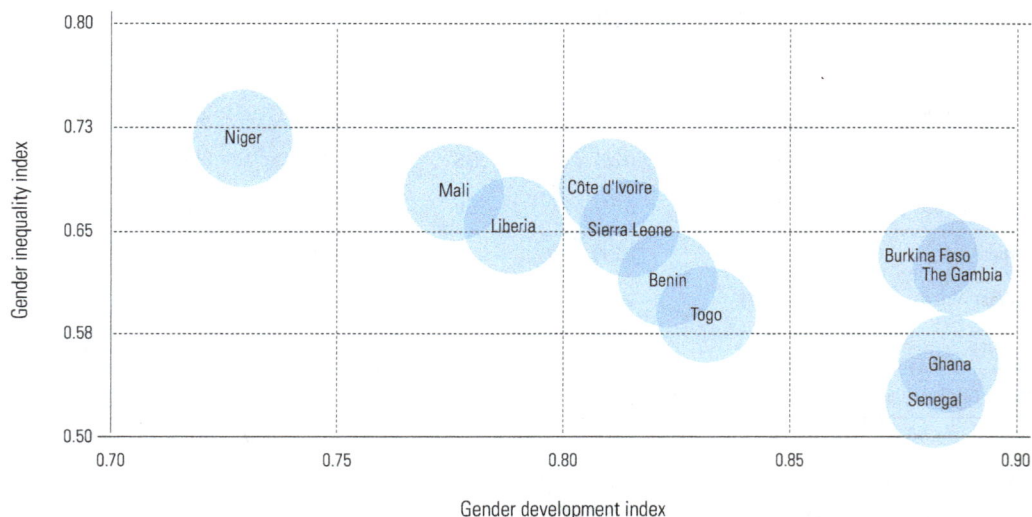

Gender inequality index

Gender development index

Niger
Mali
Liberia
Côte d'Ivoire
Sierra Leone
Benin
Togo
Burkina Faso
The Gambia
Ghana
Senegal

Source: Computed by the AfHDR Team based on data from UNDP, 2015.

and Niger, women attain less than 78 per cent of male HDI outcomes. Inequality in HDI in this sub-region is driven by unequal outcomes in education and health rather than the distribution of income across the population.

The **Gender Inequality Index** (GII) reflects gender-based inequalities in three dimensions – reproductive health, measured by maternal mortality and adolescent birth rates; empowerment, measured by the share of parliamentary seats held by women, and attainment in secondary and higher education by each gender; and economic activity, measured by the labour market participation rate for women and men. The GII can be interpreted as the loss in human development

due to inequality between female and male achievements in the three GII dimensions. Senegal and Ghana have the lowest levels of gender inequality in the sub-region, whereas Niger has the highest. Countries with higher levels of gender inequality are characterized by a high maternal mortality gap, that is, at least twice the maternal mortality rate of all developing countries, and high adolescent birth rates. In Niger, it is four times the average for all developing countries.

Countries with high gender inequality and the presence of discriminatory social institutions, as illustrated in the **Social Institutions and Gender Index** (SIGI), tend to have poorer human development outcomes for

Gender equality, social institutions and women's empowerment

	Gender Development Index	Gender Inequality Index	Social Institutions and Gender Index	Female/ male GNI per capita	Maternal mortality gap	Adolescent birth rate gap	Female share of seats in parliament	Gender gap in secondary school attainment (25+)	Labour force participation gap (15+)
	Value	Value	Value	Ratio	Ratio	Ratio	%	Ratio	Ratio
	2014	2014	2014	2014	2015	2010-2015	2016	2005–2014	2015
The Gambia	0.889	0.622	0.52	0.7	3.0	2.2	9.4	0.9	0.9
Ghana	0.885	0.554	0.30	0.7	1.3	1.1	10.9	0.9	1.0
Senegal	0.883	0.528	0.20	0.6	1.3	1.8	42.7	0.3	0.6
Burkina Faso	0.881	0.631	0.28	0.7	1.6	2.2	9.4	0.3	0.8
Nigeria	0.841	–	0.39	0.6	3.4	2.3	6.1	0.8	0.8
Togo	0.831	0.588	0.19	0.8	1.5	1.8	17.6	1.0	1.0
Benin	0.823	0.614	0.28	0.7	1.7	1.8	7.2	0.9	1.0
Sierra Leone	0.814	0.650	0.37	0.8	5.7	2.0	12.4	1.0	0.9
Côte d'Ivoire	0.810	0.679	0.25	0.5	2.7	2.5	9.2	0.6	0.6
Liberia	0.789	0.651	0.38	0.7	3.0	2.3	10.5	0.9	0.9
Guinea	0.778	–	0.32	0.7	2.8	2.5	21.9	0.8	0.9
Mali	0.776	0.677	0.52	0.4	2.5	3.4	8.8	0.6	0.6
Niger	0.729	0.713	0.44	0.4	2.3	4.0	14.6	0.4	0.4
Cabo Verde	–	–	–	0.5	0.2	1.4	23.6	0.6	0.6
Guinea-Bissau	–	–	0.21	0.7	2.3	1.9	13.7	0.9	0.9
West Africa	0.825	0.628	0.33	0.6	2.4	2.2	14.5	0.53	0.8
Africa	0.871	0.548	0.28	0.6	2.1	1.7	20.8	0.7	0.8

Source: Compiled by the AfHDR Team based on data from GDI and GII, UNDP (2015), Women in Parliament, IPU (2016), Labour force, ILO (2016), Maternal Mortality, WHO, (2016), SIGI, OECD (2015).

Notes:

a. Female and male GNI per capita, UNDP (2015).

b. Maternal mortality gap is actual deaths per 100,000 live births in each country benchmarked against developing country average of 239, WHO (2015).

c. Adolescent birth rate gap is the number of actual births per 1,000 women ages 15–19 in each country benchmarked against developing country average (2010/2015), UNDP (2015).

d. Population with at least some secondary education gap is the female to male ratio of secondary education attainment for the population aged 25 and older, UNDP (2015).

e. Female share in parliament is the average percentage of women parliamentarians in each country, across all chambers (single, lower and upper houses) at May 2016. The average for sub-Saharan Africa (SSA) is 23.1 per cent and 20.8 per cent including North Africa, IPU (2016).

f. Labour force participation gap is the female-male ratio (Ratio of female to male shares) for the female and male population aged 15 and above, ILO (2015).

References:

UNDP. 2015. Human Development Report 2015: Work for Human Development. New York.

IPU (International Parliamentary Union). 2016. International Parliamentary Union: Women in National Parliaments Database. Accessed 16 June 2016. www.ipu.org/wmn-e/world.htm

ILO (International Labour Organization). 2015. Key Indicators of the Labour Market (KILM) Database, 9th edition. Accessed 16 June 2016. www.ilo.org/global/statistics-and-databases/research-and-databases/kilm/WCMS_422090/lang--en/index.htm

WHO (World Health Organization). 2015. Trends in Maternal Mortality 1990-2015, Estimates by WHO, UNICEF, UNFPA, World Bank Group and the United Nations Population Division. www.who.int/reproductivehealth/publications/monitoring/maternal-mortality-2015/en

OECD (Organisation for Economic Co-operation and Development). 2015. Social Institutions and Gender Index 2014. OECD Development Centre. www.genderindex.org

women than men. The West Africa sub-region has a higher level than the African average level of social discriminatory institutions. The Gambia, Mali, and Niger have the highest levels of discrimination, whereas Senegal and Côte d'Ivoire have the lowest. Countries with highly discriminatory social institutions tend to have lower parliamentary representation for women. Senegal has the highest level of representation of women in parliament, followed by Guinea and Cabo Verde. Labour force participation for women is almost at par with men in almost all countries except Niger, Mali, Cabo Verde and Côte d'Ivoire, where the gender gap in secondary educational attainment is also higher. Discriminatory social institutions and practices limit women's decision-making power and status in the home, increase vulnerability to violence, and in many cases, reduce women's access to resources and decision-making platforms in public and private life.

		Human Development Index (HDI) Value							HDI rank		Average annual HDI growth %			
HDI rank	Country									Change				
		1990	2000	2010	2011	2012	2013	2014	2013	2009-2014	1990-2000	2000-2010	2010-2014	1990-2014
Very High Human Development														
High Human Development														
63	Mauritius	0.619	0.674	0.756	0.762	0.772	0.775	0.777	62	6	0.86	1.15	0.68	0.95
64	Seychelles	–	0.715	0.743	0.752	0.761	0.767	0.772	68	8	–	0.39	0.97	–
83	Algeria	0.574	0.640	0.725	0.730	0.732	0.734	0.736	84	4	1.09	1.26	0.35	1.04
94	Libya	0.679	0.731	0.756	0.711	0.745	0.738	0.724	83	-27	0.75	0.34	-1.07	0.27
96	Tunisia	0.567	0.654	0.714	0.715	0.719	0.720	0.721	96	-1	1.43	0.88	0.26	1.00
Group average		0.610	0.683	0.739	0.734	0.746	0.747	0.746	79		1.03	0.80	0.24	0.82
Medium Human Development														
106	Botswana	0.584	0.561	0.681	0.688	0.691	0.696	0.698	106	1	-0.41	1.96	0.61	0.74
108	Egypt	0.546	0.622	0.681	0.682	0.688	0.689	0.690	108	-3	1.31	0.90	0.33	0.98
110	Gabon	0.620	0.632	0.663	0.668	0.673	0.679	0.684	111	1	0.20	0.48	0.76	0.41
116	South Africa	0.621	0.632	0.643	0.651	0.659	0.663	0.666	117	4	0.17	0.18	0.87	0.29
122	Cabo Verde	–	0.572	0.629	0.637	0.639	0.643	0.646	122	2	–	0.96	0.66	–
126	Morocco	0.457	0.528	0.611	0.621	0.623	0.626	0.628	126	5	1.44	1.48	0.69	1.33
126	Namibia	0.578	0.556	0.610	0.616	0.620	0.625	0.628	128	3	-0.39	0.94	0.70	0.35
136	Rep. of the Congo	0.534	0.489	0.554	0.560	0.575	0.582	0.591	138	2	-0.87	1.25	1.61	0.42
138	Equatorial Guinea	–	0.526	0.591	0.590	0.584	0.584	0.587	137	-5	–	1.18	-0.18	–
139	Zambia	0.403	0.433	0.555	0.565	0.576	0.580	0.586	139	1	0.71	2.52	1.36	1.57
140	Ghana	0.456	0.485	0.554	0.566	0.572	0.577	0.579	140	-2	0.63	1.33	1.13	1.00
143	Sao Tome and Principe	0.455	0.491	0.544	0.548	0.552	0.553	0.555	143	-2	0.76	1.02	0.52	0.83
Group average		0.525	0.544	0.610	0.616	0.621	0.625	0.628	126	1	0.36	1.18	0.76	0.79
Low Human Development														
145	Kenya	0.473	0.447	0.529	0.535	0.539	0.544	0.548	145	0	-0.58	1.70	0.92	0.62
149	Angola	–	0.390	0.509	0.521	0.524	0.530	0.532	149	1	–	2.70	1.11	–
150	Swaziland	0.536	0.496	0.525	0.528	0.529	0.530	0.531	149	-5	-0.78	0.57	0.28	-0.04
151	Tanzania (United Republic of)	0.369	0.392	0.500	0.506	0.510	0.516	0.521	151	2	0.60	2.46	1.05	1.44
152	Nigeria	..	..	0.493	0.499	0.505	0.510	0.514	152	2	–	–	1.06	–
153	Cameroon	0.443	0.437	0.486	0.496	0.501	0.507	0.512	154	6	-0.13	1.07	1.32	0.61
154	Madagascar	–	0.456	0.504	0.505	0.507	0.508	0.510	153	-4	–	1.02	0.27	–
155	Zimbabwe	0.499	0.428	0.461	0.474	0.491	0.501	0.509	158	12	-1.53	0.75	2.50	0.08
156	Mauritania	0.373	0.442	0.488	0.489	0.498	0.504	0.506	156	1	1.71	0.98	0.92	1.28
159	Comoros	..	..	0.488	0.493	0.499	0.501	0.503	158	-1	–	–	0.75	–
161	Lesotho	0.493	0.443	0.472	0.480	0.484	0.494	0.497	161	1	-1.05	0.62	1.30	0.03
162	Togo	0.404	0.426	0.459	0.468	0.470	0.473	0.484	167	3	0.52	0.76	1.29	0.75
163	Rwanda	0.244	0.333	0.453	0.464	0.476	0.479	0.483	163	5	3.16	3.13	1.61	2.89
163	Uganda	0.308	0.393	0.473	0.473	0.476	0.478	0.483	164	-2	2.47	1.86	0.51	1.89
166	Benin	0.344	0.392	0.468	0.473	0.475	0.477	0.480	165	-2	1.33	1.78	0.64	1.40
167	Sudan	0.331	0.400	0.465	0.466	0.476	0.477	0.479	165	-5	1.90	1.52	0.74	1.55
168	Djibouti	–	0.365	0.453	0.462	0.465	0.468	0.470	168	0	–	2.17	0.97	–
169	South Sudan	–	..	0.470	0.458	0.457	0.461	0.467	171	..	–	–	-0.15	–
170	Senegal	0.367	0.380	0.456	0.458	0.461	0.463	0.466	170	-3	0.36	1.83	0.55	1.00
172	Côte d'Ivoire	0.389	0.398	0.444	0.445	0.452	0.458	0.462	172	0	0.23	1.12	0.98	0.72
173	Malawi	0.284	0.340	0.420	0.429	0.433	0.439	0.445	174	2	1.83	2.14	1.49	1.90
174	Ethiopia	–	0.284	0.412	0.423	0.429	0.436	0.442	175	2	–	3.78	1.78	–
175	The Gambia	0.330	0.384	0.441	0.437	0.440	0.442	0.441	173	-2	1.55	1.38	-0.02	1.22
176	Dem. Rep. of the Congo	0.355	0.329	0.408	0.418	0.423	0.430	0.433	176	3	-0.77	2.18	1.52	0.83
177	Liberia	–	0.359	0.405	0.414	0.419	0.424	0.430	177	1	–	1.20	1.50	–
178	Guinea-Bissau	–	..	0.413	0.417	0.417	0.418	0.420	178	-4	–	–	0.42	–
179	Mali	0.233	0.313	0.409	0.415	0.414	0.416	0.419	179	-3	2.97	2.73	0.61	2.47
180	Mozambique	0.218	0.300	0.401	0.405	0.408	0.413	0.416	180	0	3.25	2.96	0.94	2.74
181	Sierra Leone	0.262	0.299	0.388	0.394	0.397	0.408	0.413	182	0	1.32	2.63	1.59	1.91
182	Guinea	–	0.323	0.388	0.399	0.409	0.411	0.411	181	1	–	1.83	1.50	–
183	Burkina Faso	–	–	0.378	0.385	0.393	0.396	0.402	184	2	–	..	1.58	–
184	Burundi	0.295	0.301	0.390	0.392	0.395	0.397	0.400	183	0	0.20	2.62	0.66	1.28
185	Chad	–	0.332	0.371	0.382	0.386	0.388	0.392	186	1	–	1.12	1.37	–
186	Eritrea	–	–	0.381	0.386	0.390	0.390	0.391	185	-5	–	–	0.62	–
187	Central African Republic	0.314	0.310	0.362	0.368	0.373	0.348	0.350	187	0	-0.14	1.58	-0.84	0.45
188	Niger	0.214	0.257	0.326	0.333	0.342	0.345	0.348	188	0	1.85	2.40	1.69	2.05
Regional average		0.351	0.372	0.441	0.447	0.452	0.455	0.459	169	0	0.88	1.82	0.97	1.26

Source: Compiled by the AfHDR Team from UNDP (2015).

Annex I Inequality-adjusted HDI (IHDI) for African countries

Sub-Region	HDI Rank	Country	HDI Value 2014	IHDI Value 2014	Overall loss (%)	Difference from HDI Rank
High Human Development						
South	63	Mauritius	0.777	0.666	14.2	-2
East	64	Seychelles	0.772	–	–	–
North	83	Algeria	0.736	–	–	–
North	94	Libya	0.724	–	–	–
North	96	Tunisia	0.721	0.562	22.0	-2
Group average			0.746	0.614	18.1	-2
Medium Human Development						
South	106	Botswana	0.698	0.431	38.2	-23
North	108	Egypt	0.690	0.524	24.0	-5
Central	110	Gabon	0.684	0.519	24.0	-6
South	116	South Africa	0.666	0.428	35.7	-15
West	122	Cabo Verde	0.646	0.519	19.7	5
North	126	Morocco	0.628	0.441	29.7	-2
South	126	Namibia	0.628	0.354	43.6	-25
Central	136	Republic of the Congo	0.591	0.434	26.6	6
Central	138	Equatorial Guinea	0.587	–	–	–
South	139	Zambia	0.586	0.384	34.4	-6
West	140	Ghana	0.579	0.387	33.1	-3
South	143	Sao Tome and Principe	0.555	0.418	24.7	6
Group average			0.628	0.440	30.3	-6
Low Human Development						
East	145	Kenya	0.548	0.377	31.3	-3
South	149	Angola	0.532	0.335	37.0	-8
South	150	Swaziland	0.531	0.354	33.3	-2
East	151	Tanzania (United Republic of)	0.521	0.373	27.3	4
West	152	Nigeria	0.514	0.320	37.8	-9
Central	153	Cameroon	0.512	0.344	32.8	-1
Central	154	Madagascar	0.510	0.372	27.0	4
South	155	Zimbabwe	0.509	0.371	27.0	4
North	156	Mauritania	0.506	0.337	33.4	1
East	159	Comoros	0.503	0.268	46.7	-18
South	161	Lesotho	0.497	0.320	35.6	-2
West	162	Togo	0.484	0.322	33.4	1
East	163	Rwanda	0.483	0.330	31.6	4
East	163	Uganda	0.483	0.337	30.2	6
West	166	Benin	0.480	0.300	37.4	-2
East	167	Sudan	0.479	–	–	–
East	168	Djibouti	0.470	0.308	34.6	1
East	169	South Sudan	0.467	–	–	–
West	170	Senegal	0.466	0.305	34.4	1
West	172	Côte d'Ivoire	0.462	0.287	38.0	-1
South	173	Malawi	0.445	0.299	32.9	2
East	174	Ethiopia	0.442	0.312	29.4	7
West	175	The Gambia	0.441	–	–	–
Central	176	Democratic Rep. of the Congo	0.433	0.276	36.2	0
West	177	Liberia	0.430	0.280	34.8	2
West	178	Guinea-Bissau	0.420	0.254	39.6	-5
West	179	Mali	0.419	0.270	35.7	1
South	180	Mozambique	0.416	0.273	34.3	3
West	181	Sierra Leone	0.413	0.241	41.7	-4
West	182	Guinea	0.411	0.261	36.5	0
West	183	Burkina Faso	0.402	0.261	35.0	2
East	184	Burundi	0.400	0.269	32.6	5
Central	185	Chad	0.392	0.236	39.9	-1
East	186	Eritrea	0.391	–	–	–
Central	187	Central African Republic	0.350	0.198	43.5	-1
West	188	Niger	0.348	0.246	29.2	3
Group average			0.459	0.301	34.7	0
Regional average			0.524	0.440	30.3	–

Source: Compiled by the AfHDR Team from UNDP (2015).

Annex J Multidimensional Poverty Index (MPI) for African Countries

Country	MPI: Intensity of deprivation	Population near multidimensional poverty	Population in severe multidimensional poverty
	(%)	(%)	(%)
Benin	53.3	16.9	37.7
Burkina Faso	61.3	7.6	63.8
Burundi	54.0	12.0	48.2
Cameroon	54.1	17.8	27.1
Central African Republic	55.6	15.7	48.5
Chad	62.7	8.8	67.6
Comoros	48.1	23.1	14.9
Côte d'Ivoire	51.7	17.9	32.4
Democratic Rep. of the Congo	50.8	18.5	36.7
Djibouti	47.3	16.0	11.1
Egypt	37.4	5.6	0.4
Ethiopia	60.9	6.7	67.0
Gabon	43.4	19.9	4.4
Gambia	50.5	21.3	31.7
Ghana	47.3	18.7	12.1
Guinea	57.6	12.7	49.8
Guinea-Bissau	61.6	10.5	58.4
Kenya	47.0	29.1	15.7
Lesotho	45.9	20.4	18.2
Liberia	50.8	21.5	35.4
Libya	37.5	6.3	0.1
Madagascar	54.6	11.7	48.0
Malawi	49.8	24.5	29.8
Mali	58.2	10.8	55.9
Mauritania	52.4	16.8	29.9
Morocco	44.3	12.6	4.9
Mozambique	55.6	14.8	44.1
Namibia	45.5	19.3	13.4
Niger	65.0	5.9	73.5
Nigeria	54.8	18.4	30.0
Republic of the Congo	44.7	26.2	12.2
Rwanda	49.7	17.9	34.6
Sao Tome and Principe	45.5	21.5	16.4
Senegal	53.5	18.1	30.8
Sierra Leone	53.0	14.6	43.9
Somalia	61.1	8.3	63.6
South Africa	39.6	17.1	1.3
South Sudan	61.7	8.5	69.6
Sudan	54.6	17.9	31.9
Swaziland	43.5	20.5	7.4
Tanzania (United Republic of)	50.4	21.5	32.1
Togo	49.9	19.9	23.2
Tunisia	39.3	3.2	0.2
Uganda	51.1	20.6	33.3
Zambia	48.6	23.1	22.5
Zimbabwe	44.1	29.3	7.8

Note: Latest available data ranging from 2005 to 2015
Source: Compiled by the AfHDR Team from UNDP (2015).

As explained in Chapter 2, the GDI is derived by first determining the difference in female and male HDI values. With this disaggregation, the GDI is calculated as the ratio of female to male HDI values. The GDI grouping divides countries into five groups based on the absolute deviation from gender parity in HDI values:

Group 1 comprises countries with high equality in HDI achievements between women and men (absolute deviation of less than 2.5 per cent).

Group 2 comprises countries with medium to high equality in HDI achievements between women and men (absolute deviation of 2.5-5 per cent).

Group 3 comprises countries with medium equality in HDI achievements between women and men (absolute deviation of 5-7.5 per cent).

Group 4 comprises countries with medium to low equality in HDI achievements between women and men (absolute deviation of 7.5-10 per cent).

Group 5 comprises countries with low equality in HDI achievements between women and men (absolute deviation from gender parity of more than 10 per cent).

Thus, Group 1 countries have significantly higher gender parity than Group 5 countries.

What is most striking in the table is the very small number of countries, i.e. two, in Group 1 - Botswana and Namibia, and four in Group 2 - Mauritius, Libya, Lesotho and Rwanda. Twenty-eight countries are classified into Group 5, of which 23 are in the Low Human Development category. (Another seven countries lack sufficient data to make any estimates.)

Sub-Region	HDI Rank 2014	Country	GDI value 2014	GDI group 2014	HDI value Female 2014	HDI value Male 2014
High Human Development						
South	63	Mauritius	0.950	2	0.752	0.792
East	64	Seychelles	–	–	–	–
North	83	Algeria	0.837	5	0.637	0.761
North	94	Libya	0.950	2	0.699	0.736
North	96	Tunisia	0.894	5	0.671	0.751
Medium Human Development						
South	106	Botswana	0.982	1	0.691	0.704
North	108	Egypt	0.868	5	0.633	0.729
Central	110	Gabon	–	–	–	–
South	116	South Africa	0.948	3	0.646	0.681
West	122	Cabo Verde	–	–	–	–
North	126	Morocco	0.828	5	0.555	0.670
South	126	Namibia	0.981	1	0.620	0.632
Central	136	Congo (Republic of the)	0.922	4	0.561	0.609
Central	138	Equatorial Guinea	–	–	–	–
South	139	Zambia	0.917	4	0.558	0.609
West	140	Ghana	0.885	5	0.540	0.610
South	143	Sao Tome and Principe	0.891	5	0.520	0.584
Low Human Development						
East	145	Kenya	0.913	4	0.527	0.577
South	149	Angola	–	–	–	–
South	150	Swaziland	0.879	5	0.494	0.561
East	151	Tanzania (United Republic of)	0.938	3	0.504	0.538
West	152	Nigeria	0.841	5	0.468	0.556
Central	153	Cameroon	0.879	5	0.478	0.544
Central	154	Madagascar	0.945	3	0.497	0.526
South	155	Zimbabwe	0.922	4	0.487	0.529
North	156	Mauritania	0.816	5	0.446	0.546
East	159	Comoros	0.813	5	0.443	0.545
South	161	Lesotho	0.953	2	0.482	0.505
West	162	Togo	0.831	5	0.439	0.527
East	163	Rwanda	0.957	2	0.472	0.493
East	163	Uganda	0.886	5	0.452	0.510
West	166	Benin	0.823	5	0.431	0.524
East	167	Sudan	0.830	5	0.428	0.516
East	168	Djibouti	–	–	–	–
East	169	South Sudan	–	–	–	–
West	170	Senegal	0.883	5	0.436	0.494
West	172	Côte d'Ivoire	0.810	5	0.410	0.507
South	173	Malawi	0.907	4	0.423	0.467
East	174	Ethiopia	0.840	5	0.403	0.479
West	175	The Gambia	0.889	5	0.414	0.466
Central	176	Democratic Rep. of the Congo	0.833	5	0.393	0.472
West	177	Liberia	0.789	5	0.387	0.491
West	178	Guinea-Bissau	–	–	–	–
West	179	Mali	0.776	5	0.363	0.468
South	180	Mozambique	0.881	5	0.390	0.443
West	181	Sierra Leone	0.814	5	0.370	0.454
West	182	Guinea	0.778	5	0.358	0.460
West	183	Burkina Faso	0.881	5	0.376	0.427
East	184	Burundi	0.911	4	0.381	0.418
Central	185	Chad	0.768	5	0.338	0.440
East	186	Eritrea	–	–	–	–
Central	187	Central African Republic	0.773	5	0.303	0.392
West	188	Niger	0.729	5	0.287	0.394

Source Compiled by the AfHDR team from UNDP (2015).

HDI Group	HDI Rank 2014	Country	GII value 2014	GII rank 2014
North Africa				
High	83	Algeria	0.413	85
High	94	Libya	0.134	27
High	96	Tunisia	0.240	48
Medium	108	Egypt	0.573	131
Medium	126	Morocco	0.525	117
Low	156	Mauritania	0.610	139
Sub-regional average			0.416	91
East Africa				
High	64	Seychelles	–	–
Low	145	Kenya	0.552	126
Low	151	Tanzania (United Republic of)	0.547	125
Low	159	Comoros	–	–
Low	163	Rwanda	0.400	80
Low	163	Uganda	0.538	122
Low	167	Sudan	0.591	135
Low	168	Djibouti	–	–
Low	169	South Sudan	–	–
Low	174	Ethiopia	0.558	129
Low	184	Burundi	0.492	109
Low	186	Eritrea	–	–
Sub-regional average			0.525	118
West Africa				
Medium	140	Ghana	0.554	127
Low	152	Nigeria	–	–
Low	162	Togo	0.588	134
Low	166	Benin	0.614	142
Low	170	Senegal	0.528	118
Low	172	Côte d'Ivoire	0.679	151
Low	175	The Gambia	0.622	143
Low	177	Liberia	0.651	146
Low	178	Guinea-Bissau	–	–
Low	179	Mali	0.677	150
Low	181	Sierra Leone	0.650	145
Low	182	Guinea	–	–
Low	183	Burkina Faso	0.631	144
Low	188	Niger	0.713	154
Sub-regional average			0.628	141.273
Central Africa				
Medium	110	Gabon	0.514	113
Medium	136	Congo (Rep. of the)	0.593	137
Medium	138	Equatorial Guinea	–	–
Low	153	Cameroon	0.587	132
Low	154	Madagascar	–	–
Low	176	Congo (Democratic Republic of the)	0.673	149
Low	185	Chad	0.706	153
Low	187	Central African Republic	0.655	147
Sub-regional average			0.621	138.5
Southern Africa				
High	63	Mauritius	0.419	88
Medium	106	Botswana	0.480	106
Medium	116	South Africa	0.407	83
Medium	126	Namibia	0.401	81
Medium	139	Zambia	0.587	132
Medium	143	Sao Tome and Principe	–	–
Low	149	Angola	–	–
Low	150	Swaziland	0.557	128
Low	155	Zimbabwe	0.504	112
Low	161	Lesotho	0.541	124
Low	173	Malawi	0.611	140
Low	180	Mozambique	0.591	135
Sub-regional average			0.510	113
Africa-wide average			0.548	122.2

Source: Compiled by the AfHDR Team from UNDP (2015).

The table gives the GII values and rankings from a sub-regional perspective. Care must be taken, however, in putting too much emphasis on the sub-regional differences based on simple aggregations of data for the countries of each sub-region. With the exception of North Africa, all of the sub-regions' averages place them in the bottom third of all countries with GII values. North Africa's mean GII value places these countries in the middle third only because of the strength of the GII scores for Algeria, Libya and Tunisia. The final row of the table shows an average value and rank for all African countries for which data were available. The Africa-wide aggregation of the individual country estimates suggests the significance of addressing gender inequality at the regional and national levels as inequality between men and women is a drag on the social and economic fabric of the Continent.

Independent variables and statistics	HDI	HDI	GII	Life expectancy at birth	Expected years of schooling	Mean years of schooling	Female life expectancy at birth	Female adult mortality rate	Maternal mortality ratio
					Dependent variables				
GII	-0.746(7.6)*			-30.234(4.03)*	-15.072(6.66)*	-10.869(4.98)*			
GII Components									
Maternal mortality ratio		-0.0003(0.4)					-0.02(0.59)	0.183(0.56)	
Adolescent birth rate		-0.0004(2.1)**					-0.09(4.2)*	1.055(3.64)*	0.189(2.5)**
Women share of seats in parliament		0.0004(0.5)							
Population of female with at least some secondary education		0.005(4.3)*							
Population of male with at least some secondary education		0.001(1.0)							
Labour force participation rate of female		0.002(2.7)*							
Labour force participation rate of male		0.00006(0.13)							
HDI Components									
Life expectancy at birth			-0.005(2.9)*						
Expected years of schooling			-0.022(2.8)*						
Mean years of schooling			-0.009(1.3)						
GNI			0.00013(0.193)						
R-squared adjusted	0.527	0.758	0.545	0.23	0.46	0.318	0.282	0.22	0.29
F-statistic	57.88*	24.33*	13.54*	16.22*	44.4*	24.82*	11.01*	8.03*	6.27**

Notes: Figures in parenthesis represent t-statistics
* stands for significance at 1% and ** at 5%

Source: Computed by the AfHDR Team.

References

Abrahams, Yvette. 2009. *Plaiting Three Strands: Gender-Based Violence as a Cause of Global Warming*. Paper prepared for DAC/HSRC Colloquium on Social Cohesion, Durban, South Africa, 29-30 October 2009.

ActionAid. 2015. *Close the Gap! The Cost of Inequality in Women's Work.* London. www.actionaid.org.uk/sites/default/files/publications/womens_rights_on-line_version_2.1.pdf

AfDB (African Development Bank). 2014a. *Benin Economic Outlook.* Abidjan, Côte d'Ivoire.

——. 2014b. *Investing in Gender Equality for Africa's Transformation.* Abidjan, Côte d'Ivoire.

——. 2014c. *Niger Economic Outlook.* Abidjan, Côte d'Ivoire.

——. 2015. *Gender Equality Index 2015.* Abidjan, Côte d'Ivoire.

AfDB (African Development Bank), UNECA (United Nations Economic Commission for Africa), AU (African Union) and UNDP (United Nations Development Programme). 2014. Assessing progress in Africa toward the Millennium Development Goals: MDG Report 2011. Tunis, Tunisia.

Africa Renewal Online. 2015. *Women's Situation Room: Africa's Unique Approach to Reducing Electoral Violence.* www.un.org/africarenewal/magazine/april-2015/women%E2%80%99s-situation-room-africa%E2%80%99s-unique-approach-reducing-electoral-violence

African Union. 2016. *OAU/AU Treaties, Conventions, Protocols and Charters.* Addis Ababa. http://au.int/en/treaties

African Women and Peace Support Group. 2004. Liberian Women Peacemakers: Fighting for the Right to be Seen, Heard, and Counted. Trenton, New Jersey, USA: Africa World Press.

Ally, Shireen. 2008. *Domestic Workers Unionisation in Post-Apartheid South Africa.* The Ahfad Journal. Vol 23 (2).

Annan, J., C. Blattman, K. Carlson, K. and D. Mazurana. 2008. *The State of Female Youth in Northern Uganda: Phase II Uganda.* Survey of War-Affected Youth (SWAY). www.crin.org/en/docs/Survey%20of%20War%20Affected%20Youth%20II.pdf

Arbache, Jorge Saba, Alexandre Kolev and Ewa Filipiak (eds.). 2010. *Gender Disparities in Africa's Labour Market.* Washington, World Bank.

BBC News. 2012. The woman who took on Zimbabwe's security men and won, 6 July 2012.

Baird, S.,S. Chirwa, E. McIntosh and B. Özler. 2011. *The Short-term Impacts of a Schooling Conditional Cash Transfer Program on the Sexual Behavior of Young Women.* http://irps.ucsd.edu/assets/033/10615.pdf

Bandara, Amarkoon. 2015, Economic Cost of Gender Gaps: Africa's Missing Growth Reserve. *Feminist Economics,* Vol. 21, Issue 2.

Bardasi, E., K. Carlson and D. 2007. Gender, Entrepreneurship, and Competitiveness in Africa (World Bank, ed.). *Africa Competitiveness Report 2007.* Washington, D.C.

Barker, Gary and Christine Ricard. 2005. *Young Men and the Construction of Masculinity in Sub-Saharan Africa: Implications for HIV/AIDS, Conflict, and Violence.* World Bank Social Development Papers Conflict Prevention and Reconstruction, Paper No. 26. pp. 16-17. http://documents.worldbank.org/curated/en/2005/06/6022525/young-men-construction-masculinity-sub-saharan-africa-implications-hivaids-conflict-violence

Baskin, J. 1991. *Striking Back: A History of COSATU.* Johannesburg, Ravan.

Budlender, Debbie. 2008. *The Statistical Evidence on Care and Non-Care Work across Six Countries.* www.idrc.ca/EN/Documents/Care-Economy.pdf

CARE International. 2011. *Microfinance in Africa. State of the Sector Report: Closing the Gap.* www.care.org/sites/default/files/documents/MF-2011-CARE-Access-Africa-Closing-the-Gap.pdf

——. 2013. Connecting the World's Poorest People to the Global Economy: New models for linking informal savings groups to formal financial services. http://insights.careinternational.org.uk/media/k2/attachments/Connecting_the_Worlds_Poorest_People_to_the_Global_Economy.pdf

CARMMA (Campaign on Accelerated Reduction of Maternal Mortality in Africa). 2016. *Zimbabwe Country Scorecard.* Addis Ababa. www.carmma.org/scorecard/zimbabwe-0

Carrasco, Gisela. 2015. *Political Gaps: Mapping Gaps and Country Benchmarking, including Women's Empowerment for Building Peace, Security and Resilience.* Background paper prepared for 2016 African Human Development Report

Castillo Diaz, Pablo and Simon Tordjman. 2012. *Women's Participation in Peace Negotiations: Connections between Presence and Influence.* UN Women. www.unwomen.org/~/media/headquarters/attachments/sections/library/publications/2012/10/wpssourcebook-03a-womenpeacenegotiations-en.pdf

Cerise, Somali. Anna Eliseeva, Francesca Francavilla, Camila Mejia and Michele Tuccio. 2013. *How Do Maternity Leave and Discriminatory Social Norms Relate to Women's Employment in Developing Countries?* OECD Development Centre, Paris.

CNBCAfrica.com. 2015. *S. Africa's New Gender Bill Ruffles Feathers with 50% Women Quota.* 12 February. www.cnbcafrica.com/news/southern-africa/2014/02/10/safrica's-new-gender-bill-ruffles-feathers-with-50-women-quota/

De Watteville, N. 2002. *Addressing Gender issues in Demobilization and Reintegration Programs.* Africa Region Working Paper Series. No. 33. Washington, D.C. World Bank.

Deere, C.D. and C.R. Doss. 2006. *Voice and Agency: Empowering Women and Girls for Shared Prosperity.* http://ucanr.edu/blogs/food2025/blogfiles/14584.pdf. Washington, D.C.

Demirguc-Kunt and Klapper. 2012. *Measuring Financial Inclusion. Measuring Financial Inclusion: The Global Findex Database.* Policy Research Working Paper. Washington, D.C. World Bank.

DFID (Department for International Development). 2001. The Causes of Conflict in Africa. Consultation Document. London. www.gsdrc.org/document-library/causes-of-conflict-in-africa/

ECLAC (Economic Commission for Latin America and the Caribbean). 2013. *Gender Equality Observatory of LAC.* Annual Report 2012. Santiago.

EISA. 2009. *Fourth Annual Symposium: Preventing and Managing Violent Election-Related Conflicts in Africa: Exploring Best Practises,* 17-18 November 2009. Johannesburg, South Africa.

Erulkar, A.S. 2015. *Building an Evidence Base to Delay Marriage in sub-Saharan Africa.* New York, The Population Council. www.popcouncil.org/research/building-an-evidence-base-to-delay-marriage-in-sub-saharan-africa

Ezeala-Adikaibe, B., I. Onwuekwe, O. Ekenze, K. Madubuko and E. Ofoegbu. 2009. Stroke Risk Factor Profile in Nigerian African Women.*The Internet Journal of Neurology,* Vol. 13, No.1. https://ispub.com/IJN/13/1/4817

FAO (Food and Agriculture Organization of the United Nations). 2012. Sustainability dimensions. Rome. http://www.fao.org/docrep/018/i3137e/i3137e04.pdf

——. 2016. Gender and land rights database. Accessed 25 May 2016.

——. n.d. Corporate Document Repository. Rome.

Forbes. 2011. Africa's Most Successful Women: Njeri Rionge. 3 August 2011.

Fridell, M. 2009. *Consolidated Response on Gender Quotas in African Countries.* Web log message. 7 April. http://aceproject.org/electoral-advice/archive/questions/replies/165671188

Gassmann, F. and C. Behrendt. 2006. *Cash Benefits in Low-income Countries: Simulating the Effects on Poverty Reduction for Senegal and Tanzania.* www.gsdrc.org/document-library/cash-benefits-in-low-income-countries-simulating-the-effects-on-poverty-reduction-for-senegal-and-tanzania/

Gladman, K. and M. Lamb. 2013. *GMI Ratings' 2013 Women on Boards Survey.* Available at GMI Ratings website: www.boarddiversity.ca/sites/default/files/GMIRatings_WOB_042013.pdf

Goldman Sachs. n.d. *10,000 Women.* www.goldmansachs.com/citizenship/10000women.

Hein, C. and N. Cassirer. 2010. *Workplace Solutions for Childcare.* Geneva, Switzerland, ILO.

Hideg, I. and L. Ferris. 2013. *Two Sides of Sexism: How Sexist Attitudes May Undermine and Promote Gender Diversity.* In Academy of Management Proceedings, Vol. 2013, No. 1. Academy of Management.

ICF International. 2015. *The DHS Program STATcompiler.* www.statcompiler.com

ILO (International Labour Organization). 2013. Women and Men in the Informal Economy: A Statistical Picture. Second Edition. Geneva, Switzerland. www.ilo.org/wcmsp5/groups/public/---dgreports/---stat/documents/publication/wcms_234413.pdf

——. 2014. *Maternity and Paternity at Work: Law and Practice across the World.*

——. 2015a. *Key Indicators of the Labour Market (KILM) Eighth Edition.* Geneva, Switzerland.

——. 2015b. *Women in Business and Management: Gaining Momentum.* Geneva, Switzerland.

——. 2015c. *World Employment and Social Outlook.* Geneva, Switzerland.

——. 2015d. *Global Employment Trends for Youth 2015: Scaling up Investments in Decent Jobs for Youth.* Geneva, Switzerland.

INNOVATE. 2013. *Preliminary Study: Gender, Higher Education and AET.* University of Florida, USAID, Virginia Tech, Penn State, Tuskegee University. www.oired.vt.edu/innovate/documents/Cross-cutting%20Studies/9_24_13%20VT%20Gender,%20Higher%20Education%20and%20AET.pdf

IPU (International Parliamentary Union). 2016. International Parliamentary Union: Women in National Parliaments Database. Accessed 16 June 2016. www.ipu.org/wmn-e/world.htm

Klugman, Jeni, L. Hanmer, Lucia, S. Twigg, T. Hasan, J. McCleary-Sills and J. Santamaria. 2014. *Voice and Agency: Empowering Women and Girls for Shared Prosperity.* Washington, D.C., World Bank. https://openknowledge.worldbank.org/handle/10986/19036

Mama, Amina. 2008. Critical connections: feminist studies in African contexts. *In* A. Cornwall, A. Whitehead and E. Harrison (eds). *Feminisms in Development: Contradictions, Contestations and Challenges.* London, Zed Books.

Mathur, S., M. Greene and A. Malhotra. 2003. *Too Young to Wed: The Lives, Rights and Health of Young Married Girls.* Washington, D.C., International Center for Research on Women.

Mazurana, D.E. and S.R. McKay. 1999. *Women and Peace-building.* Montreal, Canada, International Centre for Human Rights and Democratic Development.

Mining.com. 2014. *Let's Talk About: Women in the Mining Industry.* 15 April. www.mining.com/lets-talk-about-women-in-the-mining-industry-31775

Modi, V, S McDade, D. Lallement and J. Saghir. 2005. *Energy Services for the Millennium Development Goals.* Achieving the Millennium Development Goals. UN Millennium Project.

Ngongo-Mbede, V. 2003. *The Traditional Mediation of Conflicts by Women in Cameroon in Women and Peace in Africa.* Paris, UNESCO. pp. 22-34.

Nguyen, M. and Q. Wodon. 2012a. Measuring Early Marriage. *Economic Bulletin.* Vol. 32 Issue 1. www.researchgate.net/publication/254407333_Measuring_child_marriage

——. 2012b. *Perceptions of Child Marriage as a Reason for Dropping out of School: Results for Ghana and Nigeria.* mimeo. The World Bank: Washington, DC

Nkosi, Bongani. 2012. A Textbook Case of Pupil Dejection. *Mail and Guardian.* 29 June 2012. http://mg.co.za/article/2012-06-29-a-textbook-case-of-pupil-dejection

Ñopo, Hugo, Nancy Daza and Johanna Ramos. 2011. Gender Earnings Gaps in the World: A study of 64 countries. Discussion Paper Series. www.emeraldinsight.com/doi/pdf/10.1108/01437721211253164

Ntahobar, J. and B. Ndayiziga. 2003. *The Role of Burundian Women in Peaceful Settlement of Conflict in Women and Peace in Africa.* Paris, United Nations Organization for Education, Science and Culture (UNESCO). pp. 11-21.

Nussbaum, Martha. 2011. *Creating Capabilities: The Human Development Approach.* Cambridge, Massachusetts, Harvard University Press.

Odejide, A. 2014. "What Can a Woman Do?" Gender Norms in a Nigerian University. www.opendemocracy.net/5050/abiola-odejide/what-can-woman-do-gender-norms-in-nigerian-university

Odusola, A. 2013. *Accelerating Progress on Maternal Health in Africa. Lessons from Emerging Policies and Institutional Innovation.* 2013 Global MDG Conference. UNDP Working Paper No. 11. New York.

OECD (Organisation for Economic Co-operation and Development). 2014. *The OECD Gender and Social Institutions Index.* www.oecd.org/dev/development-gender/theoecdsocialinstitutionsandgenderindex.htm

PACT. 2016. *WORTH's Global Reach.* Washington. www.pactworld.org/WORTH

Pungiluppi, Juliana, María Elena Castro and Ana María Muñoz-Boudet. 2010. *A Model for Promoting Gender Equity in Private Companies and in Government Agencies: The GEM Certification Process in Latin America and the Caribbean (The cases of Mexico, Chile, Argentina, and the Dominican Republic).* No. 159. http://siteresources.worldbank.org/INTLAC/Resources/257803-1269390034020/EnBreve_159_English_Printable.pdf

Powley, Elizabeth. 2014. *Case Study: Rwanda. Women Hold Up Half of the Parliament.* http://www.idea.int/publications/wip2/upload/Rwanda.pdf

PwC. 2015. *Mining for Talent. A Study of Women on Boards in the Mining Industry 2012-2014.* www.awmi.org/assets/1/7/WIM_MINING_FOR_TALENT_FINAL_2015.pdf

Reeves, S. and H. Baden. 2000. *Gender and Development: Concepts and Definitions.* Institute of Development Studies. Brighton, UK. https://books.google.it/books/about/Gender_and_Development.html?id=ZwBEAAAACAAJ&redir_esc=y

Sen, Amartya. 1999. *Development as Freedom.* Anchor Books, New York.

Soares, Fábio Veras and Clarissa Teixeira. 2010. *Impact Evaluation of the Expansion of the Food Subsidy Programme in Mozambique.* Research Brief 17, International Policy Centre for Inclusive Growth, Brasília.

Steady, F.C. 2006. *Women and Collective Action in Africa*. Palgrave Macmillan, New York.

Stoneburner, Rand and Daniel Low-Beer. 2004. Population-Level HIV Declines and Behavioural Risk Avoidance In Uganda. *Science*, 30 April 2004, Vol. 304.

Tadesse, Admassu. 2009. Private sector development: A Perspective of SME financing in Africa. www.norfund.no/.../SME%20and%20growth%20MENON%20%5BFIN

The Washington Post. 2016. *The cultural factors at play in Africa's HIV crisis*, by M. Gerson, 22 April 2016.

Thurshen, Meredith (ed.). 2010. *African Women: A Political Economy*. New York, Palgrave McMillian

Triant, Virginia A. Hang Lee, Colleen Hadigan and Steven K. Grinspoon. 2007. Increased Acute Myocardial Infarction Rates and Cardiovascular Risk Factors among Patients with Human Immunodeficiency Virus Disease. Journal of Clinical Endocrinological Metabolism, No. 92, vol. 7, July. pp. 2506–2512.

Tripp, A. 2013. *Women and Politics in Africa Today*. http://democracyinafrica.org/women-politics-africa-today

UNAIDS. 2013. *HIV and AIDS Uganda Country Progress Report 2013*. Kampala.

United Nations. 2014. *The Justice and Reconciliation Process in Rwanda: Background Note*. Department of Public Information, New York. www.un.org/en/preventgenocide/rwanda/pdf/Backgrounder%20Justice%202014.pdf

—. 2015. *The World's Women 2015: Trends and Statistics*. New York.

UNDP (United Nations Development Programme). 2000. *Human Development Report: Human Rights*. New York, Oxford University Press.

—. 2011. *Human Development Report 2011*. New York.

—. 2012a. *Africa Human Development Report 2012: Towards a Food Secure Future*. New York.

—. 2012b. *An Environment-Friendly Pilot Village to Revolutionize National Environment Protection and Poverty Reduction*. www.rw.undp.org/content/rwanda/en/home/ourwork/environmentandenergy/successstories/rubaya-an-environment-friendly-pilot-village.html

—. 2012c. *Political Economy Analysis. Institutional and Context Analysis Guidance Note*. www.undp.org/content/undp/en/home/ourwork/democraticgovernance/oslo_governance_centre/analysis_and_learning/political_economyanalysis.html

—. 2013a. *Human Development Report 2013. The Rise of the South: Human Progress in a Diverse World*. http://hdr.undp.org

____. 2013b. *Changing with the World: UNDP Strategic Plan 2014-2017*. New York. www.undp.org/content/undp/en/home/librarypage/corporate/Changing_with_the_World_UNDP_Strategic_Plan_2014_17.html

—. 2014. *Gender Equality in Public Administration*. www.undp.org/content/dam/undp/library/Democratic%20Governance/Women-s%20Empowerment/GEPA%20Global%20Report%20May%202014.pdf

—. 2015a. *Africa Policy Note*. New York, USA.

—. 2015b. *Human Development Report*. New York, USA.

—. n.d. *Political Economy Analysis*. www.undp.org/content/undp/en/home/ourwork/democraticgovernance/oslo_governance_centre/analysis_and_learning/political_economyanalysis.html

____. 2016. *UNDP's Gender Equality Seal Certification Programme: Lessons Learned in Latin America. Women Deliver*. http://womendeliver.org/2016/undps-gender-equality-seal-certification-programme-public-private-enterprises-lessons-learned-latin-america/

UNDP and The Huairou Commission. 2014. *Engendering Access to Justice. Grassroots Women's Approaches to Securing Land Rights*. www.undp.org/content/undp/en/home/librarypage/democratic-governance/access_to_justiceandruleoflaw/Engendering-access-to-justice.html

UNECA (United Nations Economic Commission for Africa). 2007. *Women in Power: Towards Democracy and Gender Equality Report*. Addis Ababa, Ethiopia.

—. 2014. *African Centre for Gender. Twenty-Year Review of the Implementation of the Beijing Declaration and Platform for Action (BPfA) + 20*. Africa Regional Review Summary Report 1995-2014. Ninth Africa Regional Conference on Women (Beijing +20). Addis Ababa, 17-19 November 2014.

UNECA (United Nations Economic Commission for Africa), AU (African Union), AfDB (African Development Bank) and UNDP (United Nations Development Programme). 2014. *Assessing Progress in Africa toward the Millennium Development Goals: Analysis of the Common African Position on the post-2015 Development Agenda*. Addis Ababa, Ethiopia.

—. 2015. *Assessing Progress in Africa toward the Millennium Development Goals: 2015 MDG Report - Lessons Learned in Implementing the MDGs*. Addis Ababa, Ethiopia.

UNFPA (The United Nations Population Fund). 2012. *By Choice, Not by Chance: Family Planning, Human Rights and Development*. The State of World Population 2012. New York, USA.

UNESCO (United Nations Educational, Scientific and Cultural Organization. 2014a. *Teaching and Learning: Achieving Quality for All. EFA*. Education for All Global Monitoring Report 2013/4. Paris. http://unesdoc.unesco.org/images/0022/002256/225660e.pdf

UNESCO. 2014b. *Progress in getting all children to school stalls but some countries show the way forward*. Policy Paper 14 / Fact Sheet 28. June 2014. Paris, France.

—. 2015. Institute for Statistics. In EdStats.

UNFPA (United Nations Population Fund) and Harvard School of Public Health. 2008. *Program on International Health and Human Rights*. UNFPA at Work: Six human rights case studies. New York.

—.2012. Marrying too young: end child marriage. New York.

—. 2014a. *Implementation of the International and Regional Human Rights Framework for the Elimination of Female Genital Mutilation*. New York.

—. 2014b. *Lessons From the First Cycle of the Universal Periodic Review: From Commitment to Action on Sexual and Reproductive Health and Rights*. New York.

UNFPA Center for Reproductive Rights. 2013. *ICPD and Human Rights: 20 years of advancing reproductive rights through UN treaty bodies and legal reform*. www.unfpa.org/sites/default/files/pub-pdf/icpd_and_human_rights_20_years.pdf

UNFPA and Guttmacher Institute. 2014. *Adding It Up: The Costs and Benefits of Investing in Sexual and Reproductive Health*, by Susheela Singh, Jacqueline E. Darroch and Lori S. Ashford. New York, USA. www.guttmacher.org/sites/default/files/report_pdf/addingitup2014.pdf

UNICEF (United Nations Children's Fund). 2016. *Factsheet Gender and Water, Sanitation and Hygiene*. Available from www.unicef.org/esaro/7310_Gender_and_WASH.html

—.2013. *Ending Child Marriage: Progress and Prospects*. New York, USA. http://www.unicef.org/media/files/Child_Marriage_Report_7_17_LR..pdf

UNSD (United Nations Statistics Division). *MDG Indicators.* Available from http://mdgs.un.org/unsd/mdg/Metadata.aspx?IndicatorId=9

UN Women. 2016. *Facts and Figures: Women's Economic Empowerment.* New York. www.unwomen.org/en/what-we-do/economic-empowerment/facts-and-figures#notes

Vanek, Joann and Martha Chen, Ralf Hussmanns and Françoise Carré. 2013. *Women and Men in the Informal Economy: A Statistical Picture.* Second ed. Geneva. International Labour Organization.

WHO (World Health Organization). 2013a. *Assisting Community Health Workers in Rwanda: MOH's Rapid SMS And Ubuzima.* http://apps.who.int/iris/bitstream/10665/92814/1/WHO_RHR_13.15_eng.pdf

—. 2013b. *Global and Regional Estimates of Violence against Women: Prevalence and Health Effects of Intimate Partner Violence and Non-Partner Sexual Violence.* Geneva.

—. 2014a. *Global Status Report on Noncommunicable Diseases.* Geneva. www.who.int/nmh/publications/ncd-status-report-2014/en

—. 2014b. *WHO Global Expenditure Atlas. September 2014. Geneva, Switzerland. http://www.who.int/health-accounts/atlas2014.pdf*

—. 2015. *Trends in Maternal Mortality: 1990 to 2015.* Geneva. http://apps.who.int/iris/bitstream/10665/194254/1/9789241565141_eng.pdf?ua=1

World Bank. 2008. *World Development Report 2008: Agriculture and Development.* Washington, D.C.

—. 2012. *2012 World Development Report on Gender Equality and Development.* Washington, D.C. http://goo.gl/Ax3vn2

—. 2014a. *Gender at Work. A Companion to the World Development Report on Jobs.* Washington, D.C.

—. 2014b. *Global Findex (Global Financial Inclusion Database).* http://datatopics.worldbank.org/financialinclusion

—. 2015a. *Women, Business and the Law.* Washington, D.C. http://wbl.worldbank.org/data

—. 2015b. *Enterprise Surveys.* Washington, D.C. www.enterprisesurveys.org/data

—. 2015c. *World Development Indicators.* Washington, D.C. www.data.worldbank.org/data-catalog/world-development-indicators

—. 2016. *Why Should Finance Ministers Care About Gender Equality? Mainstreaming Wasn't Getting Results Fast Enough.* Washington, D.C. www.worldbank.org/en/news/speech/2016/05/05/why-should-finance-ministers-care-about-gender-equality

—. n.d. Data. *The State of Education.* Washington, D.C. http://datatopics.worldbank.org/education/wStateEdu/StateEducation.aspx

—. n.d. *Third Rural Transport Project.* Washington, D.C. www.worldbank.org/projects/P075407/third-rural-transport-project?lang=en

World Bank Group. 2015. *Accessing Institutions.* Washington, D.C. http://wbl.worldbank.org/data/exploretopics/accessing-institutions.

World Bank and Elsevier. 2015. *A Decade of Development in sub-Saharan African Science, Technology, Engineering and Mathematics Research.* Washington, D.C., World Bank Group. http://documents.worldbank.org/curated/en/2014/09/20240847/decade-development-sub-saharan-african-science-technology-engineering-mathematics-research

World Economic Forum. 2014. *The Global Gender Gap Report 2014.* Cologny/Geneva Switzerland. www.weforum.org/reports/global-gender-gap-report-2014

Young, A. 2007. Preventing, Demobilizing, Rehabilitating, and Reintegrating Child Soldiers in African Conflicts. *The Journal of International Policy Solutions.* Spring, Vol. 7.

Endnotes

[1] See, for example, the pioneering work of Amartya Sen (1999) and more recently, Martha Nussbaum (2011).

[2] Mauritania is grouped with North Africa due to its close identity with the other North African states. Because of the lack of sufficient data, HD calculations for Somalia are not included in the rankings, although existing data would put Somalia in the low human development ranking categories.

[3] The education and health dimensions are each based on two indicators, while the standard of living dimension is based on six indicators. All of the indicators needed to construct the MPI for a household are taken from the same household survey. The indicators are weighted to create a deprivation score, and the deprivation scores are computed for each household in the survey. A deprivation score of 33.3 per cent (one-third of the weighted indicators) is used to distinguish between the poor and non-poor. If the household deprivation score is 33.3 per cent or greater, the household (and all members) is identified as multidimensionally poor. Households with a deprivation score greater than or equal to 20 per cent but less than 33.3 per cent are near multidimensional poverty.

[4] UNICEF (2013) provides multiple scenarios on how sub-Saharan Africa will have the largest number and global share of child brides by 2050. Nigeria, in spite of the annual decline of 1 percent in the number of child marriages over the past three decades, will lead the continent with the absolute number of child marriages unless drastic efforts are made, while Burkina Faso, due to its rapid population growth, may experience a dramatic increase in the number of child marriage by 2050.

[5] In countries with a high HIV prevalence, this has also been noted as a contributory risk factor that explains rising rates of heart disease among rural African women. See Triant et al. (2007: 2506-2512).

[6] Data are available for only six countries – Botswana, Republic of the Congo, Democratic Republic of the Congo, Ghana, Malawi, South Africa and Tanzania.

[7] ILO Convention 183 (2000), Article 4. The accompanying recommendation 191, which is aimed at providing additional (non-binding) guidance to countries, recommends a minimum of 18 weeks' paid maternity leave.

[8] Cerise et al. (2013), using 2010 data on female labour force participation and the 2012 Social Institutions Gender Index (SIGI).

[9] It is estimated that SMEs account for over 90 per cent of all enterprises, of which 70 to 80 per cent are micro and small-sized enterprises. The definition of SME is context-specific but is mostly determined by size (number of employees). Generally, micro enterprises are those with less than ten employees; small-sized, with ten to less than 50 employees; and medium-sized, with 50 to 100 employees.

[10] Castillo Diaz and Tordjman (2012); Mama (2008); Steady (2006); Ngongo-Mbede (2003); and Ntahobari and Ndayiziga (2003).

[11] These countries are Chad, Republic of the Congo, Côte d'Ivoire, Ghana, Malawi, Mali, Namibia, Rwanda, Uganda, Tanzania and Zimbabwe.

[12] The concept was first introduced by Yvette Chesson-Wureh, the Coordinator for the Liberia-based Angie Brooks International Centre, an NGO on women's empowerment. The process was first used during the 2011 elections in Liberia and has since been replicated in Kenya, Senegal and Sierra Leone. According to WSR organizers, since situations could differ in individual countries, the concept is adaptable to local conditions.

[13] UN Special Rapporteur on the Sale of Children, Child Prostitution and Child Pornography (2014, para. 67).

[14] ILO Convention 183 (2000), Article 4. The accompanying Recommendation 191, which is intended to provide additional (non-binding) guidance to countries, recommends a minimum of 18 weeks' paid maternity leave.

[15] The countries are spread across four sub-regions – Cameroon, Chad, Democratic Republic of the Congo, Gabon and Madagascar in Central Africa; Egypt and Tunisia in North North Africa; Mozambique and Zambia in Southern Africa; and Benin, Burkina Faso, Liberia, Mali, Niger, Senegal and Sierra Leone in West Africa.

SUSTAINABLE DEVELOPMENT GOALS

1 NO POVERTY	2 ZERO HUNGER	3 GOOD HEALTH AND WELL-BEING	4 QUALITY EDUCATION	5 GENDER EQUALITY	6 CLEAN WATER AND SANITATION
7 AFFORDABLE AND CLEAN ENERGY	8 DECENT WORK AND ECONOMIC GROWTH	9 INDUSTRY, INNOVATION AND INFRASTRUCTURE	10 REDUCED INEQUALITIES	11 SUSTAINABLE CITIES AND COMMUNITIES	12 RESPONSIBLE CONSUMPTION AND PRODUCTION
13 CLIMATE ACTION	14 LIFE BELOW WATER	15 LIFE ON LAND	16 PEACE, JUSTICE AND STRONG INSTITUTIONS	17 PARTNERSHIPS FOR THE GOALS	SUSTAINABLE DEVELOPMENT GOALS

www.ingramcontent.com/pod-product-compliance
Lightning Source LLC
Chambersburg PA
CBHW080423270326
41929CB00018B/3136